A BEGINNER'S GUIDE TO WRITING LESBIAN ROMANCE

A BEGINNER'S GUIDE TO WRITING LESBIAN ROMANCE

ISABELLA

SAPPHIRE BOOKS

SALINAS, CALIFORNIA

A Beginners Guide to Writing a Lesbian Romance
Copyright © 2023 by Isabella All rights reserved.

ISBN EPUB – 978-1-959929-12-3

All rights reserved. No part of this publication may be reproduced, distributed, or transmitted in any form or by any means, including photocopying, recording, or other electronic or mechanical methods, without written permission of the publisher.

Editor – Tara Young
Cover Design - Fineline Cover Design

Sapphire Books Publishing, LLC
P.O. Box 8142
Salinas, CA 93912
www.sapphirebooks.com

Produced in the United States of America
First Edition – Feb. 2024

All rights reserved under U.S. and International copyright conventions. Except for use in reviews, no part of this text may be reproduced, transmitted, downloaded, decompiled, reverse engineered, or stored in a storage and retrieval system, data base, including printing, recording either visual or audio, electronic and any future technology invented without written permission of Sapphire Books Publishing.

The author/publisher expressly prohibits any entity from using the production/publication for purposes of training A.I, artificial intelligence, to generate text that may replicate the author's style or genre similar to this work. The author retains all rights to use this work for purposes of generative AI training and development of any language learning system.

To the extent that the image on the cover of this book depicts a person or persons, such a person is merely a model and is not intended to portray any character feature in this book.

This ebook is licensed for your personal enjoyment only. This ebook may not be re-sold or given away to other people. If you would like to share this book with another person, please purchase an additional copy for each recipient. If you're reading this book and did not purchase it, or it was not purchased for your use only, then please return to your favorite ebook retailer and purchase your own copy. Thank you for respecting the hard work of this author.

This and other Sapphire Books titles can be found at www.sapphirebooks.com

Isabella's other books

Faithful Series
Always Faithful
Forever Faithful
Faithful Valor

American Yakuza Series
American Yakuza I
The Lies that Bind -American Yakuza II
Razor's Edge - American Yakuza III
Blood Honor: American Yakuza IV
American Yakuza - The Collection

Executive Series
Executive Disclosure
Surviving Reagan

Scarlet Series
Scarlet Masquerade
Scarlet Assassin

Stand Alone
Broken Shield
Dusty Road Home
Chasing Liberty
Cigar Barons: Blood isn't thicker than water, it's war.
The Gate
Twisted Deception: Love can be dangerous.

Short Stories
The Last Train
The Tinderella Chronicles: Big Sur Edition
Virgo Meets Gemini

Anthologies
Fandom to Fantasy: Volume 1
Fandom to Fantasy: Volume 2

Non- Fiction
A Beginners Guide to Writing a Crime Novel
A Beginners Guide to Writing Lesbian Romance
A Beginners Guide to Writing a Mystery

Dedication

To my wife

Table of Contents:

1. Introduction to Lesbian Romance
   - Understanding the Genre and its Audience
   - Key Elements of a Lesbian Romance Novel
   - Building Your Novel
   - Exploring Subgenres within Lesbian Romance
2. Developing Compelling Characters
   - Building Believable Lesbian Protagonists and Love Interests
   - Exploring Character Arcs and Growth
   - Writing Authentic and Engaging Dialogue
3. Creating a Compelling Plot
   - Crafting a Riveting Love Story
   - Incorporating Conflict and Tension
   - Balancing Romance with Other Plot Elements
4. Establishing a Captivating Setting
   - Choosing the Right Location and Atmosphere
   - Incorporating LGBTQ+ Spaces and Communities
   - Utilizing Descriptive Language to Bring Settings to Life
5. Writing Intimate and Emotional Scenes
   - Portraying Emotional Connection and Chemistry
   - Navigating Sexual and Romantic Tension
6. Exploring Themes in Lesbian Romance
   - Identity, Self-acceptance, and Coming Out
   - Overcoming Obstacles and Prejudices
   - Celebrating Love and Relationships
7. Editing and Polishing Your Novel
   - The Importance of Multiple Drafts
   - Self-Editing Techniques for Clarity and Coherence
   - Seeking Feedback and Professional Editing Services
8. Publishing and Marketing

- Traditional vs. Self-Publishing in the Lesbian Romance Genre
- Crafting Compelling Synopses and Blurbs
- Connecting with Lesbian Romance Reader Communities
- Building an Online Author Presence

Introduction to Lesbian Romance - Understanding the Genre and its Audience

Lesbian romance is a captivating and diverse literary genre that explores love, relationships, and emotional connections between women. As an essential subset of LGBTQ+ literature, it offers readers a chance to experience the complexities of same-sex relationships and the unique challenges faced by lesbian individuals in their pursuit of love and happiness. In this exploration, we will delve into the essence of the genre, its history, themes, and its growing significance in contemporary literature. Additionally, we will gain insight into the diverse audience that finds resonance within these stories.

Lesbian romance is a powerful genre that celebrates love, identity, and the strength of human connections. It provides a platform for diverse voices to be heard, offering readers an opportunity to explore relationships outside the traditional norm. As the genre continues to grow, it serves as a testament to the power of storytelling in fostering empathy, understanding, and acceptance among readers of all backgrounds. Whether you are a member of the LGBTQ+ community or an ally seeking heartfelt and engaging narratives, lesbian romance promises to captivate and leave a lasting impression on its audience.

Defining Lesbian Romance

Lesbian romance can be broadly defined as fictional narratives centered around romantic relationships between women. These stories can encompass a wide range of subgenres, including contemporary, historical, paranormal, fantasy, and more. The primary focus remains on the emotional and physical connections between female characters, often highlighting the challenges and triumphs they encounter as they navigate their love journeys.

The Evolution of Lesbian Romance

The origins of lesbian romance literature can be traced back to earlier works that explored same-sex relationships, albeit often through subtext and hidden narratives due to societal constraints. For example, Sappho's Poetry (c. 7th century BCE, Ancient Greece): Sappho, was an ancient Greek poet from the island of Lesbos and is often considered one of the earliest known writers to address the topic of same-sex attraction between women. Her lyric poetry often expressed deep emotional connections between women and has inspired generations of poets and writers. Over the years, the genre has evolved, and writers have become more open in their portrayal of lesbian relationships, empowering characters to embrace their identities and pursue love freely.

The history of lesbian romance literature is a journey marked by challenges, societal changes, and the gradual emergence of authentic representation. While lesbian relationships have been explored in literature for centuries, it is only in recent times that they have received more open and diverse portrayals.

Let's take a look at the key milestones that have shaped the evolution of lesbian romance:

Early Literature and Subtext: Historically, lesbian relationships were often depicted through subtext and hidden narratives in works of literature. Due to societal taboos and censorship, writers had to resort to subtle allusions and coded language to explore same-sex relationships.

- "Rebecca" by Daphne du Maurier: The intense relationship between the protagonist and Maxim's housekeeper, Mrs. Danvers, contains strong lesbian undertones. Mrs. Danvers's obsession with Rebecca, her manipulation of the protagonist, and the emotional intensity between them suggest a complex and possibly romantic connection.
- "Wuthering Heights" by Emily Brontë: The tumultuous and passionate relationship between Catherine Earnshaw and her friend, later sister-in-law, Isabella Linton, carries subtle undertones of romantic affection.
- "Little Women" by Louisa May Alcott: While the novel primarily centers around the close-knit March sisters, the particularly intense relationship between Jo March and her best friend, Laurie, raises questions about their feelings for each other. The novel portrays their deep emotional bond, with Jo describing Laurie as "her boy" and expressing a reluctance to marry him, suggesting a more complex connection.
- "The Awakening" by Kate Chopin: This novel

features a woman named Edna Pontellier who becomes increasingly dissatisfied with her traditional roles as a wife and mother. Her friendship with Adele Ratignolle is depicted with a level of emotional intimacy that some readers interpret as having lesbian undertones. Edna's yearning for freedom and self-discovery can be seen as paralleling the exploration of suppressed desires.

- "Mansfield Park" by Jane Austen: Fanny's deep emotional connection with her friend and confidante, Mary Crawford, is also notable. The intimacy of their conversations and Mary's influence on Fanny's thoughts and decisions can be interpreted as containing lesbian subtext.

- *Pulp Fiction Era*: In the early to mid-twentieth century, the emergence of pulp fiction allowed for some exploration of lesbian themes. However, these stories often sensationalized and depicted lesbian relationships as tragic or deviant.
- *Lesbian Pulp Fiction*: The mid-twentieth century saw a surge in the publication of lesbian pulp fiction novels. These novels, while still constrained by societal norms, provided lesbian readers with a sense of visibility and recognition, even if the stories were predominantly tragic or cautionary tales.
- *The Feminist Movement and Lesbian Literature*: The feminist movement of the 1960s and 1970s sparked an increase in lesbian-themed literature. Authors began to write more openly about lesbian relationships and experiences, focusing on the emotional and psychological aspects of love between women.
- *The 1980s and 1990s – Coming-Out Stories*: The 1980s and 1990s saw a rise in lesbian romance

novels that centered around coming-out stories and self-discovery. These stories highlighted the struggles and triumphs of characters as they embraced their sexual identities and sought acceptance from society and themselves.
- *Diversity and Intersectionality*: As societal attitudes evolved, lesbian romance literature started to embrace diversity and intersectionality. Authors began exploring the experiences of lesbians from various ethnic, cultural, and social backgrounds, providing a more nuanced and authentic representation of the LGBTQ+ community.
- *Mainstream Acceptance*: With the gradual acceptance of LGBTQ+ themes in mainstream culture, lesbian romance novels have gained broader recognition and readership. Major publishing houses began to publish more diverse and well-rounded lesbian romance stories, reaching a wider audience.
- *The Digital Age and Self-Publishing*: The advent of the internel and self-publishing platforms revolutionized the publishing landscape. As a result, many lesbian authors found opportunities to publish their work independently, further diversifying the genre and offering unique perspectives.
- *Modern Representation and Empowerment*: In recent years, lesbian romance literature has evolved to encompass a wide range of subgenres and themes. Modern representation focuses on empowered characters who embrace their identities and celebrate love and relationships without shame or fear.

The evolution of lesbian romance literature reflects the changing attitudes toward LGBTQ+ themes in society. From hidden subtext to vibrant representation, lesbian romance has come a long way, offering readers authentic, relatable, and empowering stories. As the genre continues to evolve, it remains an essential platform for exploring diverse love stories and amplifying the voices of lesbian authors and readers around the world.

Themes Explored in Lesbian Novels

Lesbian romance, like any other romance genre, delves into universal themes of love, passion, trust, and personal growth. However, it also addresses the unique experiences and challenges faced by lesbian individuals, such as coming out, societal acceptance, homophobia, and discrimination. These themes create an authentic and relatable reading experience for lesbian and non-lesbian readers alike. Some of the key themes explored in this book will include:

- *Self-Discovery and Coming Out*: Many lesbian romance stories revolve around characters coming to terms with their sexual orientation and embracing their identity as lesbians. These narratives often explore the emotional journey of self-discovery, the challenges of coming out to friends and family, and the empowerment that comes with accepting one's true self.
- *Acceptance and Validation*: The theme of acceptance is a prevalent and powerful aspect of lesbian romance. Characters may face internal struggles with self-acceptance or external challenges in gaining acceptance from their loved ones or society. These stories highlight the importance of validation and support in fostering healthy relationships.

- *Forbidden Love and Social Challenges*: Lesbian romance often portrays relationships that are considered taboo or face societal opposition. These stories delve into the challenges of navigating love in the face of prejudice, discrimination, and social norms that attempt to suppress authentic expression.
- *Overcoming Prejudice and Homophobia*: Addressing real-world issues, lesbian romance can depict characters confronting homophobia and prejudice. These narratives emphasize the strength and resilience needed to overcome societal barriers and celebrate love despite adversity.
- *Building Healthy Relationships*: At the core of lesbian romance lies the exploration of healthy relationships. These stories focus on communication, trust, and mutual understanding, portraying the importance of emotional connections in fostering lasting and fulfilling love.
- *Family and Community*: The theme of family and community is often present in lesbian romance. Characters may find acceptance and encouragement from their chosen family or discover allies among friends and community members who offer understanding and solidarity.
- *Empowerment and Identity*: Many lesbian romance stories showcase strong, empowered characters who embrace their identity and refuse to conform to societal expectations. These narratives encourage readers to embrace their true selves unapologetically.
- *Intersectionality and Diversity*: Diverse representation is an essential aspect of lesbian romance. These stories may feature characters from various ethnic, cultural, and social

backgrounds, addressing the intersectionality of identities and experiences within the LGBTQ+ community.
- *Emotional Intimacy and Connection*: Lesbian romance emphasizes the depth of emotional intimacy and connection between women loving women. These narratives showcase the power of emotional bonds and the transformative effect they can have on individuals.
- *Love and Personal Growth*: Ultimately, lesbian romance often explores the transformative power of love. Characters may experience personal growth and positive change as they navigate their relationships and confront their innermost desires and fears.

Lesbian romance is a genre that delves into a wide range of themes, offering readers emotional and thought-provoking narratives that go beyond romantic entanglements. By exploring themes such as self-discovery, acceptance, and empowerment, lesbian romance literature celebrates the resilience and strength of the LGBTQ+ community while providing universal lessons about love, relationships, and the human experience.

Introducing the Intersection of Identity and Diversity

One of the strengths of the lesbian romance lies in its portrayal of diverse characters and identities. Authors within the genre often depict characters from various ethnic, cultural, and social backgrounds, providing a rich tapestry of experiences that resonate with readers from all walks of life.

One of the strengths of lesbian romance literature lies in its ability to explore the intersectionality of identity and embrace diversity. By featuring characters from various ethnic, cultural, and social backgrounds, these stories provide a more authentic and inclusive representation of the LGBTQ+ community. The exploration of intersectionality not only adds depth to the narratives, but also highlights the shared struggles and unique experiences of characters within a diverse society but is relatable with its readers, as well.

Here are some key aspects you can add to your book around intersection of identity and diversity:

- *Representation of Diverse Identities*: Lesbian romance novels showcase characters with diverse identities, including but not limited to race, ethnicity, nationality, religion, and socioeconomic background. This representation allows your reader from different backgrounds to see themselves reflected in the stories and fosters a sense of belonging.
- *Embracing Cultural Nuances*: As an author of lesbian romances, you can incorporate cultural nuances, such as customs or language, into your characters' identities and experiences. By doing so, you'll create well-rounded and authentic portrayals that go beyond stereotypes, showcasing the complexities of navigating love and relationships within the context of different cultures. Oftentimes, this can also act as a conflict point for a relationship as the protagonists address their differences, mediate, and then compromise.
- *Addressing Prejudice and Discrimination*:

Intersectionality in your romance enables you to address the discrimination and prejudices faced by characters who belong to multiple marginalized communities. This exploration sheds light on the layered challenges these individuals encounter and highlights the importance of allyship and understanding.

- *Navigating Multiple Identities*: Characters in lesbian romances may grapple with the complexities of navigating multiple identities, such as being a lesbian woman of color, a queer immigrant, or a person with intersecting minority statuses. These narratives offer a glimpse into the unique experiences and resilience of individuals who face multiple societal pressures.
- *Intersectionality and Empowerment*: Through intersectionality, lesbian romance stories emphasize empowerment and solidarity within the LGBTQ+ community. Characters who embrace their multiple identities and find strength in their diversity inspire readers to embrace their whole selves and celebrate their unique qualities. Don't miss out on an opportunity to empower your characters.
- *Challenging Stereotypes*: By incorporating intersectionality, lesbian romances challenge stereotypes often associated with certain identities. These stories promote understanding and empathy, breaking down barriers and fostering appreciation for the multifaceted nature of human experiences. Sometimes we can avoid the butch-femme stereotypes or embrace them and make the stereotype something more challenging in your character development of your story.
- *Cultivating Inclusivity*: Inclusive lesbian romances contribute to creating a more

welcoming and diverse literary landscape. They invite readers of all backgrounds to engage with stories that may differ from their own experiences, promoting empathy and fostering a sense of unity.

- The intersection of identity and diversity in lesbian romance literature is a powerful force that enriches storytelling and empowers readers. By featuring characters from various backgrounds and experiences, lesbian romances celebrate the beauty and complexity of human identity. These stories encourage inclusivity, challenge stereotypes, and provide readers with a deeper understanding of the shared struggles and unique triumphs of individuals within the LGBTQ+ community. Ultimately, the intersectionality in lesbian romances contributes to a more compassionate and accepting world, both within the literary realm and beyond.

Connecting with Your Audience

Lesbian romance has garnered a devoted and passionate readership. Its appeal extends beyond the lesbian community, with many heterosexual readers appreciating the emotional depth and unique perspectives offered by these stories. Readers often find solace, inspiration, and a sense of belonging in the pages of lesbian romance novels.

For authors and creators of lesbian romance, connecting with the lesbian audience is essential to ensure that their stories resonate and leave a lasting impact. Creating meaningful connections with readers involves understanding their needs, experiences, and preferences.

Here are some keyways to connect with the lesbian audience in the context of lesbian romance:

- *Authentic Representation*: Authenticity is paramount when portraying lesbian characters and relationships. Ensure that the experiences and emotions of lesbian characters are portrayed realistically and respectfully. Avoid stereotypes and clichés, and instead, focus on creating well-rounded, relatable characters who readers can connect with on a personal level.
- *Diversity and Intersectionality*: Recognize the diversity within the lesbian community and include characters from various backgrounds, cultures, and identities. Embrace intersectionality to portray the unique experiences and challenges faced by individuals who belong to multiple marginalized communities. This inclusivity demonstrates a commitment to representation and fosters a sense of validation among readers.
- *Engaging and Empowering Storylines*: Craft compelling and empowering storylines that not only focus on romance, but also explore personal growth, self-discovery, and triumph over adversity. Lesbian readers appreciate narratives that inspire and resonate with their own journeys of love and acceptance.
- *Addressing Real-World Issues*: We don't live in a vacuum, and many lesbian readers seek stories that address real-world issues such as coming out, family acceptance, workplace discrimination, and societal prejudices. These are issues not found in your typical romance

novel sitting on the shelf at your favorite bookstore. By tackling these topics with sensitivity and authenticity, you can create a powerful connection with your audience, validating their experiences and providing a sense of understanding.

- *Creating Safe Spaces*: Incorporate safe and inclusive spaces within the story, where lesbian characters can freely express their emotions and identities without fear of judgment or harm. This allows readers to feel seen and represented in a positive light.
- *Building Emotional Connections*: You can foster emotional connections between readers and characters by portraying genuine and intimate relationships. Readers should be able to empathize with the characters' struggles, joys, and vulnerabilities, forming a strong bond that keeps them invested in the story. If they can relate to your book, then you have succeeded in telling a story that resonates with readers.
- *Engaging with the Community*: You can actively engage with the lesbian community through social media, forums, and LGBTQ+ events. Participating in discussions, listening to feedback, and being receptive to readers' perspectives can strengthen the bond between you and your audience.
- *Collaboration and Feedback*: Be involved in the community throughout the creative process through beta readers and sensitivity readers who can provide valuable feedback on representation and cultural nuances. Collaboration ensures that your story is respectful and well-received by the intended audience.
- *Sensitivity and Respect*: Approach lesbian romance with sensitivity and respect, understanding that these stories hold significant

emotional weight for readers. Acknowledge the responsibility of portraying lesbian relationships authentically and ethically. Your book may find its way into the hands of someone who has no lesbian representation in their community or comes from a family that doesn't condone the lifestyle or a community that frowns upon it. You never know where your book may end up.

Connecting with the lesbian audience in the context of lesbian romance involves genuine representation, diversity, engaging storylines, and a commitment to understanding and respecting the experiences of lesbian individuals. By fostering authentic connections with readers, you can create a positive impact, providing a platform for representation, empowerment, and a sense of belonging within the community.

Lesbian romance is a powerful genre that celebrates love, identity, and the strength of human connections. It provides a platform for diverse voices to be heard, offering readers an opportunity to explore relationships outside the traditional norm. As the genre continues to grow, it serves as a testament to the power of storytelling in fostering empathy, understanding, and acceptance among readers of all backgrounds. Whether you are a member of the LGBTQ+ community or an ally seeking heartfelt and engaging narratives, lesbian romance promises to captivate and leave a lasting impression on its audience.

Introduction to Lesbian Romance – Key Elements of a Lesbian Romance Novel

Lesbian romance is a unique and captivating genre that explores the complexities of love, relationships, and personal growth within same-sex connections between women. To craft a compelling lesbian romance novel, several key elements should be considered to create a heartfelt and engaging story. Here are some essential elements:

Authentic Representation

The portrayal of lesbian characters and relationships should be authentic and respectful. Avoid stereotypes and clichés, focusing instead on creating well-rounded, relatable characters with their own distinct personalities, hopes, and fears. Authenticity is crucial in lesbian representation as it ensures that LGBTQ+ individuals see themselves reflected accurately and respectfully in literature. Here are some key aspects of authentic portrayal you can and should have in your novel:

- *Diverse Identities:* Authentic portrayals encompass a diverse range of lesbian identities. Lesbian characters may come from various backgrounds, ethnicities, cultures, and social contexts. This diversity acknowledges the multifaceted nature of the LGBTQ+ community.

- *Multidimensional Characters*: Lesbian characters should be multidimensional, with hopes, fears, strengths, weaknesses, and complex personalities. Avoid one-dimensional stereotypes and allow characters to be fully realized individuals.
- *Realistic Experiences*: Lesbian characters' experiences should be grounded in reality, depicting the challenges and triumphs they encounter in their personal lives, relationships, and societal interactions. Realism adds depth and relatability to the characters' stories.
- *Genuine Relationships*: Authentic portrayals emphasize the genuineness of lesbian relationships. Whether it's the initial spark of attraction, the development of emotional intimacy, or navigating challenges together, the relationships should feel real and heartfelt.
- *Respectful Representation*: You must approach lesbian representation with respect and sensitivity. Avoid using LGBTQ+ identities solely for shock value or to exploit stereotypes. Instead, approach these characters and relationships with empathy and care.
- *Empowering Narratives*: Authentic portrayals can also empower readers by portraying lesbian characters as strong, resilient, and capable individuals. Showcase their agency and ability to shape their own destinies.
- *Inclusive Intersectionality*: Recognize and incorporate intersectionality in portraying lesbian characters. Acknowledge how their identities as women, and often other marginalized aspects of their lives, intersect with their lesbian identity.
- *Accurate Language and Terminology*: Use appropriate and up-to-date LGBTQ+ language and terminology when portraying characters

and relationships. Accuracy in language demonstrates respect and understanding.
- *Consultation and Sensitivity Readers*: You should seek consultation from LGBTQ+ individuals, sensitivity readers, or experts in the community to ensure an authentic portrayal and avoid unintentional mistakes or misrepresentations.
- *Impactful Storytelling*: Authentic portrayal extends beyond the surface representation. It should engage readers emotionally, allowing them to connect with the characters and empathize with their experiences.

Authentic portrayal of lesbian characters and relationships is of paramount importance in literature. By presenting diverse, multidimensional characters with realistic experiences and respectful representation, you can create meaningful and impactful stories. Through authenticity, lesbian representation becomes empowering, inclusive, and relatable, providing LGBTQ+ readers with a sense of recognition, validation, and belonging. We are members of every community and share the same hopes and dreams of heteronormative cultures, and our literature should reflect those aspirations.

Introduction to Lesbian Romance – Building your Novel

Let's talk about how to build your novel. Suggestions will be bulleted below the topic being discussed and are there to help you brainstorm and/or help you incorporate the ideas into your novel. These are the bones that will make up the body of your novel. Some may fit and some won't, but at least you have a place where you can ask yourself, "Did I build strong enough characters, plot, and story that will bring the reader to a satisfying experience reading my novel?" So let's get started.

Chemistry and Connection

The heart of any romance novel lies in the chemistry and emotional connection between the main characters. Building a strong bond between the protagonists is vital to create a love story that resonates with readers, evokes emotions, and keeps them invested in the characters' journey. Here's how to foster a powerful connection that will make readers root for their love to flourish:

- *Authenticity of Characters*: Craft authentic and relatable characters with distinct personalities, dreams, and flaws. Realistic characters make the emotional connection more genuine and compelling.
- *Meaningful Encounters*: Stage meaningful

and impactful initial encounters that leave a lasting impression on the characters. Whether it's a chance meeting or a shared interest, these moments set the foundation for their connection.
- *Shared Values and Goals*: Establish shared values and goals between the protagonists, creating a sense of alignment and understanding. This common ground strengthens the emotional bond they share.
- *Emotional Vulnerability*: Allow the characters to display vulnerability and share their fears, hopes, and dreams. Vulnerability fosters empathy and draws readers closer to the characters' emotional journey.
- *Chemistry and Tension*: Develop palpable chemistry and tension between the characters, igniting sparks in their interactions. The push and pull of their emotions keep readers engaged and invested in their evolving relationship.
- *Emotional Intimacy*: Showcase emotional intimacy through deep conversations, meaningful glances, and understanding each other's unspoken thoughts. Emotional connection enhances the readers' investment in the characters' love story.
- *Shared Experiences*: Create shared experiences and challenges that the protagonists must face together. These trials strengthen their bond and demonstrate their ability to support each other.
- *Growth and Support*: Allow the characters to grow individually and together throughout the story. They should support each other's personal development, making their love story richer and more rewarding.
- *Overcoming Obstacles*: Introduce obstacles and conflicts that test the characters' bond. Watching them overcome challenges together

- *Moments of Tenderness*: Include tender and heartfelt moments that reveal the depth of the characters' feelings for each other. These intimate moments evoke emotions in readers, making them root for the characters' love to succeed.

The chemistry and emotional connection between the main characters form the heart of the story. By building authentic characters, creating meaningful encounters, and fostering emotional intimacy, you can cultivate a strong bond that captivates readers and keeps them invested in the protagonists' journey. Through shared experiences, growth, and moments of tenderness, the connection between the characters becomes palpable, evoking emotions and making the love story resonate deeply with the readers. A well-crafted emotional connection invites readers to root for the protagonists' love to flourish, making the romance novel a fulfilling and memorable reading experience.

Emotional Depth

Explore the emotional depth of the characters' feelings for each other. Delve into their vulnerabilities, fears, and desires, allowing readers to empathize with their struggles and joys. To create a captivating and compelling romance novel, it is essential to explore the emotional depth of the characters' feelings for each other. Delving into their vulnerabilities, fears, and desires allows readers to form a profound connection with the protagonists and empathize with their struggles and joys. Here's how to showcase emotional depth in your romance novel:

- *Inner Monologues*: Offer insight into the characters' thoughts and emotions through inner monologues. By revealing their innermost feelings, readers can understand the depth of their emotional journey. We will cover more of this later in the book.
- *Past Traumas*: Address the characters' past traumas or emotional wounds, which may influence their present interactions and ability to open up to each other emotionally.
- *Authentic Dialogue*: Craft authentic and emotionally charged dialogue that reflects the characters' feelings. Dialogue should be raw and honest, revealing their vulnerabilities and hopes. We will cover more of this, with examples, later in the book.
- *Show, Don't Tell*: Instead of simply telling readers about the characters' emotions, show them through their actions, reactions, and body language. This creates a more immersive experience. This is covered later in the book.
- *Shared Confidences*: Create moments of shared confidences between the characters, where they reveal their deepest fears and desires. These intimate conversations strengthen their emotional connection.
- *Emotional Arcs*: Develop emotional arcs for the characters throughout the story. Allow them to experience a range of emotions, including love, fear, joy, and sadness, as their relationship evolves.
- *Moments of Vulnerability*: Depict moments of vulnerability, where the characters let their guards down and show their true selves to each other. These moments deepen their emotional intimacy.
- *Conflict Resolution*: Explore how the characters

navigate conflicts and misunderstandings, showing their emotional growth and willingness to work through challenges together.
- *Symbolic Gestures*: Use symbolic gestures or significant acts of affection to convey the characters' profound feelings for each other. These gestures add depth to their emotional connection.
- *Revisiting the Past*: Revisit pivotal moments from the characters' pasts that have shaped their emotional landscape. This provides context for their current feelings and actions.
- *Sensory Descriptions*: Utilize sensory descriptions to evoke emotions in readers. Describing the characters' surroundings and how they perceive them can heighten the emotional impact of the scenes. We will have more of this later in the book.
- *Impact of Love*: Illustrate how love transforms the characters' lives and perspectives. Love should not be just a plot point; it should have a profound effect on their personal growth and happiness.

Incorporating emotional depth in a romance novel is the key to creating a compelling and immersive story. By exploring the characters' vulnerabilities, fears, and desires, readers can empathize with their struggles and joys, forging a deep emotional connection with the protagonists. Through inner monologues, authentic dialogue, and moments of vulnerability, the emotional journey of the characters becomes palpable and relatable. Emotional depth enriches the romance novel, making it a powerful and memorable reading experience that lingers in the hearts of the readers long after the final page.

Well-Developed Plot

A compelling plot is crucial to keep readers engaged. While the focus is on the romance, consider incorporating other elements such as personal growth, external challenges, and obstacles that the characters must overcome together. Here's how to craft a captivating plot your romance novel:

- *Personal Growth*: Allow the characters to undergo personal growth and transformation throughout the story. As they navigate the relationship, they should learn more about themselves, confront their insecurities, and evolve as individuals.
- *External Challenges*: Introduce external challenges that test the strength of the protagonists' bond. These challenges can come from various sources such as family, society, or professional life, adding complexity to the romance.
- *Past Baggage*: Explore how the characters' past experiences and baggage influence their present actions and choices. Addressing unresolved issues from the past adds depth to the characters and their journey.
- *Shared Goals and Dreams*: Create shared goals and dreams for the characters to pursue together. This fosters a sense of teamwork and unity, making their romance feel like a partnership.
- *Subplots*: Integrate meaningful subplots that complement the central romance. Subplots can explore other relationships, friendships, or individual aspirations, enriching the overall

narrative.
- *Internal Conflicts*: Develop internal conflicts within the characters, such as conflicting desires or doubts about the relationship. These internal struggles add layers of emotional depth to the story.
- *Emotional Impact of Love*: Highlight how the characters' love for each other affects their choices and actions. Love should be a driving force behind their decisions, leading to joyful and challenging moments.
- *Climactic Moments*: Build tension and suspense throughout the story, leading to climactic moments that test the characters' commitment to each other and their emotional growth.
- *Themes of Resilience and Perseverance*: Explore themes of resilience and perseverance as the characters face obstacles and challenges. Their determination to overcome these hurdles strengthens their bond.
- *Symbolic Motifs*: Use symbolic motifs or recurring themes to tie different aspects of the plot together. This adds a layer of richness and symbolism to the story.
- *Character Arcs*: Ensure that the characters have well-defined arcs, with a clear beginning, middle, and end. Their arcs should intertwine with the progression of the romance.

A well-developed plot is the foundation of a compelling romance novel. By incorporating personal growth, external challenges, and obstacles that the characters overcome together, the story becomes multidimensional and engaging. As the protagonists face internal conflicts, pursue shared goals, and grow individually and as a couple, their journey becomes relatable and emotionally resonant for readers. A richly developed plot enhances the central romance, making the love story not only heartwarming, but also a captivating exploration of human emotions and relationships.

Conflict and Tension

Create tension and conflict that challenges the characters' relationship. This could be internal conflicts such as self-doubt or external challenges like societal prejudices or family expectations. To create a compelling and emotionally charged romance novel, introducing conflict and tension is essential. These challenges put the characters' relationship to the test, making their love story more dynamic and engaging. By incorporating both internal conflicts, such as self-doubt, and external challenges like societal prejudices or family expectations, the romance becomes a journey of growth and resilience. Here's how to create conflict and tension in your romance novel:

- *Internal Conflicts*: a. Self-Doubt: Develop internal struggles where characters doubt their worthiness of love or fear being vulnerable in a relationship. B. Fear of Rejection: Explore the characters' fear of rejection, leading them to hesitate in expressing their true feelings. C. Past Trauma: Address past traumas that impact their ability to fully open up to each other emotionally.
- *External Challenges*: a. Societal Prejudices: Introduce societal prejudices and homophobia that create obstacles for the characters, making them question the viability of their relationship. B. Family

Expectations: Depict conflicts arising from family expectations or disapproval of the characters' relationship, forcing them to choose between love and family ties. C. Workplace or Social Pressures: Explore how workplace or social pressures affect the characters' romance, potentially straining their bond.

- *Miscommunication*: Allow misunderstandings and miscommunication to arise, leading to conflicts and temporary estrangement. Resolving these issues strengthens their communication and emotional connection.
- *Rivalry or Love Triangle*: Consider introducing a rival or a love triangle that challenges the characters' commitment to each other, sparking jealousy and emotional turmoil.
- *External Threats*: Develop external threats that put the characters in dangerous or difficult situations, requiring them to support and protect each other.
- *Personal Growth*: Conflict and tension should lead to personal growth for the characters. Each challenge they face becomes an opportunity for introspection and emotional development.
- *Gradual Resolution*: Allow conflicts to be gradually resolved, showcasing the characters' ability to confront their issues and work together to overcome obstacles.
- *Compromises and Sacrifices*: Examine how the characters are willing to make compromises and sacrifices for the sake of their relationship, demonstrating the depth of their love.
- *Moments of Vulnerability*: Explore

vulnerable moments where characters must confront their deepest fears and insecurities, reinforcing their emotional bond.
- *Emotional Impact*: Highlight the emotional impact of conflicts on the characters, revealing their resilience and determination to fight for their love.

Conflict and tension are vital elements in a romance novel, as they challenge the characters' relationship and foster growth. By weaving internal conflicts, external challenges, miscommunication, and emotional turmoil, the story becomes a riveting journey of love, resilience, and personal transformation. Conflict serves to test the strength of the characters' bond, making their love story more compelling and relatable. In overcoming these obstacles, the characters emerge stronger and more deeply connected, creating a satisfying and heartfelt romance that resonates with readers.

Empowering Character Arcs

Characters should experience growth and transformation throughout the story. Show how their relationship empowers them to embrace their true selves and overcome obstacles. Empowering character arcs play a significant role in driving the narrative forward. Here's how to craft empowering character arcs in a romance novel:

- *Embracing Authenticity*: Allow the characters to discover and embrace their true selves throughout the story. Their relationship should create a safe space for them to be honest about their feelings and desires, leading to personal growth.

- *Breaking Self-Imposed Barriers*: Characters may have self-imposed barriers or limiting beliefs that hinder their happiness. Through their relationship, they learn to break free from these constraints and embrace their full potential.
- *Building Self-Confidence*: As the characters experience love and support from their partner, their self-confidence should grow. This newfound confidence enables them to face challenges with resilience.
- *Facing Fears*: The relationship should encourage the characters to confront their fears and insecurities. Together, they find strength to overcome these challenges, propelling their growth.
- *Supporting Individual Aspirations*: Show how the protagonists support each other's dreams and aspirations. Their relationship becomes a source of motivation and encouragement to pursue personal goals.
- *Empowering Each Other*: Illustrate how the characters empower each other to be the best versions of themselves. They inspire growth and self-discovery in each other.
- *Learning from Past Mistakes*: Through the relationship, characters may learn from past mistakes and take steps toward personal healing and growth.
- *Standing Up Against Adversity*: As the characters face external challenges, their relationship empowers them to stand up against adversity united. Together, they become stronger in the face of opposition.
- *Finding Inner Strength*: The love they share helps the characters tap into their inner strength and resilience, enabling them to navigate life's difficulties.
- *Emphasizing Equality*: Ensure that the

relationship is built on equality and mutual respect. Empowering character arcs involve both partners growing together as equals.
- *Defining Their Own Happiness*: The characters should learn to define their own happiness and not be limited by societal norms or expectations.

Empowering character arcs are essential in a romance novel as they contribute to the emotional depth and growth of the protagonists. Through their relationship, the characters should find the strength to embrace their true selves, face fears, and overcome obstacles together. As they support each other's individual aspirations and stand united against adversity, their love becomes a transformative force in their lives. By highlighting personal growth and the empowerment of the characters, the romance novel becomes a powerful and uplifting journey of love, self-discovery, and resilience.

Supportive Friendships and Community

Include supportive friendships and a sense of community for the characters. Show how they find acceptance and understanding within their social circles, adding depth and realism to the story. We don't live in a bubble, and it's normal to have others that aren't part of the community live in our stories, too. In a well-rounded romance novel, supportive friendships and a sense of community play a crucial role in enhancing the story's depth and realism. These elements not only provide the characters with a strong support system, but also contribute to their personal growth and the authenticity of their experiences. By showcasing acceptance and understanding within their social circles, the protagonists' love journey becomes more relatable and emotionally resonant. Here's how to incorporate supportive friendships and a sense of community in your romance novel:

- *Diverse Friendships:* Create a diverse cast of friends for the characters, representing various backgrounds, personalities, and perspectives. These friendships should reflect the richness and complexity of real-life social circles.
- *Unconditional Support:* Portray the friends as a source of unconditional support for the main characters. They are there through thick and thin, offering advice, encouragement, and a listening ear when needed.
- *Celebrating Individuality:* Emphasize how the friends celebrate the characters' individuality, including their LGBTQ+ identity. Their acceptance adds to the sense of belonging and reinforces the importance of embracing one's true self.
- *Shared Experiences:* Showcase shared experiences and traditions among the group of friends, creating a tight-knit sense of community. These shared moments strengthen their bond and create lasting memories.
- *Conflict Resolution:* Friends can play a role in helping the characters navigate conflicts in their relationships. They offer guidance and support, fostering communication and understanding.
- *Allies and Advocates:* Some friends may actively serve as allies and advocates for LGBTQ+ rights and representation, demonstrating their commitment to inclusivity and acceptance.
- *Safe Spaces:* Establish safe spaces where the characters can be themselves without fear of judgment. These spaces can be physical

locations, like LGBTQ+ venues, or virtual spaces, such as online support groups.
- *Shared Values:* Demonstrate that the characters' friendships are founded on shared values and a mutual understanding of each other's journeys.
- *Emotional Anchors:* Friends can act as emotional anchors for the characters during challenging times, providing stability and reassurance.
- *Comic Relief:* Incorporate moments of humor and lightheartedness through the characters' interactions with their friends, adding balance to the story.
- *Gradual Acceptance:* Explore how friends may take time to process and accept the characters' relationships, showcasing the complexities of human interactions.

Supportive friendships and a sense of community add depth and realism to a romance novel. By presenting diverse, accepting, and understanding social circles, the story becomes more relatable to readers. These supportive friendships serve as a source of encouragement, comfort, and celebration, enriching the main characters' love journey. As the protagonists find acceptance within their social circles, the romance novel becomes a celebration of love, friendship, and the power of genuine connections. Including these elements not only enhances the narrative, but also reinforces positive representations of LGBTQ+ relationships and experiences.

Sensual and Emotional Intimacy

Depict the physical and emotional aspects of intimacy between the characters. Striking a balance between emotional connection and sensual moments adds depth and authenticity to their love story. Here's how to skillfully incorporate sensual and emotional intimacy in your romance novel:

- *Emotional Bond:* Before delving into sensual intimacy, establish a strong emotional bond between the characters. Their connection should be rooted in mutual understanding, trust, and genuine affection.
- *Meaningful Conversations:* Use meaningful conversations to build emotional intimacy. Through these exchanges, the characters open up to each other, sharing their hopes, fears, and dreams.
- *Gestures of Affection:* Incorporate tender gestures of affection, such as hand-holding, hugging, or forehead kisses, to showcase the depth of the emotional connection between the characters.
- *Inner Thoughts and Feelings:* Reveal the characters' inner thoughts and feelings during intimate moments. This allows readers to empathize with their emotions and understand the significance of these experiences.
- *Vulnerability:* Show the characters being vulnerable with each other emotionally. Emotional vulnerability deepens their bond and creates a strong sense of intimacy.
- *Sensual Tension:* Gradually build sensual tension between the characters through meaningful glances, teasing banter, and moments of proximity.
- *Communication and Consent:* Prioritize communication and consent during intimate scenes. Characters should openly discuss their boundaries and desires, ensuring a safe and

respectful experience.
- *Unique Chemistry:* Highlight the characters' unique chemistry and how it intensifies the emotional and physical aspects of their relationship.
- *Sensory Descriptions:* Use sensory descriptions to evoke the characters' physical and emotional experiences. Describe sensations, emotions, and reactions to make the scenes more immersive.
- *Intimate Moments:* Craft intimate moments that reflect the characters' emotional connection. These scenes should be more than just physical acts; they should deepen their emotional bond.
- *Aftercare:* Depict aftercare as an essential part of intimate moments. Show the characters caring for each other's emotional well-being after experiencing intimacy.
- *Growth and Trust:* Illustrate how the characters' intimate moments contribute to their personal growth and the strengthening of trust in their relationship.

Balancing sensual and emotional intimacy is pivotal to creating a well-rounded romance novel. By building a strong emotional connection between the characters, readers become emotionally invested in their love story. Sensual moments should be meaningful, reflective of the characters' emotional bond, and depicted with care, communication, and consent. By authentically portraying both aspects of intimacy, the romance novel becomes a compelling exploration of love, trust, and vulnerability. The nuanced depiction of sensual and emotional intimacy adds depth and authenticity to the characters' relationship, making the story resonate with readers on a profound level.

Inclusivity and Intersectionality

Acknowledge the diversity within the lesbian community by featuring characters from various backgrounds and identities. Embrace intersectionality to explore the unique experiences of characters who belong to multiple marginalized communities. Here's how to incorporate inclusivity and intersectionality in your romance novel:

- *Diverse Backgrounds:* Introduce lesbian characters from different cultural, ethnic, and socioeconomic backgrounds. Acknowledge that LGBTQ+ individuals come from various walks of life.
- *Ethnic and Racial Diversity:* Ensure representation of characters from diverse racial and ethnic backgrounds. Celebrate the richness of different cultures within the lesbian community.
- *Religious and Spiritual Identities:* Portray characters with various religious or spiritual identities. Address how their beliefs intersect with their sexual orientation and the challenges they may face.
- *Gender Identity and Expression:* Explore gender diversity within the lesbian community by including characters with different gender identities and expressions. Embrace nonbinary, genderqueer, or genderfluid representations.
- *Disabled and Neurodiverse Characters:* Incorporate characters with disabilities or who are neurodiverse. Sensitively portray their experiences and challenges with authenticity and respect.
- *Socioeconomic Status:* Highlight characters from different socioeconomic backgrounds. Address how their economic circumstances may impact their experiences and access to resources.

- *Body Positivity:* Promote body positivity by depicting characters with diverse body types and challenging harmful beauty standards.
- *LGBTQ+ Allies:* Include supportive LGBTQ+ allies in the story. Allies play an important role in creating an inclusive and accepting environment for LGBTQ+ individuals.
- *Language and Terminology:* Use inclusive and up-to-date language and terminology when portraying characters' identities and experiences.
- *Intersectional Challenges:* Explore the intersectional challenges faced by characters who belong to multiple marginalized communities. Address how their identities may intersect and influence their experiences.
- *Community Support:* Showcase the importance of community support and representation. Characters may find strength and understanding through LGBTQ+ spaces and organizations.
- *Sensitivity and Authenticity:* Research and approach each character's identity with sensitivity and authenticity. Avoid stereotypes and tokenism, ensuring that their experiences are genuine and relatable.

Inclusivity and intersectionality are vital in portraying the lesbian community authentically. By featuring characters from diverse backgrounds, identities, and experiences, the romance novel becomes a celebration of the richness and complexity within the LGBTQ+ community. Embracing intersectionality allows for an exploration of unique challenges faced by characters who belong to multiple marginalized communities. Inclusive representation not only creates a more compelling and relatable narrative, but also sends a powerful message of acceptance, understanding, and empowerment to all readers.

A Satisfying Conclusion

Craft a satisfying and hopeful ending for the characters' romance. Readers should feel a sense of fulfillment and closure, knowing that the love story has reached a positive resolution. The conclusion should reflect the growth of the characters, the strength of their love, and the resolution of any conflicts or obstacles they faced. Here are ways to create a hopeful and satisfying ending:

- *Resolved Conflicts:* Ensure that any conflicts or challenges the characters faced throughout the story are resolved. This could include overcoming external obstacles, misunderstandings, or personal insecurities.
- *Emotional Catharsis:* Offer a moment of emotional catharsis, where the characters express their true feelings for each other, leading to a deepening of their emotional bond.
- *Declarations of Love:* Allow the characters to openly declare their love for each other, reinforcing the strength of their emotional connection.
- *Personal Growth:* Show how the characters have grown individually and together throughout the story, becoming stronger and more self-assured.
- *Shared Vision:* Illustrate how the characters now share a vision of their future together, filled with hope and possibility.
- *Promising Future:* Provide a glimpse of the characters' promising future, where they are

united and supportive of each other's dreams and aspirations.
- *Symbolic Gestures:* Consider incorporating symbolic gestures or callbacks to earlier moments in the story, signifying the depth of their love and growth.
- *Community Support:* Highlight the support of their friends and community, reinforcing the idea that love can flourish within a supportive and accepting environment.
- *A Moment of Triumph:* Create a moment of triumph for the characters, showcasing their ability to overcome challenges and find happiness in their love.
- *A Sense of Fulfillment:* Leave readers with a feeling of satisfaction and contentment, knowing that the characters have found their happily ever after.
- *Hopeful and Uplifting:* End the story on a hopeful and uplifting note, inspiring readers with the message that love can conquer all.
- *Epilogue (Optional):* Consider including an epilogue that offers a glimpse of the characters' lives sometime in the future, further reinforcing the positivity of their love story.

Crafting a satisfying and hopeful ending for the characters' romance is the key to leaving readers with a lasting impression. By resolving conflicts, showcasing personal growth, and reinforcing the strength of their emotional connection, the conclusion becomes a moment of fulfillment and closure. The characters' triumph over challenges and their promising future together inspires readers with hope and a sense of joy. Ultimately, a well-crafted conclusion leaves readers with the belief that love can overcome obstacles, and the romance novel becomes a gratifying and uplifting reading experience.

Sensitivity and Respect

Approach sensitive topics with care and respect, acknowledging the weight and impact they may have on readers. Be mindful of the responsibility to represent LGBTQ+ experiences authentically and ethically. It is crucial to approach sensitive topics with utmost care and respect. Here are a few ways to handle sensitive topics with care:

- *Thorough Research*: Conduct thorough research on the sensitive topics you plan to address in your novel. Understand the experiences, struggles, and nuances of LGBTQ+ individuals to portray them accurately.
- *Consultation and Sensitivity Readers*: Seek input and guidance from members of the LGBTQ+ community or sensitivity readers who can provide valuable insights. Their feedback helps ensure authentic representation and avoids harmful stereotypes.
- *Avoid Exploitation*: Resist using sensitive topics for shock value or mere plot devices. Approach them with a genuine intention to raise awareness and foster empathy.
- *Trigger Warnings*: Provide trigger warnings when the content may be distressing for some readers. This allows them to make informed decisions about their reading experience.
- *Respectful Language*: Use respectful and inclusive language when discussing sensitive topics. Be mindful of outdated or offensive terms and adopt current, affirming terminology.

- *Avoiding the Trauma Trope*: Avoid using trauma as a mere plot device. If you address traumatic experiences, do so with sensitivity and compassion, focusing on the characters' resilience and healing.
- *Empowerment and Agency*: Portray LGBTQ+ characters with agency and empowerment. Avoid victimizing them solely based on their sexual orientation or gender identity.
- *Diverse Representation*: Include diverse LGBTQ+ characters, reflecting different identities, backgrounds, and experiences within the community.
- *Sensible Storylines*: Be cautious with sensitive storylines, ensuring they contribute to the characters' growth and the overall narrative.
- *Realistic Reactions*: Portray realistic reactions from characters and society regarding sensitive topics. Address positive and negative responses, reflecting the complexity of real-life experiences.
- *Encourage Open Conversations*: Use your novel as a means to encourage open conversations about LGBTQ+ issues and experiences, fostering understanding and empathy among readers.
- *Author's Note*: Consider including an author's note at the beginning or end of the novel, expressing your commitment to respectful representation and acknowledging the significance of the topics discussed.

Handling sensitive topics with respect is essential in crafting a responsible and impactful romance novel. By conducting thorough research, seeking consultation, and using respectful language, authors can create authentic and ethical portrayals of LGBTQ+

experiences. A commitment to inclusive representation fosters empathy and understanding among readers, making the romance novel a space of acceptance and empowerment. Through thoughtful storytelling, sensitivity, and respect, we contribute to positive representations of LGBTQ+ individuals and their stories, making a meaningful impact on the literary landscape.

Lesbian romance novels are enriched by authentic representation, emotional depth, compelling plots, and a focus on empowering characters and relationships. By incorporating these key elements, you can create a captivating and meaningful story that resonates with readers, providing a platform for celebrating love and diverse identities within the lesbian community.

Introduction to Lesbian Romance – Exploring Subgenres within Lesbian Romance

Lesbian romance, like any other literary genre, encompasses various subgenres that offer unique themes, settings, and tones. These subgenres cater to different reader preferences and provide a diverse array of stories within the larger genre of lesbian romance. Here are some of the popular subgenres within lesbian romance:

- *Contemporary Romance*: This subgenre is set in modern times and focuses on romantic relationships between women in the present-day world. It explores everyday challenges, coming-of-age stories, workplace romances, and the complexities of love in contemporary settings.
- *Historical Romance*: Historical lesbian romance takes readers back in time, often featuring love stories set in various historical periods. These stories not only delve into the romantic connections, but also examine the social and cultural challenges faced by lesbian characters in the past.
- *Fantasy and Paranormal Romance*: This subgenre combines romance with elements of fantasy, magic, and the supernatural. It may feature lesbian characters with special abilities, mythical creatures, or worlds beyond reality, offering a unique and imaginative twist to

traditional romance.
- *Mystery and Thriller Romance*: Myster and thriller romance combines elements of suspense, crime, and romance. Readers are drawn into the romantic journey of the main characters, while also trying to unravel mysteries or facing dangerous situations.
- *Young Adult (YA) Romance*: YA lesbian romance is aimed at teenage readers and focuses on the challenges of love and self-discovery during adolescence. These stories often address coming-out experiences, first loves, and the emotional turbulence of youth.
- *Romantic Comedy Romance*: This subgenre infuses humor and lightheartedness into the romantic plot. It explores the ups and downs of love with comedic elements, providing readers with heartwarming and humorous moments.
- *Erotica Romance*: Erotica lesbian romance emphasizes sensuality and intimacy between women. While romance remains a core element, the focus is on exploring the characters' physical connections and desires in a more explicit manner.
- *Inspirational Romance*: Inspirational lesbian romance centers on characters finding love while overcoming personal challenges or life obstacles. These stories often highlight personal growth, resilience, and the power of love to heal and transform.
- *Second Chance Romance*: This subgenre features characters who reconnect after a significant period of time apart. It explores the themes of forgiveness, redemption, and the possibility of finding love again.
- *Holiday and Seasonal Romance*: Holiday-themed lesbian romance takes place during specific holidays or seasons, adding a festive

atmosphere to the love story. These stories celebrate love amid the backdrop of special occasions and traditions.

The diverse subgenres within romance provide readers with a wide range of storytelling experiences, from contemporary love stories to historical adventures, from heartwarming comedies to thrilling mysteries. Each subgenre offers a unique lens through which to explore the complexities of lesbian relationships and personal journeys. Whether readers prefer a touch of magic, historical authenticity, or heartwarming contemporaries, there is a romance subgenre to suit every literary taste.

Developing Compelling Characters – Building Believable Lesbian Protagonists and Love Interests

Creating believable and authentic lesbian protagonists and love interests is essential to crafting a compelling lesbian romance novel. These characters are at the heart of the story, and their development plays a crucial role in engaging readers and fostering emotional connections. In creating a compelling romance novel, it is essential to develop well-rounded and multifaceted personalities for the protagonist and love interest. One-dimensional characters can feel unrealistic and less relatable, whereas diverse interests, passions, strengths, weaknesses, and unique backstories add depth and authenticity to the narrative. Here's how to craft dynamic characters:

- *Unique Backstories*: Provide each character with a unique and compelling backstory that shapes their personality and motivations. These backgrounds can influence their desires, fears, and values.
- *Multifaceted Personalities*: Develop well-rounded and multifaceted personalities for the protagonist and love interest. Avoid one-dimensional characters by giving them diverse interests, passions, strengths, weaknesses, and unique backstories.
- *Diverse Interests and Passions*: Give characters a range of interests and passions. Whether it's a hobby, career, or creative

pursuit, these diverse aspects of their lives add complexity to their personalities.
- *Strengths and Weaknesses*: Balance characters' strengths with weaknesses. No one is perfect, and acknowledging their flaws makes them more relatable and human.
- *Complex Emotions*: Explore a wide range of emotions within each character. Allow them to experience joy, fear, anger, and vulnerability, showcasing their emotional depth.
- *Moral Ambiguity*: Challenge characters with moral dilemmas, blurring the lines between right and wrong. This complexity adds realism to their decision-making process.
- *Growth and Development*: Create opportunities for characters to grow and develop throughout the story. Their experiences should lead to personal growth and transformative moments.
- *Relationships Beyond Romance*: Develop meaningful relationships for the characters beyond their romantic connection. Friends, family, or mentors contribute to their personal development.
- *Internal Conflicts*: Introduce internal conflicts that characters grapple with, such as self-doubt, insecurities, or conflicting desires. These conflicts add layers to their personalities.
- *Individual Agency*: Show characters exercising their agency and making decisions that shape the course of their lives. Avoid making them solely defined by their relationship.
- *Believable Dialogue*: Craft authentic and distinct dialogue for each character, reflecting their personalities and unique

voice. We cover this more in depth later in the book.
- *Realistic Reactions*: Portray characters reacting to situations in ways consistent with their personalities and backgrounds.
- *Growth and Learning*: Illustrate how characters learn from their experiences and interactions, changing and evolving over time.

Developing well-rounded and multifaceted personalities for characters is essential in creating an engaging romance novel. By giving them unique backstories, diverse interests, passions, strengths, weaknesses, and complex emotions, they become relatable and realistic. Through internal conflicts, growth, and meaningful relationships, characters evolve into dynamic individuals who resonate with readers. Crafting dynamic characters adds depth and authenticity to the romance, making the love story more compelling and immersive.

Individual Goals and Motivations

Give each character her own distinct goals, dreams, and motivations that drive her actions throughout the story. This adds depth to her personality and helps readers connect with her desires and aspirations. Giving each character her own distinct goals, dreams, and motivations is essential for creating well-rounded and relatable personalities. Here's how to develop distinct goals and motivations for the characters:

- *Personal Ambitions*: Explore each character's personal ambitions, whether they are career-

related, creative pursuits, or personal growth goals. These aspirations shape their identities and choices.
- *Dreams and Passions*: Identify the characters' dreams and passions, which can range from achieving a lifelong dream to pursuing a specific hobby or interest.
- *Overcoming Challenges*: Introduce obstacles that challenge the characters in achieving their goals. Their determination to overcome these challenges reveals their resilience and determination.
- *Conflicting Desires*: Showcase conflicting desires that the characters may grapple with, adding complexity to their decision-making process.
- *Aligning with Values*: Ensure that the characters' goals align with their core values and beliefs, deepening their authenticity.
- *Personal Growth*: Demonstrate how working toward their goals contributes to the characters' personal growth and development throughout the story.
- *Influence on Relationship*: Explore how each character's goals and motivations impact the development of their romantic relationship. Their individual journeys can enrich the overarching love story.
- *Interests Beyond Romance*: Give the characters interests and motivations beyond their romantic relationship, showing them as fully realized individuals with diverse passions.
- *Overarching Themes*: Tie the characters' goals and motivations to the overarching themes of the novel, reinforcing the central message and emotional impact.
- *Emotional Investment*: Illustrate the characters' emotional investment in their goals, making

their triumphs and setbacks more resonant with readers.
- *Inner Conflict*: Address inner conflicts that arise when pursuing their goals, highlighting the internal struggles they must overcome.
- *Authentic Resolutions*: Ensure that the characters' journeys toward their goals lead to authentic and satisfying resolutions, regardless of the outcome.

Developing individual goals, dreams, and motivations for each character elevates the romance novel, creating depth and relatability. By exploring personal ambitions, dreams, and passions, readers connect with the characters on a deeper level. Introducing challenges, conflicting desires, and opportunities for personal growth adds complexity to their personalities and emotional journeys. Balancing individual aspirations with the development of the romantic relationship makes the love story more enriching and authentic. Ultimately, crafting well-defined goals and motivations for characters enhances the narrative and fosters a strong emotional connection between readers and the story's protagonists.

Realistic Flaws and Vulnerabilities

Make your characters human by giving them realistic flaws and vulnerabilities. Nobody is perfect, and flaws add depth and authenticity to characters, making them more relatable and endearing to readers. Here are some examples to think about when developing characters with realistic flaws and vulnerabilities:

- *Internal Conflicts*: Introduce internal conflicts

within each character, such as self-doubt, insecurities, or past traumas. These struggles make them multidimensional and relatable.
- *Relatable Insecurities:* Give characters relatable insecurities that reflect common human fears, like fear of failure, rejection, or not being good enough.
- *Character Growth:* Ensure that the characters' flaws create opportunities for growth and self-discovery. Overcoming these imperfections can be a significant part of their emotional journey.
- *Making Mistakes:* Allow characters to make mistakes and face the consequences of their actions. This shows their fallibility and adds depth to their personalities.
- *Vulnerable Moments:* Create vulnerable moments for the characters, where they reveal their true selves, fears, and emotions. These moments foster empathy from readers.
- *Impact on Relationships:* Showcase how their flaws and vulnerabilities impact their relationships, adding complexity and realistic dynamics to the romance.
- *Balanced Attributes:* Balance their strengths with weaknesses, so they are not overshadowed by an overly idealized image.
- *Realistic Reactions:* Portray the characters' flaws in a way that elicits realistic reactions from others. Friends and love interests may support or challenge them, reflecting how real relationships unfold.
- *Self-Awareness:* Explore how characters grapple with their flaws and strive to better themselves. Some may display self-awareness and actively work on personal growth.
- *Overcoming Barriers:* Address how their flaws and vulnerabilities can act as barriers to achieving their goals, making their journeys

- *Character Arcs:* Allow characters' flaws and vulnerabilities to be an integral part of their character arcs, contributing to their development and transformation.
- *Acceptance and Growth:* Highlight moments of self-acceptance and growth, where characters learn to embrace their imperfections and find strength in vulnerability.

Realistic flaws and vulnerabilities are essential in making characters relatable and human. By exploring internal conflicts, insecurities, and the impact of their imperfections on relationships, characters become multidimensional and endearing to readers. Balancing strengths with weaknesses and allowing characters to make mistakes fosters empathy and understanding. As they grow and overcome their flaws, the romance novel becomes a poignant and relatable exploration of human experiences. Embracing the imperfect aspects of characters adds depth and authenticity to the narrative, leaving readers with a lasting emotional connection to the story and its protagonists.

Understanding Their Sexual Identity

When building lesbian characters, explore their journey of understanding and accepting their sexual identity. Show how their self-discovery and acceptance have shaped their experiences and emotions, making them more authentic and relatable. This exploration adds depth and authenticity to the characters. Here's how to portray the process of self-discovery and acceptance for lesbian characters:

- *Introspection:* Allow the characters to engage in introspection and self-questioning as they begin to recognize their attraction to the same gender. This internal exploration is the first step in understanding their sexual identity.
- *Uncertainty and Confusion:* Address the uncertainties and confusion that may accompany the characters' realization of their same-gender attraction. This phase can be emotionally tumultuous and challenging to navigate.
- *Seeking Guidance:* Show how characters may seek guidance and support from trusted friends, family members, or LGBTQ+ communities. These interactions can be pivotal in their journey of self-discovery.
- *Emotional Struggles:* Portray the emotional struggles characters face as they come to terms with their sexual identity. These struggles can include fear of rejection, internalized homophobia, or concerns about societal acceptance.
- *Finding Representation:* Highlight the importance of representation and how discovering other LGBTQ+ individuals can help the characters feel less isolated and more understood.
- *Exploring Relationships:* Explore how characters navigate romantic relationships as they come to understand their sexual identity. These relationships can provide moments of clarity and growth.
- *Acceptance and Self-Love:* Illustrate the process of self-acceptance and self-love as characters embrace their lesbian identity. This acceptance is a transformative and empowering moment in their journey.
- *Empowerment through Connection:* Show how

connections with other LGBTQ+ individuals empower the characters to be proud of their identity and stand up against discrimination.
- *Overcoming Internal Struggles:* Address the internal struggles characters face during their acceptance journey. This may include letting go of internalized shame and embracing their authentic selves.
- *Supportive Relationships:* Highlight the significance of supportive relationships in helping characters embrace their sexual identity. These relationships can offer emotional support and understanding.
- *Building Resilience:* Show how the characters' journey of self-discovery and acceptance contributes to their resilience and strength.
- *Advocacy and Empathy:* Portray characters becoming advocates for LGBTQ+ rights and expressing empathy for others on similar journeys, fostering a sense of community.

Remember exploring the journey of understanding and accepting their sexual identity is a fundamental aspect of crafting authentic and relatable characters. By delving into introspection, uncertainty, emotional struggles, and the transformative moments of self-acceptance, the characters become multidimensional and compelling. The portrayal of their experiences adds depth and authenticity to the romance novel, making it a poignant exploration of the complexities of sexual identity. As readers witness the characters' journey toward self-discovery and acceptance, they connect with the emotional depth of the story and its protagonists, leaving a lasting impact on their hearts and minds.

Developing Chemistry

Establish a strong emotional and physical chemistry between the protagonist and love interest. Their interactions should be genuine and evocative, creating a palpable connection that tugs at the heartstrings of readers. Here are some things to consider in building irresistible chemistry:

- *Authentic Dialogue:* Craft authentic and engaging dialogue that reflects the characters' personalities and emotions. Conversations should flow naturally, revealing their thoughts and feelings.
- *Meaningful Glances:* Use meaningful glances and body language to convey unspoken emotions and create a sense of intimacy between the characters.
- *Shared Vulnerabilities:* Allow the characters to share their vulnerabilities with each other, fostering a sense of trust and emotional intimacy.
- *Emotional Resonance:* Create situations that evoke strong emotions in the characters, bringing them closer together and deepening their connection.
- *Shared Interests:* Give the characters shared interests or hobbies that provide opportunities for bonding and memorable interactions.
- *Playful Banter:* Incorporate playful banter and teasing exchanges that showcase their chemistry and affection for each other.
- *Physical Touch:* Use subtle physical touches, such as a gentle touch on the arm or a lingering hand-hold, to heighten the sense of intimacy between the characters.
- *Intimate Moments:* Craft intimate moments

that reveal the characters' emotional connection and the depth of their feelings for each other.
- *Understanding and Empathy:* Show the characters demonstrating understanding and empathy for each other's experiences, creating a sense of emotional resonance.
- *Heightened Tension:* Build tension and anticipation between the characters, allowing their chemistry to simmer and grow throughout the story.
- *Shared Experiences:* Create opportunities for the characters to share meaningful experiences or face challenges together, forging a stronger bond.
- *Emotional Conflicts:* Introduce emotional conflicts that challenge the characters' connection, making their chemistry even more compelling as they work through the issues.

Developing a strong emotional and physical chemistry between the protagonist and love interest is essential to crafting an irresistible romance. By using authentic dialogue, meaningful glances, and shared vulnerabilities, readers become invested in the characters' journey. The emotional resonance, playful banter, and intimate moments add depth and authenticity to their connection. As tension builds and emotional conflicts arise, the chemistry between the characters becomes all the more captivating. Ultimately, the palpable connection draws readers into the romance novel, making their hearts race and emotions soar as they experience the irresistible chemistry between the protagonists.

Respectful Representation

Respectfully represent lesbian relationships, avoiding stereotypes and clichés. Portraying the characters' love story with the same depth, authenticity, and respect as any other romantic relationship is essential. This approach emphasizes mutual respect, consent, and a profound emotional connection between the characters. Here are a few options to achieve respectful representation:

- *Diverse Personalities*: Create diverse and multidimensional lesbian characters, avoiding monolithic portrayals. Represent individuals with varying backgrounds, interests, and personalities.
- *Avoiding Stereotypes*: Steer clear of harmful stereotypes or generalizations about lesbian individuals. Instead, focus on the uniqueness and complexity of each character.
- *Genuine Emotions*: Portray the characters' emotions authentically, ensuring their feelings are portrayed with sincerity and depth.
- *Respectful Dialogue*: Craft respectful and inclusive dialogue that reflects the characters' mutual respect and understanding for each other.
- *Equal Partnership*: Illustrate the relationship as an equal partnership, where both characters contribute to the love story's development and growth.
- *Consent and Communication*: Emphasize the importance of consent and open communication in the characters' interactions, both emotionally and physically.
- *Emotional Intimacy*: Highlight the emotional intimacy and connection between the characters, as it is a vital aspect of any romantic

relationship.
- *Realistic Struggles*: Address realistic challenges faced by lesbian couples, without overly dramatizing or stereotyping these issues.
- *Healthy Conflict Resolution*: Demonstrate healthy conflict resolution, where the characters work through their differences with respect and empathy.
- *Supportive Relationships*: Include supportive friendships and relationships within the characters' social circles, reflecting a sense of community and acceptance.
- *Authentic Love Story*: Treat the love story between the lesbian characters as authentic and meaningful, without sensationalizing or fetishizing their relationship.
- *Celebrating Love*: Celebrate the love shared between the characters, emphasizing that love is a universal and beautiful emotion regardless of gender or sexual orientation.

Respectful representation of lesbian relationships is crucial in crafting an inclusive and authentic romance novel. By avoiding stereotypes and clichés and focusing on genuine emotions, consent, and mutual respect, the love story becomes relatable and endearing to readers. Emphasizing emotional intimacy, equal partnership, and healthy communication reinforces the idea that love knows no boundaries, and lesbian relationships are as valid and meaningful as any other romantic connection. By portraying the characters' love story with respect and authenticity, the romance novel becomes a celebration of love, fostering understanding, empathy, and acceptance among all readers.

Realistic Dialogue

Craft natural and believable dialogue for your characters. Pay attention to their unique voices, speech patterns, and expressions, ensuring that their interactions feel genuine and reflective of their personalities. Here's how to develop realistic dialogue:

- *Character Voice*: Develop distinct voices for each character, reflecting their personality, background, and upbringing. Their speech should be consistent with their traits and motivations.
- *Tone and Emotion*: Convey the characters' emotions through their dialogue, using appropriate tones and expressions to match their feelings in various situations.
- *Avoiding Monologues*: Keep the dialogue engaging by avoiding overly long monologues. Instead, incorporate back-and-forth exchanges to create a dynamic conversation.
- *Natural Flow*: Ensure that the dialogue flows naturally, replicating how people talk in real-life conversations. Avoid overly formal or stilted language unless it suits a particular character. We talk about this later in the book and give a few examples.
- *Unfinished Sentences*: Include occasional unfinished sentences or interruptions to mimic the interruptions and overlaps that occur in natural conversations.
- *Subtle Subtext*: Incorporate subtext in the dialogue, allowing characters to communicate underlying emotions or hidden meanings without explicitly stating them. We talk about this later in the book.
- *Age and Generation*: Consider the characters' ages and generations when crafting their

dialogue. Younger characters might use more contemporary language and slang, while older characters might have more formal speech patterns.
- *Regional Dialects*: Use regional dialects sparingly and with care. Excessive use of dialects may become distracting, but subtle hints can add depth to a character's background.
- *Character Development*: Allow the characters' dialogue to evolve as they undergo personal growth or experience significant events. Their speech may change based on their experiences.
- *Context and Setting*: Adapt the dialogue to fit the story's context and setting. Characters' speech might differ depending on whether they are at home, work, or in a social setting.
- *Show, Don't Tell*: Use dialogue to show the characters' personalities, beliefs, and motivations rather than explicitly telling the reader about them. We talk about this later in the book and give a few examples.
- *Read Aloud*: Read the dialogue aloud to ensure its authenticity and natural flow. This practice helps identify any awkward phrasing or dialogue that doesn't sound true to the characters.

Realistic dialogue brings characters to life, making them relatable and engaging for readers. By crafting distinct voices, paying attention to emotions, and avoiding monologues, the dialogue becomes natural and believable. Showcasing character development through speech patterns, regional dialects, and appropriate context enhances the authenticity of the narrative. As readers immerse themselves in genuine and dynamic conversations, they form deeper connections with the characters and the story as a whole. Realistic dialogue is a powerful tool in breathing life into characters and making the romance novel a captivating and relatable experience.

Incorporating Diversity

Explore diverse identities and backgrounds for your characters. Represent characters from different ethnicities, cultures, and walks of life to reflect the richness and complexity of real-world experiences. Here's how to incorporate diversity into your characters:

- *Diverse Ethnicities*: Create characters from various ethnic backgrounds, reflecting the diverse tapestry of cultures and traditions in the real world.
- *Cultural Nuances*: Pay attention to cultural nuances and practices unique to each character's heritage. This adds depth to their identity and authenticity to the story.
- *Avoiding Stereotypes*: Steer clear of harmful stereotypes and generalizations associated with different ethnicities or cultures. Instead, focus on portraying well-rounded individuals with diverse personalities.
- *Intersectionality*: Embrace intersectionality by exploring characters who belong to multiple marginalized communities. This can lead to unique and profound storytelling opportunities.
- *Representing Different Walks of Life*: Include characters from different walks of life, such as various socioeconomic backgrounds, professions, or life experiences. This broadens the scope of the narrative.
- *Language and Speech*: Incorporate linguistic

- *Family and Traditions*: Explore the impact of family dynamics and cultural traditions on the characters' lives and relationships, highlighting the significance of heritage.
- *Celebrating Differences*: Celebrate the characters' differences and use them to foster empathy and understanding among readers.
- *Mutual Respect and Learning*: Showcase how characters from diverse backgrounds learn from and respect each other's cultures, fostering meaningful connections.
- *Shared Values*: Emphasize shared values and emotions that transcend cultural or ethnic differences, highlighting the universal aspects of love and relationships.
- *Inclusive Relationships*: Portray inclusive relationships where characters from different backgrounds form meaningful and supportive connections.
- *Realistic Representation*: Conduct thorough research and consult with individuals from the represented communities to ensure authentic and respectful portrayal.

Incorporating diversity into characters enriches the romance novel, offering a more inclusive and relatable narrative. By representing characters from various ethnicities, cultures, and walks of life, the story reflects the vibrant and complex tapestry of real-world experiences. Avoiding stereotypes and embracing intersectionality allows for well-rounded and authentic portrayals. Celebrating differences, shared values, and inclusive relationships promotes understanding and empathy among readers. Thorough research and respectful representation ensure that the diverse identities and backgrounds are portrayed with integrity and accuracy. Ultimately, embracing diversity in characters fosters a sense of inclusivity and authenticity, making the romance novel a more enriching and immersive reading experience.

Addressing Internal and External Conflicts

Create compelling and realistic internal and external conflicts for the protagonist and love interest. These challenges should be integral to their character development and growth, making their journey toward love and self-discovery more engaging and emotionally resonant. Here's how to address internal and external conflicts effectively:

- *Internal Conflicts*: Explore the characters' inner struggles, such as fears, insecurities, or past traumas, that hinder their ability to open up to love and embrace vulnerability.
- *Emotional Baggage*: Address emotional baggage that affects the characters' relationships, delving into unresolved issues from their past that must be confronted and healed.
- *Self-Doubt and Insecurities*: Showcase self-doubt and insecurities that plague the protagonist and love interest, revealing their human vulnerability.
- *Conflicting Desires*: Introduce conflicting desires that challenge the characters' commitment to their goals and, at times, to each other.
- *Fear of Vulnerability*: Explore the fear of vulnerability and intimacy that might push the characters to maintain emotional distance from each other.

- *Family Expectations*: Examine how family expectations and societal pressures influence the characters' decisions and affect their relationship.
- *Communication Barriers*: Develop communication barriers that hinder the characters from expressing their true feelings, leading to misunderstandings and conflicts.
- *Past Heartbreaks*: Address past heartbreaks that may make the characters hesitant to enter into a new relationship, requiring them to confront and heal from these wounds.
- *External Obstacles*: Incorporate external obstacles that stand in the way of the characters' love story, such as opposition from others or circumstances beyond their control.
- *Pursuit of Dreams*: Show how pursuing individual dreams and aspirations can create tension in the relationship, testing their commitment and compatibility.
- *Reconciling Differences*: Demonstrate the characters' efforts to reconcile their differences and find common ground, fostering growth and understanding.
- *Personal Growth*: Use conflicts as opportunities for personal growth and development, allowing the characters to learn from their experiences and evolve.

Compelling internal and external conflicts drive the characters' development and shape their journey toward love and self-discovery in a romance novel. By exploring their internal struggles, emotional baggage, and fears of vulnerability, the characters become multidimensional and relatable. Addressing communication barriers, past heartbreaks, and external obstacles creates tension and depth in the narrative, keeping readers engaged in the protagonists' emotional journey. The conflicts should be intricately woven into the characters' growth, highlighting the transformative power of love and self-awareness. Ultimately, the resolution of these conflicts allows the characters to embrace vulnerability and find love, making the romance novel a powerful and emotionally resonant tale of growth and connection.

Showcasing Growth

Allow your characters to grow and evolve throughout the story. Demonstrate their personal growth, particularly in how their romantic relationship influences their development as individuals. In a captivating romance novel, allowing characters to grow and evolve is essential for creating a compelling narrative. Here's how to showcase growth in your characters:

- *Establishing a Starting Point*: Introduce the characters at the beginning of the story, highlighting their strengths, weaknesses, and personal struggles.
- *Reflecting on Past Choices*: As the characters embark on their romantic journey, incorporate moments where they reflect on past choices and experiences, showing a willingness to learn from their mistakes.
- *Overcoming Internal Conflicts*: Address the characters' internal conflicts and fears that might hinder the growth of their relationship. Show them working through these issues with maturity and self-awareness.
- *Supporting Each Other*: Illustrate how the characters support and encourage each other's

personal goals and dreams, demonstrating their investment in each other's growth.
- *Emotional Resilience*: Explore how their love and emotional connection make the characters more resilient in facing challenges and setbacks.
- *Challenging Perspectives*: Allow the romantic relationship to challenge the characters' perspectives and beliefs, prompting them to reevaluate their values and priorities.
- *Pursuing Personal Interests*: Encourage the characters to pursue personal interests and hobbies outside the relationship, showcasing their individuality and personal growth.
- *Communicating Effectively*: Show them learning to communicate openly and honestly, addressing conflicts with empathy and understanding.
- *Empowering Each Other*: Highlight moments where the characters empower each other to embrace their true selves, fostering personal growth and acceptance.
- *Learning from Mistakes*: Demonstrate how the characters learn from their mistakes and take responsibility for their actions, showcasing their maturity and growth.
- *Embracing Vulnerability*: As the relationship deepens, showcase how the characters become more comfortable with vulnerability and emotional intimacy.
- *Celebrating Milestones*: Celebrate significant milestones in the characters' personal growth and the evolution of their relationship, allowing readers to witness their transformative journey.

Showcasing growth in characters throughout a romance novel is a powerful storytelling tool. By establishing a starting point, addressing internal conflicts, and supporting each other's personal growth, the characters become multidimensional and relatable. Through their emotional resilience, effective communication, and willingness to learn from mistakes, readers witness their evolution as individuals. As the romantic relationship influences their personal development, the characters become more authentic and endearing to readers. Emphasizing the importance of embracing vulnerability and celebrating milestones in their growth adds depth and richness to the narrative. Ultimately, showcasing growth in characters enhances the love story, making it a poignant and relatable exploration of personal development and the transformative power of love.

Sensitivity and Research

Approach writing lesbian characters with sensitivity and respect. Conduct thorough research to understand the experiences and challenges faced by lesbian individuals, seeking input from beta readers or sensitivity readers if possible. Conveying their experiences and challenges accurately requires thorough research and understanding. To ensure authenticity and empathy in your portrayal, consider the following:

- *Respectful Language*: Use inclusive and respectful language when discussing topics related to sexual orientation and LGBTQ+ identities. Avoid derogatory terms or offensive language.
- *LGBTQ+ Resources*: Educate yourself about LGBTQ+ issues and experiences by reading books, articles, and resources written by and for lesbian individuals. This will deepen your understanding of their perspectives.

- *Engaging Sensitivity Readers*: Consider working with sensitivity readers from the lesbian community who can provide valuable feedback and insights on your character's portrayal. Their input ensures cultural accuracy and sensitivity.
- *Avoiding Stereotypes*: Steer clear of harmful stereotypes or clichés associated with lesbian individuals. Each character should be unique and free from overly simplistic portrayals.
- *Diverse Perspectives*: Remember that lesbian individuals come from diverse backgrounds, cultures, and experiences. Reflect this diversity in your characters to avoid monolithic representations.
- *Empathetic Interviewing*: If possible, conduct interviews with lesbian individuals to gain a firsthand understanding of their perspectives and experiences.
- *Understanding Struggles*: Be aware of the challenges faced by lesbian individuals, such as discrimination, homophobia, and societal pressures. Incorporate these sensitively into your character's narrative.
- *Nuanced Relationships*: Portray lesbian relationships as nuanced, loving, and authentic, with mutual respect, consent, and emotional connection.
- *Normalizing Representation*: Normalize the presence of lesbian characters in various genres and settings, making them a natural part of the narrative landscape.
- *Respecting Privacy*: Remember that not all individuals are comfortable sharing their personal experiences, and that's okay. Respect their privacy and boundaries.
- *Realistic Narratives*: Craft realistic narratives that accurately reflect the experiences of lesbian individuals without sensationalizing or

fetishizing their identities.
- *Being Open to Feedback*: Be open to feedback from the LGBTQ+ community and engage in constructive conversations about your portrayal of lesbian characters.

Writing lesbian characters with sensitivity and respect is vital to creating authentic and relatable portrayals. Conducting thorough research, engaging sensitivity readers, and avoiding stereotypes are crucial steps in developing well-rounded and respectful characters. Embrace diverse perspectives and experiences, ensuring your portrayal accurately reflects the richness and complexity of lesbian individuals' lives. By approaching the task with empathy and openness to feedback, your romance novel can become a compassionate and inclusive exploration of love and identity. Building believable lesbian protagonists and love interests requires a balance of authentic characterization, chemistry, and emotional depth. By creating well-rounded characters with diverse backgrounds, individual motivations, and realistic flaws, and treating their romantic relationship with sensitivity and respect, authors can craft a compelling and relatable lesbian romance that resonates with readers on an emotional level.

Developing Compelling Characters – Exploring Character Arcs and Growth

Character arcs and growth are fundamental elements of storytelling, and in lesbian romance novels, they play a vital role in depicting the emotional journeys of the protagonists. A well-crafted character arc allows readers to witness the transformation and personal development of the characters throughout the story. Introduce the protagonists and provide insight into their personalities, desires, motivations, strengths, weaknesses, and the conflicts they may be facing. This sets the foundation for their character development and the journey toward love. Here's how to establish the starting point for the protagonists:

- *Establishing the Starting Point:* Introduce the protagonists at the beginning of the story, providing insight into their personalities, desires, and motivations. Identify their strengths, weaknesses, and the internal or external conflicts they may be facing.
- *Character Descriptions:* Offer vivid descriptions of the protagonists' physical appearances, as well as their demeanor and mannerisms. These details help readers visualize the characters.
- *Personality Traits:* Outline their key personality traits, such as being adventurous, introverted, ambitious, compassionate, or witty. Show how these traits shape their

actions and decisions.
- *Desires and Goals:* Reveal the protagonists' desires and long-term goals. What do they want to achieve in life, professionally or personally?
- *Internal Conflicts:* Explore the internal conflicts they may be grappling with, such as fears, self-doubt, insecurities, or past traumas that have shaped their emotional landscapes.
- *External Conflicts:* Identify external challenges they are facing, like family expectations, societal pressures, or career dilemmas that may influence their choices.
- *Backstories:* Offer glimpses into their pasts, giving readers insight into the events and experiences that have shaped their characters.
- *Motivations:* Uncover the driving forces behind their actions and decisions. What motivates them to pursue specific goals or relationships?
- *Strengths and Weaknesses:* Highlight their strengths, which propel them forward, and their weaknesses, which they may need to overcome or navigate.
- *Emotional Landscape:* Delve into their emotional landscapes, showcasing their hopes, dreams, and the fears that may inhibit them from pursuing love or personal growth.
- *Interactions with Others:* Illustrate their interactions with family, friends, and colleagues, as these relationships provide context for their interpersonal dynamics.
- *Current Circumstances:* Present their current circumstances in life, such as their job, social circle, or personal projects, to

establish the setting for their romantic journey.
- *Setting the Tone:* Use the starting point to set the tone of the story, giving readers an understanding of what to expect from the protagonists' personal growth and romantic development.

Establishing the starting point for the protagonists is a crucial aspect of a romance novel. By providing insight into their personalities, desires, motivations, strengths, weaknesses, and conflicts, readers become invested in their journey toward love and self-discovery. The starting point serves as the groundwork for character development, setting the stage for emotional growth and transformative relationships. As the story unfolds, readers will eagerly follow the protagonists' progress, hoping for a heartfelt and fulfilling conclusion to their romantic and personal journey.

Defining Goals and Obstacles

Give each character specific goals or desires they wish to achieve throughout the story. These goals can be related to their relationship, personal growth, or overcoming obstacles. Introduce challenges and obstacles that stand in their way, forcing them to confront their fears and vulnerabilities. Giving each character specific goals or desires is crucial to driving the narrative forward. Here's how to define goals and obstacles for the characters:

- *Protagonist's Goals*: Clearly outline the primary goals or desires of the protagonist. These can include finding true love, pursuing a dream

career, or overcoming past traumas.
- *Love Interest's Goals*: Identify the love interest's goals or desires, which might align or conflict with those of the protagonist. Their individual goals create tension and complexity in the relationship.
- *Relationship Milestones*: Set relationship milestones that the characters aim to achieve, such as going on their first date, expressing their feelings, or overcoming a major relationship hurdle.
- *Personal Growth Objectives*: Establish objectives for personal growth and development that both characters pursue throughout the story. This might involve overcoming insecurities or becoming more open to vulnerability.
- *Internal Obstacles*: Explore internal obstacles that hinder the characters from achieving their goals, such as fear of commitment, low self-esteem, or unresolved emotional baggage.
- *External Challenges*: Introduce external challenges and conflicts that the characters must face together. This can include external pressures from family, career-related obstacles, or unexpected life events.
- *Communication Barriers*: Incorporate communication barriers that create misunderstandings between the protagonists, leading to conflicts and challenges in their relationship.
- *Past Wounds*: Address past wounds and traumas that resurface, affecting the characters' ability to move forward in their love story.
- *Fear of Vulnerability*: Examine how the fear of vulnerability impacts the protagonists' ability to fully open up to each other and trust in the relationship.
- *Balancing Priorities*: Highlight moments when

the characters must balance their personal goals with their commitment to the relationship, leading to moments of tension and growth.
- *Facing Difficult Choices*: Present situations where the characters must make difficult choices that test their commitment to their goals and the relationship.
- *Learning from Setbacks*: Show how the characters learn from setbacks and obstacles, leading to personal growth and strengthened bonds with each other.

Defining specific goals and obstacles for the characters is essential to crafting a compelling romance novel. By establishing their desires, personal growth objectives, and relationship milestones, the narrative gains direction and purpose. Introducing internal and external obstacles challenges the characters to confront their fears and vulnerabilities, fostering meaningful character development. As the protagonists navigate through the challenges and setbacks, readers become emotionally invested in their journey of love and self-discovery. Ultimately, it is the pursuit of these goals and the resolution of obstacles that make the romance novel a poignant and unforgettable tale of growth, connection, and triumph.

Conflict and Growth

Conflict is a driving force behind character growth. As the protagonists face challenges and conflicts, they are pushed out of their comfort zones, leading to personal growth and self-discovery. Allow them to confront their flaws and fears and show how these experiences shape their growth. These experiences shape their journey of love and transformation. Here's how to weave conflict and growth into the narrative:

- *Challenging Their Comfort Zones*: Introduce conflicts that challenge the protagonists' comfort zones, pushing them to confront their fears and insecurities.
- *Internal Struggles*: Explore internal struggles, such as self-doubt, guilt, or a fear of vulnerability, which inhibit the characters from fully embracing the relationship.
- *External Obstacles*: Incorporate external obstacles and conflicts that force the protagonists to work together and rely on each other's strengths.
- *Making Tough Choices*: Present the characters with difficult choices that test their values and priorities, leading to profound character development.
- *Confronting Flaws*: Allow the characters to confront their flaws and shortcomings, fostering self-awareness and growth.
- *Overcoming Past Traumas*: Show how the protagonists' past traumas impact their present relationship and how facing these traumas becomes a catalyst for healing and growth.
- *Resolving Misunderstandings*: Create misunderstandings and conflicts between the characters, showcasing their journey toward resolving these issues and deepening their bond.
- *Learning from Setbacks*: Illustrate how the characters learn from setbacks and failures, providing opportunities for growth and resilience.
- *Embracing Vulnerability*: Explore how the characters' journey toward love involves embracing vulnerability and opening up to each other.

- *Self-Discovery*: Allow the conflicts to lead the characters on a path of self-discovery, helping them understand their desires, passions, and values.
- *Supportive Relationships*: Highlight the role of supportive friendships and communities in the protagonists' growth and development.
- *Celebrating Progress*: Celebrate the protagonists' progress and growth, showing how their journey toward love and self-discovery has transformed them into stronger individuals.

Conflict is an indispensable element in driving character growth in a romance novel. By challenging the protagonists' comfort zones, exploring internal struggles, and introducing external obstacles, the characters experience transformative personal growth. Through the journey of facing flaws, embracing vulnerability, and overcoming past traumas, the characters evolve into stronger and more self-aware individuals. The resolution of conflicts and the growth that emerges from these experiences deepens the emotional connection between the protagonists and adds depth to their love story. Ultimately, the intertwining of conflict and growth shapes the romance novel into a powerful and emotionally resonant narrative of love, transformation, and self-discovery.

Internal and External Transformation

Character arcs involve internal and external transformation. Internal growth is reflected in their emotional and psychological development, while external growth can manifest through changes in their actions, beliefs, and relationships. Here's how to create dynamic character arcs:

- *Internal Transformation:* Illustrate the protagonists' emotional journey, delving into their evolving thoughts, feelings, and beliefs. Show how their experiences in the romance influence their self-awareness and emotional growth.
- *Overcoming Insecurities:* Portray the characters working to overcome their insecurities and fears, gradually gaining confidence and self-acceptance.
- *Resolving Emotional Baggage:* Address past traumas and emotional baggage, allowing the characters to heal and move forward in their relationship.
- *Evolving Perspectives:* Showcase shifts in the protagonists' perspectives, as they learn from their experiences and begin to view the world and relationships differently.
- *Empathy and Understanding:* Demonstrate how the characters' emotional growth leads to greater empathy and understanding, fostering deeper connections with others.
- *Acceptance and Forgiveness:* Explore the themes of acceptance and forgiveness as the characters learn to let go of grudges and embrace compassion.
- *Self-Discovery:* Allow the protagonists to embark on a journey of self-discovery, exploring their desires, passions, and true selves.
- *External Transformation:* Examine how the characters' actions, behaviors, and relationships change as a result of their internal growth.
- *Bold Actions:* Portray the characters taking bold actions and making brave decisions, driven by newfound confidence and emotional clarity.
- *Reassessing Priorities:* Show how the characters

- *Strengthened Relationships:* Illustrate how the protagonists' external transformation leads to strengthened relationships with others, including their love interest and supportive friends.
- *Becoming Agents of Change:* Position the characters as agents of change in their own lives and the lives of those around them, leaving a positive impact through their growth.

Character arcs involving internal and external transformation enrich the romance novel, creating multidimensional and relatable protagonists. By delving into their emotional and psychological development, readers witness the characters' internal growth as they overcome insecurities, resolve emotional baggage, and embrace self-discovery. The external transformation is equally important as the characters' actions, beliefs, and relationships change as a result of their internal journey. Strengthened relationships and becoming agents of change demonstrate the impact of their growth on the narrative. The interplay of internal and external transformation fosters dynamic character arcs that resonate deeply with readers, making the romance novel an emotional and memorable exploration of love, growth, and self-discovery.

Learning from Relationships

In lesbian romance, the relationship between the protagonists is central to their growth. As the characters navigate their romantic journey, allow them to learn from each other, supporting each other's personal development, and fostering a deep emotional connection that enriches their individual character arcs. Here's how to cultivate growth and emotional connection through their relationship:

- *Shared Experiences*: Create opportunities for the protagonists to share experiences, allowing them to gain insights and perspectives from each other's lives.
- *Emotional Support*: Illustrate how the characters offer emotional support to each other during challenging times, providing a safe space for vulnerability and healing.
- *Encouraging Personal Growth*: Show how the protagonists encourage each other's personal growth, inspiring them to pursue their dreams and overcome obstacles.
- *Learning from Differences*: Explore how the characters learn from their differences, gaining a broader understanding of the world and the people in it.
- *Vulnerability and Trust*: Demonstrate how the characters' emotional connection encourages them to be vulnerable and trust each other with their deepest fears and desires.
- *Celebrating Each Other's Success*: Celebrate moments where the protagonists cheer each other on, celebrating their individual achievements and milestones.
- *Challenging Limiting Beliefs*: Use the relationship as a catalyst for challenging limiting beliefs or self-doubt, helping the characters see their true potential.
- *Offering Perspective*: Allow the characters to offer each other valuable perspectives, guiding each other toward personal insights and self-discovery.

- *Strengthening Resilience*: Show how the emotional connection between the protagonists strengthens their resilience in the face of challenges.
- *Mutual Growth*: Portray the relationship as a space for mutual growth, where both characters evolve and mature throughout the course of the story.
- *Emotional Intimacy*: Develop emotional intimacy between the protagonists, where they can communicate openly and honestly, deepening their connection.
- *Facing Obstacles Together*: Illustrate how the characters face obstacles together, learning from each other's strengths and weaknesses.

In lesbian romance, the relationship between the protagonists is a transformative force. By allowing them to learn from each other, support each other's personal growth, and cultivate a deep emotional connection, the characters' individual character arcs are enriched. Through shared experiences, emotional support, and vulnerability, the relationship becomes a source of strength and inspiration for both protagonists. As they navigate their romantic journey together, they learn, evolve, and mature, making the romance novel a powerful exploration of love, growth, and emotional connection. The authentic and emotional bond between the characters resonates with readers, leaving a lasting impact and making the story a heartfelt and unforgettable experience.

Overcoming Adversity

As characters encounter challenges and adversity,

showcase their resilience and determination to overcome them. Highlight the strength they draw from their romantic bond and how it empowers them to face obstacles together. Here's how to portray the protagonists overcoming adversity:

- *Introducing Adversity*: Present the characters with significant challenges that test their relationship and individual strength.
- *Embracing Resilience*: Highlight the protagonists' resilience as they confront adversity, demonstrating their ability to bounce back from setbacks and difficulties.
- *Supporting Each Other*: Illustrate how the characters support and uplift each other during challenging times, providing emotional fortitude and encouragement.
- *Finding Solutions*: Show them working together to find solutions to their problems, using their unique strengths and perspectives to navigate through difficulties.
- *Communication and Teamwork*: Emphasize effective communication and teamwork as they face adversity, strengthening their bond and ability to overcome obstacles.
- *Drawing Strength from Love*: Demonstrate how the romantic bond between the characters empowers them with a sense of hope, love, and determination.
- *Learning from Setbacks*: Illustrate how the protagonists learn from setbacks, using them as opportunities for growth and deeper connection.
- *Mutual Support*: Portray the relationship as a source of mutual support, where they lean on each other during difficult times.
- *Celebrating Triumphs*: Celebrate the characters'

triumphs over adversity, showcasing the rewards of their resilience and determination.
- *Encouraging Individual Growth*: Show how facing adversity together fosters individual growth and emotional maturity in both characters.
- *Bonding through Shared Challenges*: Explore how overcoming challenges together strengthens the emotional connection between the protagonists.
- *Empowerment in Unity*: Highlight how their unity and commitment to each other empower them to face any obstacle that comes their way.

Portraying characters overcoming adversity is a powerful storytelling element. By showcasing their resilience, determination, and unwavering support for each other, the protagonists demonstrate the strength they draw from their romantic bond. The relationship becomes a source of hope and empowerment, helping them face challenges together and emerge stronger and more connected. Their ability to communicate, work as a team, and support each other fosters growth and deepens their emotional bond. Ultimately, the portrayal of their triumphs over adversity reflects the enduring power of love and resilience, making the romance novel an inspiring and unforgettable tale of love's ability to conquer all obstacles.

Realistic Progression

Character growth should be gradual and realistic, not instantaneous. Let their transformation evolve organically, allowing readers to witness the step-by-step development of the characters as they navigate their love journey. Here are a few ways to achieve realistic progression:

- *Establishing Baseline Personalities*: Introduce the characters with their initial traits, beliefs, and motivations, creating a baseline for their growth.
- *Identifying Areas for Growth*: Identify specific areas where each character can grow, both individually and within the relationship.
- *Growth Through Experience*: Allow growth to occur through experiences, interactions, and challenges the characters face as the story unfolds.
- *Learning from Mistakes*: Show how the characters learn from their mistakes and use those lessons to make better choices.
- *Incremental Change*: Depict gradual shifts in their behaviors, beliefs, and emotions, rather than abrupt changes.
- *Showing Effort*: Illustrate the characters' efforts to grow, emphasizing the work they put into their personal development and relationship.
- *Self-Reflection*: Incorporate moments of self-reflection where the characters consider their progress and acknowledge their areas of growth.
- *Realistic Timelines*: Give character growth realistic timelines, acknowledging that personal development takes time and dedication.
- *Balancing Setbacks and Triumphs*: Present a balance of setbacks and triumphs, as both are essential in shaping character growth.
- *Supporting Characters*: Show how supporting characters play a role in influencing and supporting the protagonists' growth.
- *Consistency*: Maintain consistency in their growth, ensuring it aligns with their personalities and the events in the story.

- *Culmination of Growth*: Let character growth culminate in a satisfying resolution that reflects the authentic journey they've undertaken.

Realistic progression is key to creating relatable and engaging characters. By allowing growth to evolve organically, readers can witness the step-by-step development of the protagonists as they navigate their love journey. Showcasing their efforts, learning from mistakes, and embracing incremental changes contribute to the depth and authenticity of their personal growth. As they face challenges and celebrate triumphs, the characters' realistic timelines reflect the complexity of personal development. Balancing setbacks and growth adds depth to their journey, and the support of other characters fosters a rich narrative. Ultimately, the culmination of their growth leads to a satisfying resolution, leaving readers with a heartfelt and genuine portrayal of love, transformation, and personal development.

Facing Past Traumas or Insecurities

Integrating past traumas or insecurities that influence the characters' actions and decisions adds depth to their journey. As they confront these issues, depict how the power of love and support helps them heal and grow. Here's how to handle this sensitive aspect of their character arcs:

- *Introducing Past Traumas*: Reveal the characters' past traumas or insecurities, ensuring they are portrayed with sensitivity and empathy.
- *Impact on Present Behavior*: Show how these

past experiences influence the characters' current actions, choices, and relationships.
- *Emotional Baggage*: Explore the emotional baggage carried by the protagonists, which may hinder them from fully embracing love and vulnerability.
- *Trigger Moments*: Introduce trigger moments that resurface past traumas, causing emotional turmoil and inner conflicts.
- *Healing Process*: Depict the protagonists' journey toward healing, as they confront their past and work through their insecurities.
- *Supportive Love Interest*: Illustrate how the love interest serves as a source of unwavering support, offering comfort and understanding during difficult times.
- *Vulnerability and Trust*: Show the gradual development of trust and vulnerability between the characters as they open up about their pasts.
- *Communication and Compassion*: Highlight the importance of open communication and compassion, fostering a safe space for emotional healing.
- *Encouragement to Seek Help*: Incorporate instances where the characters encourage each other to seek professional help or therapy for their traumas.
- *Shared Healing*: Portray how the power of their love and support aids in each other's healing process, forming a strong emotional bond.
- *Celebrating Progress*: Celebrate moments of progress and growth as the characters overcome their insecurities and traumas.
- *Aiding Each Other's Recovery*: Show how the protagonists aid each other's recovery by facing their pasts together and providing unwavering support.

Integrating past traumas or insecurities into the characters' journeys enhances the emotional depth of a lesbian romance novel. Sensitively portraying the impact of past experiences on their present behavior creates relatable and multidimensional protagonists. By depicting the healing process through the power of love and support, readers witness the characters' growth and transformation. The love interest's role in providing understanding, encouragement, and emotional safety reinforces the strength of their bond. As they navigate through their pasts together, the characters' emotional journey becomes a powerful narrative of healing, love, and growth. Ultimately, the novel becomes an uplifting and authentic exploration of the resilience of the human spirit and the transformative power of love.

Embracing Identity and Acceptance

The journey of embracing sexual identity and self-acceptance is often a significant part of the characters' arcs. Showcasing how their relationship fosters self-acceptance and empowers them to be true to themselves is a powerful narrative thread. Here's how to portray this empowering aspect of their character development:

- *Initial Self-Doubt:* Introduce the characters with initial self-doubt or struggles related to their sexual identity, reflecting the challenges many individuals face.
- *Emotional Connection:* Illustrate how the emotional connection between the protagonists creates a safe space for vulnerability and self-expression.
- *Understanding and Support:* Show how the love

interest's understanding and support play a pivotal role in the characters' journey toward self-acceptance.
- *Encouragement to Explore:* Depict the characters encouraging each other to explore and embrace their sexual identity without judgment or fear.
- *Challenging Prejudices:* Address societal prejudices and the characters' internalized fears, portraying how their relationship empowers them to challenge these notions.
- *Empowering Conversations:* Include empowering conversations that allow the characters to open up about their identity and experiences.
- *Breaking Free from Expectations:* Explore how the protagonists break free from societal expectations and embrace their authentic selves within their relationship.
- *Defying Stereotypes:* Challenge stereotypes commonly associated with lesbian characters, showcasing the complexity of their identities.
- *Supporting Each Other's Journeys:* Illustrate how the characters support and uplift each other during moments of self-discovery and self-acceptance.
- *Celebrating Individuality:* Celebrate moments where the characters celebrate and embrace their individuality, fostering a sense of pride in who they are.
- *Unconditional Love:* Highlight the power of unconditional love as the characters' bond strengthens through acceptance and authenticity.
- *Becoming Agents of Change:* Portray how their self-acceptance empowers them to be agents of change, positively impacting their lives and relationships.

Embracing sexual identity and self-acceptance are transformative themes in a lesbian romance novel. By sensitively portraying the characters' initial self-doubt and struggles, the narrative becomes relatable and meaningful to readers. Through the emotional connection, understanding, and support within the relationship, the protagonists find the courage to explore and embrace their authentic selves. The love interest's role in empowering the characters' journeys fosters a deep emotional bond and a sense of pride in their identities. As the characters defy stereotypes and challenge societal prejudices, their love story becomes an empowering narrative of self-discovery and acceptance. Ultimately, the novel celebrates the power of love in fostering self-acceptance, making it a heartfelt and empowering exploration of identity, love, and personal growth.

Resolution and Reflection – aka The Happy Ending or Happy for Now

At the end of the story, provide a satisfying resolution to the characters' arcs. Allow them to reflect on their growth and how their experiences have shaped them, leaving readers with a sense of fulfillment and closure. This leaves readers with a sense of fulfillment and closure. Here's how to craft a meaningful resolution and reflection:

- *Resolution of Conflict:* Resolve any lingering conflicts or obstacles that the characters faced throughout the story, providing a sense of closure.
- *Relationship Milestones:* Celebrate significant

relationship milestones that signify the characters' growth and commitment to each other.
- *Emotional Reconciliation:* Portray emotional reconciliation, where the characters express their feelings and thoughts openly and honestly.
- *Reflecting on Growth:* Allow the characters to reflect on their personal growth and the transformative journey they've undertaken.
- *Acknowledging Change:* Show how the experiences they shared in the relationship have influenced their perspectives and attitudes.
- *Gratitude and Appreciation:* Illustrate moments of gratitude and appreciation between the characters for the love and support they received.
- *Learning from the Past:* Depict how the characters have learned from their past mistakes and experiences, leading to personal growth.
- *Embracing Self-Acceptance:* Celebrate the characters' journey toward self-acceptance as they embrace their true selves.
- *Emotionally Resonant Moments:* Include emotionally resonant moments where the characters recognize the impact of their love on each other's lives.
- *Looking Toward the Future:* Convey a sense of hope and anticipation for the future as the characters embark on a new chapter together.
- *Strength of Their Bond:* Highlight the strength of the emotional bond between the protagonists, which has grown through their experiences.
- *Leaving Readers Fulfilled:* Conclude the novel with a sense of fulfillment, leaving readers satisfied with the characters' growth and the love story's resolution.

A satisfying resolution and reflection in a lesbian

romance novel provide readers with a profound sense of closure. By resolving conflicts, celebrating relationship milestones, and allowing the characters to reflect on their growth, the narrative achieves a meaningful conclusion. As the protagonists acknowledge the impact of their experiences and embrace self-acceptance, the novel becomes a powerful exploration of love, growth, and personal transformation. Leaving readers fulfilled and hopeful for the characters' future, the resolution and reflection elevate the romance novel into an emotionally resonant and unforgettable tale of love's enduring power.

Character arcs and growth are essential elements that breathe life into the protagonists of a lesbian romance novel. By crafting compelling character journeys filled with challenges, self-discovery, and personal growth, authors create emotionally resonant stories that captivate readers and leave a lasting impact. The exploration of character arcs allows readers to connect with the protagonists on a deeper level and celebrate the transformative power of love in the context of lesbian relationships.

Developing Compelling Characters – Writing Authentic and Engaging Dialogue

Writing authentic and engaging dialogue is crucial in creating a captivating lesbian romance novel. Dialogue not only advances the plot, but also reveals the personalities, emotions, and relationships of the characters.

Establish Individual Voices

Each character should have a distinct voice and manner of speaking. Their backgrounds, personalities, and experiences should shape their dialogue, creating a rich tapestry of diverse voices that helps readers differentiate between characters and adds realism to their interactions. Here's how to achieve individuality in their voices:

- *Background and Upbringing:* Consider each character's background and upbringing when crafting their dialogue. Characters from different cultural or social backgrounds may use unique expressions and phrases.
- *Personality Traits:* Tailor dialogue to reflect the personalities of the characters. An extroverted character might be more outspoken, while an introverted character might speak more thoughtfully.

- *Emotional Range:* Take into account the emotional range of each character. Their dialogue should convey their feelings, whether it's excitement, vulnerability, anger, or joy.
- *Speech Patterns:* Develop specific speech patterns for each character, including their use of slang, regional dialects, or verbal quirks.
- *Education and Vocabulary:* Consider the characters' education levels and vocabulary. A highly educated character might use more sophisticated language, while a character with a different background might have a more casual way of speaking.
- *Personal History:* Incorporate the characters' personal history and experiences into their dialogue. Past traumas or joyful memories may influence their choice of words and tone.
- *Role in the Story:* Differentiate the dialogue of main characters, secondary characters, and supporting characters. Their roles in the story may influence their communication styles.
- *Consistency:* Maintain consistency in each character's voice throughout the novel. Readers should recognize their unique manner of speaking in various situations.
- *Internal Dialogue:* Use internal monologues to provide deeper insights into the characters' thoughts and emotions, further enriching their individual voices.
- *Dialogue Tags:* Vary dialogue tags to match the characters' voices. For example, one character might "shout," while another might "murmur."
- *Subtle Differences:* Craft subtle differences in language and tone, particularly during conversations between characters. This attention to detail enhances the realism of the interactions.
- *Beta Readers' Feedback:* Seek feedback from

beta readers to ensure the dialogue resonates authentically and captures the uniqueness of each character's voice.

In a lesbian romance novel, individual voices and diverse dialogue create a dynamic and authentic narrative. By considering each character's background, personality, and experiences, you can craft dialogue that reflects their uniqueness. These distinct voices help readers differentiate between characters and immerse themselves in the story. By using varied speech patterns, emotional range, and vocabulary, the characters come to life and engage readers on a deeper level. The result is a richly woven tapestry of voices that contributes to the realism and emotional resonance of the lesbian romance, making it a captivating and memorable reading experience.

Use Natural Language

Dialogue should sound natural and conversational. The characters should sound like real people, and you should avoid overly formal or stilted language unless it suits a specific character's personality or background. Using contractions, slang, and colloquialisms can mirror real-life conversations and make the dialogue feel more authentic. Here's an example of natural language dialogue:

Character A: Hey, I was thinking of checking out that new café that opened up downtown. Wanna join me?
Character B: Sure thing! I heard they have some amazing pastries there. When do you wanna go?
Character A: How about tomorrow afternoon? Say

around 3 p.m.?
Character B: Sounds good to me! See you there.
In this example, the characters speak in a casual and friendly manner, using phrases like "I was," "I heard," and "I wanna," as well as the informal greeting "Hey" and the colloquial phrase "sounds good to me." This natural language helps to create a relatable and authentic atmosphere, making the dialogue more engaging for readers. Remember to tailor the dialogue to each character's unique personality and background, allowing their individual voices to shine through in their conversations.

A few more examples.

Example (Casual Conversation):

Character A: Hey, are you going to the Pride parade this weekend?
Character B: Totally! Wouldn't miss it for the world. You coming, too?

Example (Emotional Exchange):

Character A: I just wanted to say...I really like you. Like, *really* like you.
Character B: Wow, I feel the same way. I've been trying to find the right words to tell you, too.

Example (Playful Banter):

Character A: You're such a troublemaker, you know that?
Character B: Guilty as charged! But you love me for it,

right?

Example (Internal Monologue):

Character A: I can't believe I'm feeling this way. It's like my heart's doing somersaults whenever she's around.

Example (Confrontation):

Character A: Why didn't you tell me about your past? I thought we were open with each other.
Character B: I was scared, okay? Scared you'd judge me or run away.

Example (Supportive Encouragement):

Character A: I'm thinking of coming out to my family, but I'm so nervous.
Character B: You've got this! Be true to yourself, and I'll be right by your side.

Example (Humorous Interaction):

Character A: Did you see the way she tripped on that curb?
Character B: I know, right? Graceful as a newborn giraffe!

Example (Intimate Moment):

Character A: I want to be with you every step of the way.
Character B: Me too. You make my heart feel so full.

Example (Expressions of Affection):

Character A: Hey, beautiful, you ready to go?
Character B: Ready when you are, gorgeous.

Example (Nervous Confession):

Character A: I've been trying to find the right moment to tell you...I love you.
Character B: You have no idea how long I've been waiting to hear that.

In your novel, using natural language in the dialogue is crucial for creating authentic and engaging interactions between characters. Embrace contractions, slang, and colloquialisms to make the conversations mirror real-life exchanges. Whether it's casual banter, emotional exchanges, or intimate moments, natural language enhances the characters' authenticity and helps readers connect with their emotions and experiences. By avoiding overly formal or stilted language, the dialogue becomes approachable and relatable, inviting readers to immerse themselves fully in the captivating world of the lesbian romance.

Show, Don't Tell

Dialogue is an excellent way to show emotions and character dynamics without explicitly stating them. Instead of telling the reader how a character feels, let their words and reactions reveal their emotions and inner thoughts. Here's how to effectively implement "Show, Don't Tell" in the dialogue:

Example (Love and Affection):

Telling: "I love you," she said affectionately.
Showing: "You make my heart feel so full," she

whispered, looking into her lover's eyes.

Example (Anger and Frustration):

Telling: "He was angry at her for keeping secrets."
Showing: "How could you not tell me? Do you know how much that hurt?" he exclaimed, his fists clenched in frustration.

Example (Sadness and Vulnerability):

Telling: "She was heartbroken."
Showing: "I...I can't do this anymore," she said, her voice trembling.

Example (Playfulness and Teasing):

Telling: "She teased her playfully."
Showing: "Oh, come on, don't be such a tease!" she said, a playful grin spreading across her face.

Example (Nervousness and Excitement):

Telling: "She was nervous about the upcoming event."
Showing: "I can't believe it's almost here! I'm so excited but also a little nervous," she admitted.

Example (Confusion and Curiosity):

Telling: "He was confused by her actions."
Showing: "I don't understand. Why did you do that?" he asked, genuine curiosity in his eyes.

Example (Support and Encouragement):

Telling: "She supported her during a difficult time."
Showing: "You're strong, and I know you can get through this," she said, offering a reassuring hug.

Example (Intimacy and Connection):

Telling: "They felt a strong connection."
Showing: Their gazes met, and in that moment, it was like the rest of the world faded away.

Example (Pride and Self-Confidence):

Telling: "She was proud of her accomplishments."
Showing: "I did it! Can you believe it?" she exclaimed, her face beaming with pride.

Example (Disappointment and Regret):

Telling: "He regretted his actions."
Showing: "I messed up. I wish I could go back and do things differently," he said.

"Show, Don't Tell" is a powerful technique to reveal emotions and character dynamics through dialogue in a lesbian romance novel. By allowing the characters' words and reactions to convey their feelings and thoughts, the narrative becomes more immersive and emotionally resonant. Through the subtleties of their interactions, readers gain a deeper understanding of the characters' emotions, desires, and conflicts. By embracing this approach, the dialogue becomes a rich tapestry of emotions, adding depth and authenticity to the lesbian romance, and leaving readers captivated by the characters' heartfelt journey of love and self-discovery.

Be Concise and Purposeful

Every line should contribute to character development, plot progression, or adding depth to the story. Avoid lengthy monologues or excessive exposition to keep the narrative engaging and impactful. Here's how to achieve focused dialogue:

Example (Character Development):

Concise: "I've never felt this way before," she admitted, her heart pounding.
Less Concise: "I've been trying to understand my feelings, and I must confess that I've never experienced anything like this. It's as if my heart is doing somersaults whenever I'm around you."

Example (Plot Progression):

Concise: "We need to find a way to stop them," she said, determined.
Less Concise: "We're facing a challenging situation, and it's up to us to find a solution. We can't let them get away with what they're planning."

Example (Adding Depth):

Concise: "I know it's not easy, but I'll support you no matter what," she reassured.
Less Concise: "I understand that you're going through a difficult time, but I want you to know that I'll always be here for you. You can count on me no

matter what happens."

Example (Revealing Emotions):

Concise: "I can't stop thinking about you," she confessed, blushing.
Less Concise: "I've been trying to push these thoughts away, but I can't. You're always on my mind, and it's becoming harder to hide my feelings."

Example (Advancing Relationship):

Concise: "I want to be with you," she said, her voice unwavering.
Less Concise: "I've thought about it a lot, and I've come to the conclusion that I want to be with you. I can't imagine my life without you in it."

Example (Creating Tension):

Concise: "Why did you do that?" she asked, her eyes narrowing.
Less Concise: "I need to understand your actions. It's important to me, so please, tell me why you did that."

Example (Humorous Interaction):

Concise: "You're such a troublemaker," she teased, laughing.
Less Concise: "You always manage to find yourself in the middle of trouble. It's like you're a magnet for chaos!"

Example (Intimacy and Vulnerability):

Concise: "I trust you," she whispered, her gaze softening.
Less Concise: "I've been hurt in the past, but I want you to know that I trust you. I believe in you and in us."

Example (Self-Reflection):

Concise: "I need to figure this out on my own," she said, determined.
Less Concise: "I've realized that I need some time to myself to sort through my thoughts. It's essential for me to figure things out on my own."

Example (Resolution):

Concise: "I love you," she said, smiling.
Less Concise: "I've been holding this in for so long, but I can't keep it to myself anymore. I love you, and I want you to know that."

Keeping dialogue concise and purposeful is crucial in your romance novel. Each line should contribute to character development or plot progression or add depth to the story. By avoiding lengthy monologues or excessive exposition, the narrative remains engaging and impactful. Focused dialogue reveals emotions, advances relationships, and creates tension, making the lesbian romance a captivating and compelling journey of love, growth, and self-discovery.

Use Subtext

Subtext in dialogue adds depth and complexity to conversations. Characters may not always say exactly what they mean, leaving room for readers to interpret their underlying thoughts and feelings. Subtext enriches the narrative and allows for a more nuanced exploration of emotions and relationships. Here's how to effectively incorporate subtext into the dialogue:

Example (Unspoken Attraction):

Text: "You look nice today," she said, blushing.
Subtext: Her compliment carried a hint of nervousness, revealing her unspoken attraction to the other woman.

Example (Hesitation and Doubt):

Text: "I'm not sure if this is the right decision," she admitted.
Subtext: Her words masked the uncertainty she felt, grappling with doubts about the choices ahead.

Example (Hidden Vulnerability):

Text: "I'm fine," she replied, avoiding eye contact.
Subtext: Her defensive response hinted at underlying vulnerability she didn't want to reveal.

Example (Unresolved Tension):

Text: "We should talk about what happened," she suggested.
Subtext: The suggestion held an unspoken weight, reflecting the lingering tension between the

characters.

Example (Concealed Longing):

Text: "I'm happy for you," she said, smiling.
Subtext: Beneath the smile, a trace of sadness betrayed her concealed longing for something more.

Example (Unacknowledged Regret):

Text: "It's all in the past now," she stated firmly.
Subtext: Despite her firm words, a trace of regret lingered, hinting at unresolved feelings.

Example (Unspoken Support):

Text: "You'll be great," she said, offering a reassuring hug.
Subtext: The hug conveyed unspoken support, letting the other know she believed in her abilities.

Example (Fear of Rejection):

Text: "I don't want to ruin our friendship," she confessed.
Subtext: Her confession masked the fear of potential rejection if she revealed her true feelings.

Example (Longing for Connection):

Text: "I miss you," she whispered, her voice soft.
Subtext: The whispered words carried a depth of longing, reflecting her desire for emotional closeness.

Example (Masked Heartache):

Text: "I'm used to it," she said, her smile forced.
Subtext: Her forced smile concealed the heartache of past disappointments.

Example (Unspoken Attraction):

Character A: "You're spending a lot of time with her lately."
Character B: "She's just a friend."
Subtext: Character A hints at her attraction to Character B, but Character B dismisses it to avoid revealing her true feelings.

Example (Hidden Vulnerability):

Character A: "I'm fine, don't worry about me."
Character B: "You don't have to put up a front with me."
Subtext: Character A conceals her vulnerability, but Character B sees through the façade and offers support and understanding.

Example (Indirect Confession):

Character A: "I heard you went out last night."
Character B: "Yeah, I had a great time."
Subtext: Character A looks like she is fishing for information about Character B's love life, hoping for a hint that she might be interested in someone.

Example (Mixed Feelings):

Character A: "I'm happy for you and your new job."
Character B: "Thanks, but I'll miss spending time with you."
Subtext: Character B is subtly expressing her mixed feelings about leaving, implying that she values her time with Character A.

Example (Resentment Disguised as Humor):

Character A: "You always have the perfect answer, don't you?"
Character B: "Well, someone's got to have all the answers!"
Subtext: Character A's sarcastic remark hides her annoyance with Character B's know-it-all attitude.

Example (Longing and Uncertainty):

Character A: "I'm going to the party tonight."
Character B: "Have fun."
Subtext: Character B hides her disappointment at not being invited to the party; perhaps she's unsure of her place in Character A's life.

Example (Jealousy and Insecurity):

Character A: "I ran into your ex yesterday."
Character B: "Oh, how was that?"
Subtext: Character B is subtly checking for signs of jealousy in Character A, fearing she might still have unresolved feelings for her ex.

Example (Unspoken Understanding):

Character A: gazes at Character B with a smile
Character B: returns the smile, without saying a word
Subtext: Their silent exchange reveals a deep connection and understanding that goes beyond words.

Example (Hidden Intentions):

Character A: "Let me help you with that."
Character B: "I've got it, thanks."
Subtext: Character B refuses help to assert her independence, but she secretly appreciates the gesture from Character A.

Example (Longing for Reassurance):

Character A: "I'm just not sure if I'm doing the right thing."
Character B: "You're doing great. I believe in you."
Subtext: Character A seeks reassurance, and Character B provides it, showing her support and care.

As you can see in the above examples, subtext in dialogue adds layers of depth and complexity to conversations. Characters may not always speak directly about their thoughts and feelings, leaving room for readers to interpret their unspoken emotions. Subtext allows for nuanced interactions, revealing hidden desires, insecurities, and unspoken connections between characters. By skillfully weaving subtext into the dialogue, the lesbian romance becomes an emotionally resonant and immersive experience, inviting readers to explore the subtleties of the characters' inner worlds and the complexity of their relationships.

Subtext in dialogue is a powerful tool in a lesbian romance novel, and we've seen it used quite famously in that show with a warrior princess and her blond sidekick. It enriches conversations with depth and complexity. By allowing characters to not say everything they mean, the narrative becomes more emotionally resonant and engaging. Readers are invited to interpret the characters' underlying thoughts and feelings, creating a more immersive and nuanced experience. Subtext adds layers of complexity to interactions, unveiling unspoken attractions, doubts, vulnerabilities, and longings. Through the artful use of subtext, the lesbian romance becomes a poignant exploration of emotions, relationships, and the intricacies of love.

Introduce Conflict

Engaging dialogue often involves conflict and tension between characters. Introduce disagreements, misunderstandings, or differing perspectives to create engaging and dynamic interactions. Here's how to effectively introduce conflict in the dialogue:

Example (Disagreement):

Character A: "I think we should take a break from each other for a while."
Character B: "What? Why would you even suggest that?"
Conflict: Character A's suggestion creates tension and disagreement between them, leading to a heated exchange of differing opinions.

Example (Misunderstanding):

Character A: "I can't believe you said that about me!"
Character B: "No, that's not what I meant. Let me explain."
Conflict: Character A misunderstands something Character B said, leading to hurt feelings and the need for clarification.

Example (Differing Perspectives):

Character A: "I want to move to a new city and start fresh."
Character B: "But what about our life here? This is where our family is."
Conflict: Character A and Character B have different perspectives on their future, leading to a conflict of desires and priorities.

Example (Jealousy):

Character A: "I saw you talking to her. Is there something going on between you?"
Character B: "No, it was just a friendly conversation."
Conflict: Character A's jealousy causes tension between her and Character B, who tries to reassure her.

Example (Past Resentment):

Character A: "I can't believe you didn't tell me about that!"
Character B: "It happened a long time ago, and I didn't think it mattered."

Conflict: Character A brings up a past event that Character B didn't disclose, leading to unresolved resentment and tension.

Example (Conflicting Values):

Character A: "I can't believe you lied for your friend."
Character B: "She needed my support, and I couldn't let her down."
Conflict: Character A and Character B clash over their differing values and priorities.

Example (Hidden Secrets):

Character A: "Why won't you tell me what's really going on?"
Character B: "It's complicated, and I don't want to burden you."
Conflict: Character B's reluctance to share her secrets creates tension and frustration between her and Character A.

Example (External Obstacles):

Character A: "We can't be together, not with everything going on."
Character B: "I don't care about the obstacles. I want to fight for us."
Conflict: Character A and Character B face external obstacles that challenge their relationship and force them to confront their feelings.

Example (Conflicting Loyalties):

Character A: "You're always putting your family before us!"
Character B: "They need me right now, and I can't just abandon them."
Conflict: Character A feels neglected, while Character B grapples with conflicting loyalties between family and her relationship.

Example (Complicated History):

Character A: "I can't forget what you did in the past."
Character B: "I've changed, but I can't erase my mistakes."
Conflict: Character A struggles to move past Character B's past actions, and Character B grapples with the weight of her history.

Introducing conflict in dialogue adds depth and intensity to the interactions between characters. Disagreements, misunderstandings, differing perspectives, and external obstacles create engaging and dynamic scenes that fuel the emotional journey of the story. The conflicts allow for growth, self-discovery, and the exploration of the characters' true desires and values. By navigating the complexities of conflict in the dialogue, the romance becomes a compelling and realistic exploration of love, challenges, and the strength of relationships in the face of adversity.

Balance Dialogue Tags

Use dialogue tags (e.g., "she said," "he replied") to attribute speech, but avoid overusing them. Instead, incorporate action beats and character reactions to break up dialogue and add visual cues to the scene. This technique creates a more immersive and engaging reading experience. Here are a few examples on how to achieve this balance:

Example:

Dialogue Tag: "I can't believe you did that," Character A said.
Action Beat: Character B's eyes widened in surprise. "I didn't mean to, it just happened."

Example:

Dialogue Tag: "You're right," Character A replied, nodding.
Action Beat: Character B took a deep breath, relieved to hear the agreement.

Example:

Dialogue Tag: "I'm sorry," Character A said, looking down.
Action Beat: Character B reached out and gently lifted Character A's chin. "There's no need to apologize."

Example:

Dialogue Tag: "I don't know what to do," Character A said, feeling overwhelmed.
Action Beat: Character B wrapped her arms around Character A, offering comfort without saying a word.

Example:

Dialogue Tag: "I missed you," Character A said with a smile.
Action Beat: Character B's face lit up, and she hugged Character A tightly.

Example:

Dialogue Tag: "I can't believe we did it," Character A said, laughing.
Action Beat: Character B high-fived Character A, celebrating her accomplishment.

Example:

Dialogue Tag: "I'm scared," Character A admitted, biting her lip.
Action Beat: Character B held Character A's hand, offering reassurance.

Example:

Dialogue Tag: "I'll always be here for you," Character A said sincerely.
Action Beat: Character B leaned in and placed a gentle kiss on Character A's forehead.

Example:

Dialogue Tag: "You mean the world to me," Character A said softly.
Action Beat: Character B's heart swelled with emotion, unable to respond in words.

Example:

Dialogue Tag: "I love you," Character A whispered.
Action Beat: Character B's eyes filled with tears, and she pulled Character A into a tight embrace.

Balancing dialogue tags with action beats and character reactions is essential in your novel. Using dialogue tags sparingly and incorporating visual cues through action beats adds depth and realism to the scenes, making them more immersive for readers. Visual cues allow readers to feel the emotions and connect with the characters on a deeper level, enhancing the overall reading experience. By carefully weaving dialogue tags, action beats, and character reactions, the romance becomes a vivid and emotionally resonant journey, capturing the hearts of readers and leaving them fully immersed in the characters' captivating love story.

Reflect the Setting and Tone

Dialogue should be in harmony with the setting and tone of the story. For example, dialogue in a lighthearted romantic comedy will differ from that in a serious, emotional drama. Tailoring dialogue to match the setting and tone adds authenticity and depth to the narrative. Here's how to achieve this reflection:

Lighthearted Romantic Comedy:

Dialogue Example 1: Character A: "I can't believe you talked me into this crazy adventure!"
Character B: "Hey, it's all about living in the moment, right?"

Dialogue Example 2: Character A: "I have a date tonight!"
Character B: "Ooh, spill the details! Where are you going? What are you wearing?"

Dialogue Example 3: Character A: "Do you believe in love at first sight?"
Character B: "I didn't before, but now I'm not so sure."

Dialogue Example 4: Character A: "You make me laugh like no one else."
Character B: "Well, we are a match made in comedy heaven."

Serious, Emotional Drama:

Dialogue Example 1: Character A: "I can't keep pretending everything's fine when it's not."
Character B: "I know, but we have to face this together."

Dialogue Example 2: Character A: "I wish I could change the past."
Character B: "We can't change what happened, but we can learn from it."

Dialogue Example 3: Character A: "I need some time alone to figure things out."
Character B: "I understand. Take all the time you need."

Dialogue Example 4: Character A: "I've never felt this

vulnerable before."
Character B: "I'm here for you, and I won't let anything hurt you."

Mystery/Thriller:

Dialogue Example 1: Character A: "We need to be careful. I think someone's watching us."
Character B: "Are you sure? Let's stick together and stay alert."

Dialogue Example 2: Character A: "I can't trust anyone."
Character B: "You can trust me. We're in this together."

Dialogue Example 3: Character A: "I've got a bad feeling about this place."
Character B: "Let's get out of here before something happens."

Dialogue Example 4: Character A: "I found something suspicious in the old files."
Character B: "We need to investigate further but be cautious."

Reflecting the setting and tone through dialogue is crucial. Tailoring the characters' speech and interactions to match the atmosphere, whether it's a lighthearted romantic comedy, a serious emotional drama, or a mysterious thriller, enhances the reader's immersion and emotional connection to the story. By carefully crafting dialogue that aligns with the setting and tone, the lesbian romance becomes a captivating and authentic journey of love, challenges, and personal growth, resonating with readers on multiple levels. Here's how to reflect the setting and tone through dialogue:

Example – Lighthearted Romantic Comedy:

Setting: A bustling coffee shop with upbeat music playing in the background.
Dialogue: Character A: "Your latte art skills are on point!"
Character B: "Well, I have to impress my number one customer."
Tone: The dialogue is light and playful, mirroring the fun and carefree ambiance of the coffee shop.

Example – Serious, Emotional Drama:

Setting: A quiet park during sunset, with soft, melancholic music in the background.
Dialogue: Character A: "I can't keep pretending everything is okay."
Character B: "I know, but we can work through this together."
Tone: The dialogue is serious and heartfelt, echoing the emotional intensity of the scene and the characters' struggles.

Example – Quirky Urban Setting:

Setting: An art gallery with unconventional and colorful artwork displayed.
Dialogue: Character A: "What do you think about this painting?"

Character B: "It's...unique. Definitely thought-provoking."
Tone: The dialogue has a touch of quirkiness, reflecting the eclectic and artsy atmosphere of the gallery.

Example – Intimate Café Scene:

Setting: A cozy, dimly lit café with soft jazz music in the background.
Dialogue: Character A: "I've never met someone like you before."
Character B: "And I've never felt this way with anyone else."
Tone: The dialogue exudes intimacy and romance, perfectly matching the ambiance of the candlelit café.

Example – Beach Retreat:

Setting: A sandy beach with the sound of waves crashing and seagulls calling.
Dialogue: Character A: "This sunset is breathtaking."
Character B: "Not as breathtaking as you."
Tone: The dialogue is sweet and romantic, capturing the beauty of the beach setting and the characters' affection for each other.

Example – Emotional Confrontation:

Setting: An empty room with dim lighting, adding to the somber mood.
Dialogue: Character A: "I can't keep living a lie."
Character B: "I never wanted to hurt you."
Tone: The dialogue is tense and emotional, reflecting

the seriousness of the confrontation and the characters' internal turmoil.

Example – Playful Road Trip:

Setting: Inside a car, driving through scenic countryside.
Dialogue: Character A: "Do you have a playlist for this road trip?"
Character B: "Of course! Get ready for some epic tunes."
Tone: The dialogue is playful and excited, reflecting the adventurous spirit of the road trip.

Example – Historical Drama:

Setting: A grand ballroom with elegant decorations and classical music.
Dialogue: Character A: "May I have this dance?"
Character B: "I'd be honored."
Tone: The dialogue is formal and elegant, fitting the historical setting and the characters' refined manners.

Reflecting the setting and tone through dialogue is crucial in a lesbian romance novel. By tailoring the dialogue to match the atmosphere of the scene, the story becomes more authentic, allowing readers to fully immerse themselves in the world of the characters. Whether it's a lighthearted romantic comedy, a serious emotional drama, or any other setting, well-crafted dialogue enhances the overall reading experience and complements the story's tone, making the lesbian romance a captivating and resonant journey of love and self-discovery.

Avoid Exposition Dumps in Dialogue

Resist the temptation to use dialogue solely for delivering exposition. Instead, sprinkle necessary information throughout the story to maintain a natural flow. Exposition dumps, where characters provide large amounts of information all at once, can disrupt the natural flow of the story and feel forced. Instead, sprinkle necessary information throughout the narrative to maintain a smooth and authentic reading experience. Here's how to achieve this:

Example (Exposition Dump):

Character A: "I can't believe you're leaving for college tomorrow. We've been best friends since we were kids, and now everything is changing. Remember that time we got lost in the woods together and had to find our way back home?"

Example (Avoiding Exposition Dump):

Character A: "I can't believe you're leaving for college tomorrow."
Character B: "I know, it's bittersweet. But we'll always be best friends, no matter the distance."

In this revised example, the essential information about the characters' long-lasting friendship is conveyed without an excessive exposition dump. Instead, it flows naturally within their conversation, maintaining a realistic and engaging interaction.

Example (Exposition Dump):

Character A: "I'm nervous about meeting your family. Are they accepting of your sexuality? What if they don't like me because I'm a musician?"

Example (Avoiding Exposition Dump):

Character A: "I'm nervous about meeting your family."
Character B: "They're supportive and open-minded. You have nothing to worry about."

Here, the necessary information about Character B's family's acceptance and the protagonist's concern about her music career is subtly interwoven into the dialogue, avoiding a lengthy exposition dump.

Example (Exposition Dump):

Character A: "I've always loved painting and dreamed of becoming an artist. My mom used to take me to art galleries when I was a child, and it inspired me to pursue this passion. I took art classes throughout high school and won several competitions. Now I'm hoping to get into a prestigious art school in the city."

Example (Avoiding Exposition Dump):

Character A: "I've always loved painting and dreamed of becoming an artist. Now I'm hoping to get into a prestigious art school in the city."

By omitting unnecessary details about Character

A's past experiences, the dialogue remains focused and avoids becoming an exposition dump while still conveying the protagonist's passion for art and aspirations.

Example with rewrites (Exposition Dump):

Character A: "I can't believe we've known each other since high school, where we were both part of the drama club. Remember that time we performed *Romeo and Juliet*? That's when we first realized we had feelings for each other. After that, we went to different colleges, but somehow, fate brought us back together in this small town where we both decided to pursue our dreams of becoming writers."

Example with rewrites (Natural Flow):

Character A: "Hey, remember back in high school when we were both part of the drama club?"
Character B: "Of course! Those were some fun times."
Character A: "And do you recall that one performance of *Romeo and Juliet*? It was unforgettable."
Character B: "Oh, yes! That's when we first realized we had feelings for each other."
Character A: "Life took us on different paths after that, but somehow, fate brought us back together in this small town. I'm grateful we both followed our dreams of becoming writers."

Example (Exposition Dump):

Character A: "I come from a traditional family, and they have always been skeptical of same-sex relationships.

It was a difficult journey for me to accept my identity, and I faced numerous challenges in the process. Now I'm finally at a point where I'm comfortable with who I am and ready to embrace love."

Example with rewrites (Natural Flow):

Character A: "You know, growing up in a traditional family wasn't easy. They had certain expectations and were skeptical of same-sex relationships."
Character B: "I can imagine that must have been tough."
Character A: "It was a journey of self-acceptance, with its fair share of challenges. But now I'm at a point where I'm comfortable with who I am and ready to embrace love."

Example (Exposition Dump):

Character A: "I work as an architect for a renowned firm in the city. It's demanding, but I love designing buildings and creating spaces that inspire people. I've been passionate about architecture since I was a child, and my parents were always supportive of my career choice."

Example with rewrites (Natural Flow):

Character A: "You know, I work as an architect for a renowned firm in the city."
Character B: "That's impressive! It must be demanding but fulfilling."
Character A: "Absolutely. Designing buildings that inspire people has been my passion since I was a

child. Fortunately, my parents were always supportive of my career choice."

In your novel, it's crucial to avoid exposition dumps in dialogue. Instead, gradually sprinkle necessary information throughout the story, maintaining a natural flow and allowing the readers to connect with the characters and their journey authentically. By crafting dialogue that organically reveals essential details, the lesbian romance becomes a captivating and immersive experience, drawing readers into a world of love, growth, and self-discovery.

Edit and Revise your Dialogue

Review and revise your dialogue to ensure it aligns with the character's voice and the overall narrative. Consider reading the dialogue aloud to assess its authenticity and flow.

Original Dialogue:
Character A: "I can't believe you're leaving for college tomorrow."
Character B: "I know, it's bittersweet. But we'll always be best friends, no matter the distance."

Revised Dialogue:
Character A: "You're really leaving for college tomorrow?"
Character B: "Yeah, it's happening. It's bittersweet, you know? But no matter where we are, we'll always be best friends."

In the revised dialogue, I made some subtle changes to

better align with the characters' voices and the overall narrative. Character A's response now reflects surprise and emotion, while Character B's reply acknowledges the bittersweet nature of their departure and emphasizes the enduring nature of their friendship. The revised dialogue feels more authentic and maintains a natural flow between the characters.

Dialogue with characters and situations we've used before:
Character A: "I can't believe you're leaving for college tomorrow."
Character B: "I know, it's bittersweet. But we'll always be best friends, no matter the distance."

Revised Dialogue:
Character A: "Leaving for college tomorrow, huh?"
Character B: "Yeah, it's bittersweet. But no matter the distance, we'll always be best friends."

In the revised dialogue, the characters' voices remain authentic, but the phrasing is adjusted slightly to flow more naturally. The use of "Leaving for college tomorrow, huh?" in Character A's response adds a sense of familiarity and casualness, reflecting their close relationship. Character B's response maintains the bittersweet sentiment and emphasizes the unbreakable bond between them.

Original Dialogue:
Character A: "I'm nervous about meeting your family. Are they accepting of your sexuality? What if they don't like me because I'm a musician?"
Character B: "They're supportive and open-minded.

You have nothing to worry about."

Revised Dialogue:
Character A: "Meeting your family makes me nervous. Are they accepting of your sexuality?"
Character B: "They're supportive and open-minded. Trust me, they'll love you, musician and all."

In the revised dialogue, the characters' voices remain intact, but some information is rephrased to sound more natural. Character A's concern about meeting the family is expressed more concisely, and Character B's reassurance emphasizes that she will be accepted for who she is, including her career as a musician.

Original Dialogue:
Character A: "I've always loved painting and dreamed of becoming an artist. My mom used to take me to art galleries when I was a child, and it inspired me to pursue this passion. I took art classes throughout high school and won several competitions. Now I'm hoping to get into a prestigious art school in the city."

Revised Dialogue:
Character A: "I've always loved painting and dreamed of becoming an artist. I'm hoping to get into a prestigious art school in the city."

In the revised dialogue, the character's voice remains consistent, but unnecessary details about past experiences are removed to maintain a smoother flow. The dialogue still conveys Character A's passion for art and her aspiration to attend art school in the city.

Reviewing and revising dialogue is essential to ensure it aligns with the character's voice and the overall narrative. By reading the dialogue aloud, you can assess its authenticity, flow, and naturalness. In the revised dialogue, characters' voices remain intact, and the phrasing is adjusted for a smoother, more engaging conversation. By crafting dialogue that sounds realistic and purposeful, the lesbian romance becomes a compelling and authentic tale of love and self-discovery, drawing readers into the characters' world and emotions.

Remember, when reviewing and revising dialogue, consider the characters' personalities, emotions, and the context of the scene. Reading the dialogue aloud can help assess its authenticity and flow, ensuring that it resonates with readers and enhances their experience of the lesbian romance story.

Be Open to Feedback

Seek feedback from beta readers or sensitivity readers, especially if you are writing about diverse identities or experiences. Listening to their insights can help you refine the dialogue and ensure respectful representation. Here's why feedback is valuable and how to embrace it:

- *Understanding Diverse Identities*: As an author, it is essential to recognize that no single perspective can fully encompass the breadth of diverse identities and experiences within the lesbian community. Beta readers or sensitivity readers can offer valuable perspectives that may

enrich and validate your portrayal of characters and relationships.
- *Ensuring Authenticity*: Feedback from individuals with lived experiences similar to your characters allows you to ensure authenticity and accuracy in your portrayal. This ensures that the emotions, struggles, and triumphs of the characters resonate with readers from diverse backgrounds.
- *Challenging Stereotypes*: Constructive feedback helps identify and challenge potential stereotypes or clichés that may unintentionally find their way into the narrative. Sensitivity readers can guide you in avoiding harmful tropes and promoting respectful representation.
- *Refining Dialogue*: Dialogue is a powerful tool for conveying emotions and character dynamics. Beta readers can provide valuable insights into whether the dialogue feels authentic and aligned with diverse voices, cultures, and experiences.
- *Cultivating Empathy*: Being open to feedback fosters empathy and a willingness to learn from others' experiences. This empathy translates into more nuanced and compassionate storytelling, making the lesbian romance novel relatable to a broader audience.
- *Addressing Unintended Biases*: No writer is immune to unconscious biases. Feedback from sensitivity readers helps identify and address any unintentional biases, creating a more inclusive and respectful narrative.
- *Celebrating Diverse Experiences*: Embracing feedback allows you to celebrate the richness and complexity of diverse identities within the lesbian community. It showcases a commitment to giving each character an authentic and unique voice.
- *Continuous Improvement*: Writing is a

continuous learning process. By embracing feedback, you grow as a writer, elevating your storytelling and creating a more impactful lesbian romance novel.

Incorporating diverse identities and experiences in a lesbian romance novel requires openness to feedback. Seeking insights from beta readers or sensitivity readers is a valuable step in refining the dialogue and ensuring respectful representation. Listening to diverse perspectives enhances authenticity, challenges stereotypes, and cultivates empathy, making your lesbian romance a compelling and inclusive journey of love, growth, and self-discovery. Embrace feedback as an opportunity to create a more profound and resonant connection with readers, showcasing the beauty and complexity of diverse identities within the lesbian community.

Writing authentic and engaging dialogue is an art that brings characters to life and enhances the reader's connection to the story. By focusing on individual voices, natural language, subtext, and purposeful interactions, authors can create compelling conversations that drive the plot forward and reveal the complexities of the characters' emotions and relationships. Well-crafted dialogue elevates the overall quality of the novel and leaves readers immersed in the world of the characters' love journey.

Creating a Compelling Plot – Crafting a Riveting Love Story

Creating a riveting love story is a delightful and rewarding challenge for any writer, especially in the context of a lesbian romance novel. To captivate readers and evoke powerful emotions, consider incorporating the following elements into your storytelling:

Compelling Protagonists

Introducing relatable and well-developed protagonists is essential to creating a deep emotional connection with readers. To make their love journey compelling, craft protagonists with clear goals, distinct personalities, and relatable struggles. Give readers a reason to invest in their love journey by making them likable, flawed, and easy to root for. Here's how to achieve this:

- *Clear Goals*: Each protagonist should have specific and meaningful goals that drive their actions throughout the story. Whether it's pursuing a career, finding self-acceptance, or overcoming past traumas, these goals add depth to their characters and create a sense of purpose in the narrative.
- *Distinct Personalities*: Develop protagonists with unique personalities that shine through their dialogue, actions, and thoughts. Diverse personalities create a rich tapestry of characters that readers can connect with on various levels.
- *Relatable Struggles*: Give protagonists struggles

and challenges that readers can empathize with. These struggles may include navigating identity, dealing with heartbreak, or balancing personal and professional aspirations. Relatable challenges make the protagonists more human and their journey more captivating.

- *Likability and Flaws*: Make the protagonists likable by highlighting their positive traits, such as kindness, wit, or resilience. However, don't shy away from giving them flaws and vulnerabilities. Imperfections make characters more relatable and endearing, allowing readers to root for their growth and happiness.
- *Emotional Depth*: Dive into the protagonists' emotions and inner thoughts. Show their fears, desires, and doubts, allowing readers to understand their motivations and connect with their emotional journey.
- *Backstories*: Provide meaningful backstories that shape the protagonists' identities and actions. Past experiences influence their current behavior, motivations, and approach to relationships.
- *Growth and Development*: Throughout the story, allow the protagonists to experience personal growth and transformation. Their romantic relationship should empower them to embrace their true selves and overcome obstacles, reinforcing the theme of self-discovery and acceptance.
- *Chemistry and Connection*: Establish a strong emotional and physical chemistry between the protagonists. Their interactions should be genuine and evocative, creating a palpable connection that draws readers into their love story.
- *Relatable Relationships*: Explore the protagonists' relationships with friends,

family, and the LGBTQ+ community. These relationships add depth and dimension to their characters, showing different facets of their personalities and values.
- *Resilience and Determination*: As the protagonists face challenges and adversity, showcase their resilience and determination to overcome them. Their love for each other should serve as a source of strength, empowering them to face obstacles together.

Crafting compelling protagonists is vital to captivating readers and immersing them in a journey of love, growth, and self-discovery. By introducing protagonists with clear goals, distinct personalities, and relatable struggles, readers can connect with their emotional journey on a profound level. Make the protagonists likable, flawed, and easy to root for, showcasing their growth, resilience, and determination as they navigate their love story. Through well-developed characters and their emotional connection, the lesbian romance becomes an unforgettable and heartfelt exploration of love, identity, and the triumph of the human spirit.

Establishing Chemistry

Building a strong emotional and physical chemistry between the protagonists is essential to create a captivating love story. From the very beginning, their interactions should be authentic, engaging, and filled with a genuine connection and attraction. Here's how to establish chemistry between the protagonists:

- *Authentic First Meeting*: Craft a memorable and authentic first meeting for the protagonists.

Whether it's a chance encounter, a shared interest, or a meaningful introduction, make the moment feel special and significant.
- *Sparks of Attraction*: Infuse their initial interactions with subtle sparks of attraction. Show them looking into each other's eyes, nervous glances, or the warmth in their smiles when they are around each other.
- *Shared Interests and Passions*: Develop common interests or passions that the protagonists can bond over. Sharing hobbies or dreams creates an immediate connection and sets the foundation for their chemistry to grow.
- *Meaningful Conversations*: Allow their conversations to be meaningful and filled with depth. Encourage them to share their thoughts, fears, and aspirations, creating an emotional bond that goes beyond superficial attraction.
- *Emotional Vulnerability*: Explore moments of vulnerability where the protagonists reveal their fears and insecurities to each other. Sharing vulnerability deepens their connection and makes the chemistry more profound.
- *Moments of Tension*: Introduce moments of tension and conflict in their interactions. These can be playful banter, heated discussions, or instances where their perspectives differ, adding depth and dynamics to their chemistry.
- *Emotional Resonance*: Show how their emotions mirror each other's. When one character feels joy, the other shares it, and when one character experiences sorrow, the other empathizes. This emotional resonance strengthens their bond.
- *Physical Gestures*: Incorporate meaningful physical gestures, such as a gentle touch, a lingering glance, or a subtle brush of hands. These small but intimate actions speak volumes about their attraction to each other.

- *Shared Laughter*: Showcase moments of shared laughter and joy. Humor and laughter create an intimate and lighthearted atmosphere that allows the chemistry to flourish.
- *Building Anticipation*: Develop a sense of anticipation in their interactions. Let readers feel the underlying tension and excitement as the protagonists' feelings for each other deepen.

Building a strong emotional and physical chemistry between the protagonists is the heart of a compelling romance. Through authentic interactions, shared interests, emotional vulnerability, and genuine attraction, readers become invested in their love story. As the protagonists' chemistry evolves and intensifies, the romance becomes a powerful and immersive journey of connection, self-discovery, and passionate love. By crafting a tale of authentic attraction, the lesbian romance captivates readers' hearts and leaves them rooting for the protagonists' love to flourish.

Realistic Obstacles

Introduce obstacles and conflicts that test the protagonists' relationship. These challenges can be internal, such as self-doubt or fear of vulnerability, or external, like societal prejudices or family opposition. Overcoming these obstacles should be a central theme of the story. Setting realistic obstacles and conflicts is essential to test the protagonists' relationship and add depth to the narrative. Here's how to craft realistic obstacles in the narrative:

- *Internal Struggles*: Explore the protagonists' internal struggles, such as grappling with past traumas, fears of commitment, or self-acceptance. Their inner conflicts should be relatable and resonate with readers, adding layers to their character arcs.

- *Fear of Vulnerability*: Showcase how the protagonists' fear of being vulnerable and getting hurt affects their willingness to fully open up to each other. This fear can create emotional distance, leading to challenges in their relationship.
- *External Prejudices*: Confront the couple with external challenges like societal prejudices, homophobia, or discrimination they face due to their sexual orientation. This allows you to address important real-world issues and highlight the strength of their love amid adversity.
- *Family Opposition*: Develop conflicts arising from family opposition or unsupportive relatives. Show how the protagonists navigate the complexities of family dynamics while staying true to their love for each other.
- *Communication Breakdown*: Introduce moments of miscommunication or misunderstandings that strain the protagonists' relationship. These conflicts can arise from different communication styles or past baggage.
- *Time and Distance*: Explore how external factors like time and physical distance can put a strain on the couple's relationship. Long-distance challenges or time-consuming commitments can lead to feelings of isolation and doubt.
- *Personal Growth and Priorities*: Show how personal growth and shifting priorities can lead to conflicts in the relationship. As the protagonists evolve individually, they may face challenges in aligning their paths.
- *Temptations and External Influences*: Present

situations where the protagonists are tempted or influenced by others, potentially leading to conflict and testing the strength of their commitment.
- *Facing the Past*: Bring the protagonists face-to-face with unresolved past issues that impact their present relationship. Addressing these unresolved matters allows for growth and healing.
- *Overcoming Together*: Emphasize the importance of overcoming obstacles as a team. By facing challenges together, the protagonists demonstrate the depth of their love and the power of their bond.

Don't forget that realistic obstacles provide a crucible for testing the protagonists' relationship. By exploring internal struggles, external prejudices, family opposition, and other challenges, the love journey becomes a powerful narrative of resilience and triumph. As the protagonists navigate through these obstacles and emerge stronger together, the story becomes a testament to the enduring power of love and the unwavering spirit of the human heart. Crafting realistic obstacles and central conflicts ensures that your novel will resonate deeply with readers and leaves a lasting impression of hope, acceptance, and the transformative power of love.

Emotional Depth

Delving into the emotional depth of the characters' feelings for each other is vital to creating a profound and unforgettable love story. Showcasing the progression of their love, from the initial spark to the deep emotional bond they develop over time, adds layers of authenticity and resonance to their relationship. Here's how to explore emotional depth in the narrative:

- *Initial Spark*: Introduce the protagonists' first encounters, where the spark of attraction ignites between them. Use vivid imagery and evocative language to portray the butterflies, heart flutters, and heightened senses that accompany the early stages of attraction.
- *Growing Connection*: Illustrate the protagonists' growing connection as they spend more time together. Showcase shared experiences, meaningful conversations, and moments of vulnerability that strengthen their emotional bond.
- *Vulnerable Moments*: Allow the characters to open up about their fears, insecurities, and past wounds. These vulnerable moments create emotional intimacy and foster a deeper understanding of each other's inner worlds.
- *Shared Dreams and Aspirations*: Explore how the protagonists support each other's dreams and aspirations. Their shared vision for the future strengthens their emotional connection and reinforces their commitment to each other.
- *Empathy and Understanding*: Demonstrate moments of empathy and understanding between the characters. As they become attuned to each other's feelings and needs, their emotional bond deepens.
- *Overcoming Obstacles Together*: Showcase how the protagonists face and overcome obstacles as a team. The challenges they conquer together forge an unbreakable emotional bond and a sense of unity.
- *Intimate Moments*: Write intimate scenes that

reveal the characters' vulnerability, passion, and emotional connection. These moments of physical and emotional intimacy strengthen their bond and convey the depth of their love.
- *Weathering Storms*: Confront the characters with conflicts and hardships that test their relationship. How they navigate these storms together highlights the resilience and depth of their love.
- *Reaffirming Love*: Create heartwarming scenes where the characters reaffirm their love for each other, expressing it through words and actions. These gestures solidify their emotional connection and reaffirm their commitment.
- *Profound Declarations*: Allow the protagonists to make profound declarations of love that encapsulate the depth of their emotions. These declarations can be simple yet heartfelt, leaving readers moved and invested in their love story.

The depth of feelings the characters have for each other is the soul of a compelling lesbian romance. As their love progresses from the initial spark to a deep emotional bond, readers become captivated by the authenticity and resonance of their relationship. By depicting vulnerable moments, shared dreams, and intimate connections, the love journey becomes a powerful exploration of the human heart's capacity for love and growth. Crafting emotional depth in the narrative ensures that the lesbian romance leaves readers with a profound and heartwarming experience, celebrating the transformative power of love and the beauty of a love that unfolds with genuine emotional depth.

Evocative Setting

The setting plays a crucial role in setting the stage for the love story. Crafting an evocative and immersive backdrop enhances the atmosphere of the romance, enveloping readers in a world that beautifully complements the protagonists' emotional journey. The setting becomes a canvas for love's enchantment whether it's a bustling city, a picturesque countryside, or a fantastical realm. Here's how to create an evocative setting in the narrative:

- *Cityscape Charms*: If the story takes place in a bustling city, vividly describe the sights, sounds, and energy of urban life. Illuminate the busy streets, twinkling city lights, and the hum of a buzzing metropolis, which reflects the protagonists' dynamic lives and passions.
- *Rustic Romance*: For a picturesque countryside setting, paint a serene landscape of rolling hills, lush meadows, and quaint cottages. Use sensory details to evoke the fragrance of wildflowers, the gentle rustle of leaves, and the tranquility of nature, mirroring the protagonists' journey of self-discovery and finding solace in simplicity.
- *Enchanting Fantasy Realm*: If your love story unfolds in a fantastical realm, weave a tapestry of magical landscapes and otherworldly wonders. Describe mystical forests, cascading waterfalls, and ethereal creatures, embodying the protagonists' extraordinary love amid the enchantment.
- *Coastal Serenity*: Set the romance against the backdrop of a tranquil coastal setting. Describe the rhythmic crash of waves, the feel of sand beneath bare feet, and the salty ocean breeze, symbolizing the ebb and flow of the protagonists' emotions and the enduring nature of their love.

- *Historic Charm*: Transport readers to a setting rich in history and charm. Use descriptive language to evoke the grandeur of old castles, cobblestone streets, and ornate architecture, which mirrors the depth and timeless quality of the protagonists' love.
- *Sensory Immersion*: Engage the senses to immerse readers in the setting. Describe the tastes of local cuisine, the feel of the sun on skin, the sounds of laughter, and the warmth of a crackling fireplace, enveloping readers in the ambiance of the romance.
- *Seasonal Enchantment*: If the story spans across seasons, showcase the transformative beauty of nature. Each season can reflect different phases of the protagonists' relationship, from the budding romance of spring to the cozy intimacy of winter.
- *Cultural Richness*: Embrace the cultural aspects of the setting to add depth and authenticity. Incorporate traditions, festivals, and customs that resonate with the characters' backgrounds and experiences.

An evocative and immersive setting in your novel serves as a mesmerizing backdrop for the love story, enhancing its atmosphere and emotional resonance. Whether it's a bustling city, a picturesque countryside, or a fantastical realm, the setting becomes a living entity that reflects the protagonists' emotions, growth, and unfolding romance. By masterfully painting the canvas of love's enchantment through vivid descriptions and sensory immersion, the lesbian romance becomes an unforgettable journey of love and self-discovery, transporting readers to a world where the heart's desires bloom and love's magic weaves its spell.

Well-Paced Plot

A well-paced plot is the key to keeping readers engaged and eager to journey alongside the protagonists. Balancing moments of tension and conflict with tender and heartwarming scenes creates a roller coaster of emotions, making the love story unforgettable. Here's how to craft a well-paced plot that captivates readers:

- *Engaging Introduction*: Begin the story with an engaging and intriguing introduction that hooks readers from the first page. Introduce the protagonists and their world in a way that sparks curiosity and sets the tone for the emotional journey ahead.
- *Initial Spark*: Build tension and excitement as the protagonists' initial attraction sparks. Create moments of anticipation and longing, leaving readers eager to see how their relationship unfolds.
- *Developing Connection*: Allow the relationship to blossom gradually, giving room for the emotional bond between the protagonists to deepen. Balance heartfelt conversations and shared experiences that strengthen their connection.
- *Moments of Tension*: Introduce conflicts and obstacles that test the relationship. These moments of tension add drama and keep readers invested in the protagonists' journey of overcoming challenges.
- *Heartwarming Scenes*: Offset moments of tension with heartwarming scenes that showcase the protagonists' affection and tenderness for each other. These moments of intimacy and

support resonate with readers and reinforce the strength of their love.
- *Emotional Turmoil*: Explore the protagonists' emotional turmoil as they confront their internal struggles. Allow readers to empathize with their fears, doubts, and vulnerabilities, making the characters more relatable.
- *External Challenges*: Bring in external challenges that impact the relationship, such as societal prejudices or family opposition. Addressing these challenges adds depth to the plot and highlights the resilience of the protagonists' love.
- *Climactic Moments*: Build anticipation toward climactic moments where the protagonists face their biggest obstacles. These moments should be emotionally charged and transformative for the characters.
- *Resolution and Growth*: Offer a satisfying resolution to the conflicts, allowing the protagonists to grow individually and as a couple. Showcase their personal development and how their love has transformed them.
- *Emotional Catharsis*: End the story with an emotional catharsis that leaves readers with a profound sense of fulfillment and closure. A well-paced plot ensures that readers are emotionally invested until the very last page.

Crafting a well-paced plot ensures that readers are enthralled by the emotional journey of the protagonists. By balancing moments of tension, conflict, and emotional turmoil with heartwarming scenes of love and tenderness, the plot becomes a roller coaster of emotions that keeps readers eager to turn the pages. A carefully crafted plot invites readers to experience the protagonists' challenges, growth, and triumphs, making the love story a truly immersive and unforgettable experience.

Moments of Intimacy

Add emotional and physical intimacy to your story. Thoughtful and intimate conversations can be just as powerful as sensual scenes, adding depth and authenticity to the protagonists' connection. Here's how to include emotional and physical intimacy in the story:

- *Emotional Vulnerability*: Show the protagonists sharing their fears, dreams, and past traumas, creating a profound bond of trust and understanding.
- *Heartfelt Conversations*: Develop thoughtful and heartfelt conversations that delve into the characters' feelings and motivations. These intimate dialogues allow readers to witness the growth of their emotional connection.
- *Shared Dreams and Aspirations*: Explore moments where the protagonists share their dreams and aspirations with each other. Supporting each other's goals adds depth to their emotional intimacy.
- *Comfort in Silence*: Showcase the comfort the characters find in each other's presence, even in moments of silence. This unspoken understanding reinforces the strength of their emotional connection.
- *Physical Gestures*: Include tender physical gestures that convey affection and care. A gentle touch, a hand on the shoulder, or an embrace can speak volumes about their emotional intimacy.

- *Sensory Details*: Use sensory details to heighten the emotional intimacy of a scene. Describe the warmth of their touch, the softness of their voice, or the way they look into each other's eyes, deepening the readers' emotional engagement.
- *Private Moments*: Craft scenes of private and intimate moments between the protagonists. These secluded moments provide the space for vulnerability and emotional honesty.
- *Sensual and Meaningful*: When incorporating sensual scenes, ensure they are meaningful and add depth to the emotional connection. Focus on the characters' emotions and their emotional bond during these moments.
- *Building Anticipation*: Create a sense of anticipation in emotional and sensual scenes. Let readers feel the emotional tension and the tender vulnerability, heightening the impact of these moments.
- *Aftermath of Intimacy*: Show the aftermath of intimate moments, where the characters reflect on the depth of their feelings for each other. These introspective moments add richness to the emotional journey.

Remember moments of intimacy in emotional and physical aspects weave the threads of a profound connection in a lesbian romance. Thoughtful and intimate conversations, along with meaningful and sensual scenes, build a multidimensional relationship that readers can truly invest in. By depicting emotional vulnerability, shared dreams, and tender physical gestures, the love story becomes a tapestry of emotional and physical intimacy that resonates with readers' hearts. A skillful blend of these moments ensures that the protagonists' connection feels authentic and enduring, leaving readers deeply immersed in a love story that celebrates the beauty and power of emotional and physical intimacy in its most genuine form.

Character Growth

Allow your protagonists to experience personal growth throughout the story. Their journey together should inspire positive change and lead to self-discovery and empowerment. Character growth is a pivotal element that adds depth and authenticity to the protagonists' journey. Here's how to craft a narrative that celebrates the blossoming of the characters:

- *Initial Flaws and Insecurities*: Introduce the protagonists with relatable flaws and insecurities that hinder their emotional growth. These imperfections make them human and relatable to readers.
- *Learning from Each Other*: As the characters' love journey progresses, show how they learn from each other's strengths and weaknesses. Their interactions become opportunities for growth and self-reflection.
- *Facing Past Traumas*: Confront the protagonists with their past traumas and unresolved issues. Through the support of their relationship, allow them to heal and overcome these emotional barriers.
- *Challenging Comfort Zones*: Push the characters out of their comfort zones, prompting them to face their fears and embrace new experiences. Growth often happens when they are willing to step into the unknown.
- *Encouraging Self-Acceptance*: As the relationship develops, depict how the protagonists find

acceptance of themselves and their sexual identity. Love becomes a catalyst for embracing who they truly are.
- *Supporting Dreams and Aspirations*: Let the characters support each other's dreams and aspirations, encouraging personal growth and empowerment. Their relationship becomes a safe space for pursuing their passions.
- *Embracing Vulnerability*: Showcase the protagonists' willingness to be vulnerable with each other. This emotional openness fosters growth and strengthens their emotional bond.
- *Evolving Priorities*: Explore how their priorities evolve throughout the story. As they grow together, their goals and desires may shift, reflecting their personal growth.
- *Facing Adversity Together*: Allow the characters to face challenges and adversity as a team. Their ability to support and uplift each other in difficult times demonstrates their emotional maturity and growth.
- *Reflecting on Growth*: Toward the end of the story, provide moments of introspection where the characters reflect on their personal growth and how their relationship empowered them to become better versions of themselves.

Character growth is a vital aspect of a compelling lesbian romance, shaping the protagonists' journey of self-discovery and empowerment. As they navigate through challenges, face their past traumas, and support each other's dreams, their love story becomes a testament to the transformative power of love. By embracing vulnerability and pushing past comfort zones, the characters bloom into more confident, empowered, and self-accepting individuals. Character growth is a powerful aspect of a lesbian romance, inspiring readers with the protagonists' journey of self-discovery and empowerment. By allowing them to confront their flaws, heal from past wounds, and overcome internal barriers, the love story becomes a testament to the transformative power of love and understanding. As they empower each other, support personal goals, and navigate challenges together, the protagonists blossom into stronger, more authentic individuals. Ultimately, the characters' growth serves as a profound message of hope and empowerment, celebrating the beauty of love's capacity to ignite positive change and lead to self-discovery, acceptance, and a brighter future.

Showcasing Vulnerability – Embracing Hearts, Shared Souls

Displaying vulnerability in characters adds layers of authenticity and emotional depth to their relationship. Allowing them to share their fears and insecurities with each other creates a profound sense of trust and intimacy. Here's how to portray vulnerability to strengthen the emotional bond between the protagonists:

- *Opening Up*: Craft scenes where the characters open up about their deepest fears and insecurities. Let them share their past traumas, doubts, and vulnerabilities, creating an emotional connection built on honesty and understanding.
- *Fear of Rejection*: Explore the fear of rejection that may accompany coming out or embracing their true selves. Delve into how they navigate these anxieties together, reinforcing the trust

between them.
- *Moments of Uncertainty*: Create moments of uncertainty and self-doubt, where the characters question their feelings or their place in the relationship. These moments of vulnerability mirror real-life struggles and make the characters more relatable.
- *Comfort in Each Other*: Showcase how the protagonists find comfort and solace in each other's arms during moments of vulnerability. Their willingness to be vulnerable with each other strengthens their emotional bond.
- *Shared Support*: Illustrate how they support each other through moments of vulnerability, offering a safe space to express their deepest emotions without judgment or fear.
- *Emotional Closeness*: As the characters share their fears and insecurities, demonstrate how this emotional closeness fosters a sense of trust and understanding that enhances their connection.
- *Healing from Past Wounds*: Show how their vulnerability allows them to heal from past wounds and experiences. Together, they find the strength to face their inner demons and emerge stronger.
- *Reassurance and Affirmation*: Write scenes where they offer reassurance and affirmation to each other, reinforcing their love and commitment despite vulnerabilities.
- *Growth Through Vulnerability*: Highlight how vulnerability becomes a catalyst for personal growth and transformation. As they embrace their vulnerabilities, the characters evolve into more self-aware and confident individuals.
- *Unconditional Acceptance*: Ultimately, depict how vulnerability becomes a pillar of their relationship, paving the way for unconditional

acceptance and love.

Vulnerability in characters creates a profound and intimate emotional journey. Allowing the protagonists to share their fears, insecurities, and past traumas strengthens their emotional bond and nurtures trust. As they support each other through moments of uncertainty, their relationship becomes a haven of acceptance and understanding. Vulnerability becomes a powerful tool for personal growth and healing, leading the characters to embrace their true selves and find solace in each other's arms. By showcasing vulnerability, the love story becomes a celebration of the courage to be vulnerable and the transformative power of love to mend broken hearts and create an enduring connection.

Evoking Emotion

A riveting love story should evoke a range of emotions in readers, from joy and excitement to heartache and catharsis. Think of it as creating a symphony of feelings, the music of emotions. Tap into the universal themes of love, longing, and belonging to create an emotional resonance. The ability to evoke a range of emotions in readers is the heart of its power. Here's how to craft a love story that stirs the soul:

- *Joyful Beginnings*: Infuse the early stages of the protagonists' relationship with moments of delight and exhilaration. Their blossoming love should spark joy in readers, making them share in the thrill of new beginnings.
- *Tender Intimacy*: Create intimate scenes filled

with tenderness and vulnerability. These moments of emotional connection allow readers to feel the depth of the characters' love.
- *Longing and Desire*: Explore the yearning and longing the characters experience when they are apart. The ache of separation heightens the intensity of their emotions, resonating with readers who have experienced the same emotions.
- *Heartache and Conflict*: Introduce moments of heartache and conflict that test the protagonists' relationship. These emotional lows draw readers deeper into the story, invested in the characters' emotional journey.
- *Empathy and Understanding*: Develop scenes that elicit empathy from readers as they witness the characters' struggles and vulnerabilities. Fostering understanding between readers and characters strengthens the emotional bond.
- *Courage and Resilience*: Showcase the protagonists' courage and resilience as they face challenges and adversities. Readers will admire their strength and root for their triumph over obstacles.
- *Cathartic Moments*: Build toward cathartic moments where emotions run high, leading to emotional release and relief. These pivotal scenes provide readers with a powerful emotional experience.
- *Moments of Belonging*: Illustrate how the love between the characters fulfills their need for belonging. The sense of home and connection resonates deeply with readers' own desire for love and acceptance.
- *Bittersweet Farewells*: Craft bittersweet moments of farewell and reunion. The emotional complexity of these scenes tugs at readers' hearts, leaving them with a profound

sense of emotion.
- *Satisfying Closure*: Provide a satisfying resolution that leaves readers with a sense of fulfillment and hope. The emotional journey culminates in a cathartic and uplifting conclusion.

Evoking emotion is powerful and brings the readers along on the journey, the essence of its enchantment. By weaving universal themes of love, longing, and belonging, the narrative becomes a tapestry of feelings that resonate with readers' own experiences and emotions. From joy and excitement to heartache and catharsis, readers embark on an emotional journey that mirrors the complexities of love and relationships. By tapping into the core of human emotions, the love story becomes a timeless symphony that captures the hearts of readers, leaving them with a profound sense of connection and resonance with the characters' emotions.

Satisfying Resolution

Craft a satisfying and meaningful resolution to the love story. Give readers a sense of closure and fulfillment as they witness the protagonists' growth and triumph over obstacles, culminating in a powerful and heartwarming conclusion. Think of it as a journey of triumph and a heartwarming conclusion that the readers are begging for. Their happy-ever-after, or at least their happy-for-now, ending. Here's how to create a resolution that leaves a lasting impact:

- *Emotional Catharsis*: Build toward emotional catharsis, where the characters confront their

deepest fears and vulnerabilities. Allow them to express their emotions openly, paving the way for healing and growth.
- *Overcoming Obstacles*: Showcase how the protagonists confront and overcome the challenges that tested their love. Their resilience and determination to face obstacles together symbolize the strength of their bond.
- *Personal Growth*: Illustrate how the love story has influenced the protagonists' personal growth and transformation. Readers should witness their journey toward self-discovery and empowerment.
- *Empowering Love*: Emphasize how the love between the characters empowers them to embrace their true selves and find happiness. Their love becomes a beacon of hope and acceptance.
- *Fulfilled Desires*: Bring the characters' individual goals and desires to fruition. Seeing their dreams fulfilled adds a sense of accomplishment and closure to their personal journeys.
- *Stronger Together*: Highlight how the protagonists are stronger together, having faced and overcome challenges as a united front. Their bond becomes unshakable, and readers celebrate their love's triumph.
- *Meaningful Declarations*: Craft heartfelt declarations of love and commitment between the characters. These declarations solidify their emotional connection and leave readers with a warm feeling of love and contentment.
- *Celebration of Love*: End the story with a celebration of love and happiness. Whether it's a tender moment shared between the characters or a heartwarming event, it reinforces the beauty of their journey.
- *Hope and Promise*: Conclude the story with a

sense of hope and promise for the future. Let readers envision a life of love and happiness for the protagonists beyond the final page.
- *Emotional Resonance*: Ensure that the resolution resonates emotionally with readers, leaving a lasting impact on their hearts and minds. A satisfying conclusion is one that lingers with readers long after the story ends.

A satisfying and meaningful resolution is the culmination of an emotional journey filled with growth and triumph. By providing closure and fulfillment, readers are left with a heartwarming conclusion that celebrates the protagonists' triumph over obstacles and their profound emotional connection. Through personal growth, empowering love, and heartfelt declarations, the resolution leaves readers with a warm feeling of hope and happiness. The love story becomes a powerful testament to the resilience of love and the triumph of the human spirit, making it a truly satisfying and memorable experience for readers.

Crafting a riveting love story in the context of a romance novel involves a delicate balance of character development, chemistry, emotional depth, and realistic challenges. By immersing readers in a rich and captivating world, connecting them to compelling protagonists, and evoking a range of emotions, authors can create a love story that lingers in readers' hearts long after the final page is turned. Ultimately, a well-crafted love story has the power to inspire, uplift, and resonate with readers, celebrating the transformative and empowering nature of love in all its forms.

Creating a Compelling Plot – Incorporating Conflict and Tension

Conflict and tension are essential elements in any engaging story, including lesbian romance novels. They add depth, excitement, and emotional intensity to the narrative, making the love story more compelling and memorable. Each protagonist carries their own personal baggage and insecurities, which shape their journey toward love. Delve into their past traumas, fears, and past relationship disappointments to create internal conflicts and obstacles that challenge their ability to fully open up to love. Here's how to explore their emotional complexities and craft a heartfelt narrative:

- *Traumatic Experiences*: Unveil the protagonists' traumatic experiences from their past. It could be heartbreak, loss, or painful memories that haunt their hearts and create emotional barriers.
- *Fear of Vulnerability*: Explore their fear of vulnerability and intimacy. Delicate moments of hesitation reveal the characters' struggle to trust and open up emotionally.
- *Emotional Walls*: Illustrate how they have built emotional walls around their hearts as a defense mechanism. These walls protect them from potential hurt but also hinder their ability to embrace love fully.
- *Past Relationship Disappointments*: Reveal past relationship disappointments that still linger in their hearts. The wounds of the past cause them

to be cautious about diving into new love.
- *Fear of Rejection*: Portray their fear of rejection, particularly related to their sexual identity. The societal pressure to conform adds complexity to their emotional journey.
- *Overcoming Internal Conflicts*: Allow the characters to grapple with their internal conflicts as they navigate their feelings for each other. Their emotional growth becomes intertwined with their ability to confront these conflicts.
- *Healing Through Love*: As the love story progresses, show how their emotional bond becomes a source of healing and empowerment. The protagonists discover the courage to confront their insecurities, knowing they have each other's support.
- *Patience and Understanding*: Demonstrate how patience and understanding play a vital role in breaking down the walls around their hearts. The gradual opening up creates a sense of hope and anticipation.
- *Supportive Encounters*: Introduce supportive encounters with friends or mentors who encourage the protagonists to confront their insecurities. These interactions act as catalysts for emotional growth.
- *Triumph of Love*: The resolution should celebrate the protagonists' triumph over their personal baggage and insecurities. As they choose love and vulnerability, their emotional liberation becomes a powerful and heartwarming conclusion.

Exploring each protagonist's personal baggage and insecurities is essential to crafting a layered and emotionally resonant lesbian love story. By delving into their past traumas, fears, and relationship disappointments, readers witness the complexity of their emotional journey. As they overcome internal conflicts, embrace vulnerability, and choose love over fear, the protagonists' emotional growth becomes a testament to the transformative power of love. Ultimately, the love story becomes a heartwarming celebration of healing, liberation, and the unyielding strength of the human heart.

External Obstacles

Think of external obstacles as triumphing against adversity. Introducing external challenges adds depth and tension to the protagonists' relationship. These obstacles are external factors that stand in the way of their love, testing their commitment and resilience. These could include societal prejudices against same-sex couples, disapproving family members, or professional conflicts that strain their ability to be together. Here's how to create impactful external obstacles that shape their emotional journey:

- *Societal Prejudices*: Address societal prejudices against same-sex couples. Explore how the characters navigate discrimination, judgment, and misunderstanding from the world around them.
- *Familial Disapproval*: Introduce disapproving family members who challenge the protagonists' relationship. The characters must confront the pain of familial rejection and find strength to be true to themselves.
- *Professional Conflicts*: Depict professional conflicts that strain their ability to be together.

Balancing careers and personal lives becomes a challenge as they strive to make their relationship work.
- *Homophobia and Bigotry*: Confront instances of homophobia and bigotry that the protagonists encounter in their daily lives. These instances add tension and emotional depth to the story.
- *Long-Distance Relationship*: Consider a long-distance relationship as an external obstacle. The geographical distance tests the characters' commitment and communication.
- *Social Stigma*: Address the social stigma and misconceptions surrounding same-sex relationships. The characters may struggle with the weight of these misconceptions on their love.
- *Legal Battles*: Introduce legal battles or challenges related to same-sex relationships. This external obstacle adds a layer of complexity to their journey.
- *Fear of Outing*: Explore the fear of being outed or the pressure to remain closeted due to external circumstances. This internal conflict can affect their ability to fully embrace their love.
- *Workplace Discrimination*: Illuminate workplace discrimination against same-sex couples. This obstacle challenges the characters' professional lives and their sense of security.
- *Supporting Each Other*: As they face external challenges, show how the protagonists support and uplift each other. Their unwavering love and determination become powerful tools to overcome adversity.

Introducing external obstacles in a lesbian love story enriches the narrative, showcasing the protagonists' resilience in the face of adversity. Addressing societal prejudices, familial disapproval, and professional conflicts adds depth to the characters' emotional journey. By triumphing against homophobia, social stigma, and legal battles, the love story becomes a powerful celebration of love's ability to conquer all odds. The characters' commitment to each other, despite external challenges, leaves readers inspired by their strength and love's unwavering power. Ultimately, the love story becomes a poignant reminder of the importance of love, acceptance, and the triumph of the human spirit over external adversities.

Miscommunication and Assumptions

Miscommunication and misunderstandings between the protagonists can create tension and drama. Play with the idea of characters making assumptions or failing to communicate effectively, leading to conflicts that need to be resolved. These misunderstandings create tension and conflicts that test their emotional bond and highlight the importance of effective communication. A word of caution here—how often have you read a novel and thought, "If only the character's said something, all of this could have been avoided," make sure you don't fall into this trap, too. Here's how to play with miscommunication and assumptions to craft a captivating narrative:

- *Unspoken Feelings*: Establish moments where the characters have unspoken feelings for each other. Their failure to express their emotions creates underlying tension and sparks curiosity in readers.
- *Assumptions about Intentions*: Let the

protagonists make assumptions about each other's intentions or actions. These assumptions may lead to misunderstandings and emotional turmoil.
- *Misinterpretations*: Show how innocent actions or gestures can be misinterpreted, leading to confusion and conflict. The characters' misinterpretations fuel the story's emotional arc.
- *Fear of Rejection*: Illustrate how the fear of rejection inhibits the characters from communicating their true feelings. This fear becomes a barrier they must overcome to connect deeply.
- *External Influences*: Introduce external influences or third parties who manipulate or distort the characters' understanding of each other. These influences contribute to the drama and tension.
- *Reluctance to Confront*: Demonstrate their reluctance to confront the truth or address the misunderstandings. Their hesitance prolongs the emotional conflict and keeps readers invested in their resolution.
- *Emotional Distance*: Depict emotional distance between the characters due to miscommunication and assumptions. This distance adds depth to their emotional journey.
- *Healing through Clarity*: As the story progresses, show how clarity and effective communication become the pathway to healing and resolution. The characters learn the importance of honesty and vulnerability.
- *Vulnerable Conversations*: Craft vulnerable conversations where the protagonists finally address their misunderstandings. These heart-to-heart conversations lead to emotional breakthroughs.

- *Strengthened Bond*: Through overcoming miscommunication, illustrate how their bond deepens and their love becomes more profound. The resolution brings a satisfying sense of emotional growth.

Miscommunication and assumptions are potent elements in a lesbian love story, creating tension and emotional depth. By exploring unspoken feelings, misunderstandings, and fear of rejection, readers are drawn into the protagonists' emotional journey. As the characters confront their assumptions and communicate effectively, the resolution becomes a celebration of emotional growth and the triumph of love. The love story serves as a reminder of the significance of honest and vulnerable communication in nurturing a strong and enduring bond. Ultimately, the unraveled hearts find healing and clarity, leading to a heartfelt and fulfilling conclusion that resonates with readers.

Love Triangles

Introduce a love triangle where one or both protagonists have to choose between two potential love interests. This adds complexity and heightened emotions to the story as they navigate their feelings and make difficult decisions. As one or both protagonists find themselves torn between two potential love interests, their feelings and loyalties are tested. Another word of caution here—we aren't talking about adultery or cheating, both taboo with most readers. Here's how to craft a compelling love triangle that keeps readers engaged:

- *First Love Rekindled*: Reintroduce a former love interest from the protagonist's past, creating a nostalgic connection that reignites old feelings.
- *New and Exciting*: Introduce a new love interest who brings excitement and novelty into the protagonist's life, stirring a sense of curiosity and attraction.
- *Emotional Tug-of-War*: Illustrate the internal tug-of-war the protagonist experiences as they grapple with their feelings for both love interests.
- *Shared History*: Develop the history and shared experiences between the protagonist and their former love interest. These memories evoke emotions and challenge the protagonist's present relationship.
- *Strong Connection*: Highlight the strong emotional connection between the protagonist and the new love interest. Their bond adds depth to the love triangle and fuels the protagonist's dilemma.
- *Emotional Vulnerability*: Show the emotional vulnerability of the protagonists as they struggle to make a decision that impacts their hearts and lives.
- *Friendship vs. Romance*: Explore how the protagonist's existing friendship with one love interest complicates their decision-making process.
- *Conflicting Desires*: Illuminate the conflicting desires the protagonist has for each love interest, leaving readers torn along with the protagonist.
- *Internal Growth*: As the love triangle unfolds, allow the protagonist to experience internal growth and self-discovery, paving the way for their eventual choice.
- *Resolution and Closure*: Bring the love triangle to a satisfying resolution, where the protagonist

makes a heartfelt decision that honors their emotional journey.

A well-crafted love triangle in a lesbian love story adds layers of complexity and heartfelt emotions to the narrative. As the protagonists navigate their feelings and make difficult decisions, readers become emotionally invested in their journey. The internal tug-of-war, shared history, and emotional vulnerability draw readers into the heart of the love triangle. Ultimately, the resolution of the love triangle becomes a pivotal moment of growth and self-discovery for the protagonist. The love story serves as a reminder of the intricacies of the human heart and the power of love to shape our lives and choices.

Internal Conflict Over Identity – Embracing the True Self

In a poignant lesbian love story, exploring the internal conflict over sexual identity adds a layer of emotional depth to the characters and their romantic relationships. The protagonists' journey of self-acceptance and self-discovery becomes a powerful narrative arc. Here's how to address this internal conflict with sensitivity and authenticity:

- *Self-Doubt*: Illustrate the characters' self-doubt about their sexual identity. They may grapple with questions of self-worth and struggle to accept themselves fully.
- *Fear of Rejection*: Depict the fear of rejection, both from others and from themselves. The characters may hesitate to embrace their

true selves due to societal pressures or past experiences.
- *Navigating Society's Expectations*: Explore the internal conflict of living up to societal expectations and norms. The pressure to conform can create inner turmoil as the characters strive to find their authentic selves.
- *Reluctance to Open Up*: Show how the characters' internal conflict impacts their ability to open up emotionally in their romantic relationships. They may fear judgment or rejection from their partners.
- *Supportive Relationships*: Introduce supportive relationships with friends or mentors who encourage the characters to embrace their true selves. These relationships become catalysts for growth.
- *Emotional Growth*: Allow the characters to experience emotional growth and self-acceptance throughout the story. The journey toward embracing their identity becomes intertwined with their romantic relationships.
- *Overcoming Shame*: Address the characters' struggle with feelings of shame surrounding their sexual identity. Overcoming this shame becomes a significant milestone in their emotional journey.
- *Moments of Self-Discovery*: Craft tender moments of self-discovery where the characters begin to recognize and embrace their true identity. These moments evoke powerful emotions.
- *Trust and Vulnerability*: Show how the characters' journey toward self-acceptance impacts their ability to trust and be vulnerable in their romantic relationships.
- *Celebration of Identity*: Ultimately, celebrate the characters' acceptance and embracing of

their sexual identity. Their journey becomes an inspiring testament to the power of self-love.

Addressing the internal conflict over sexual identity in a lesbian love story adds emotional depth and authenticity to the characters' journey. Through self-doubt, fear of rejection, and societal expectations, the characters' emotional struggles are brought to life. As they navigate their path toward self-acceptance, their romantic relationships become a space of vulnerability and growth. The resolution becomes a celebration of their true selves, inspiring readers with the importance of embracing one's identity and finding love in its purest form. The love story serves as a reminder of the resilience of the human spirit and the beauty of embracing one's authentic self.

Secrets and Reveals

Incorporate secrets or undisclosed information that can alter the course of the relationship. Revealing these secrets at pivotal moments can heighten tension and bring the protagonists closer or create additional conflicts to resolve. They can add intrigue and emotional intensity to the narrative. Here's how to skillfully integrate secrets and reveals into the story:

- *Unspoken Pasts*: Establish unspoken pasts that one or both protagonists carry. These undisclosed experiences contribute to their emotional complexity.
- *Fear of Vulnerability*: Depict the characters' fear of vulnerability, which leads them to withhold important information from each other.
- *Pivotal Moments of Revelation*: Strategically

reveal the secrets at pivotal moments in the story, where their disclosure has significant emotional impact.
- *Conflict or Connection*: The revelation of secrets can lead to either conflict or a deeper emotional connection between the protagonists, depending on the nature of the truth.
- *Trust and Forgiveness*: Show how the characters grapple with trust and forgiveness as they navigate the aftermath of the reveals.
- *Impact on the Relationship*: Illustrate how the disclosed information alters the course of their relationship. It can lead to self-discovery, strengthened bonds, or additional conflicts to overcome.
- *Unraveling Hearts*: The disclosure of secrets can unravel the characters' hearts, forcing them to confront their true emotions and desires.
- *Emotional Roller Coaster*: The moments of revelation can create an emotional roller coaster for the characters and readers, heightening the stakes of the love story.
- *Growth and Empowerment*: As the characters face the truth and its consequences, allow them to experience personal growth and empowerment.
- *Resolution and Healing*: The resolution of the secrets should offer healing and closure, culminating in a transformative and satisfying conclusion.

Incorporating secrets and reveals into a lesbian love story adds depth and tension to the characters' emotional journey. The unspoken pasts, fear of vulnerability, and pivotal moments of revelation keep readers engaged and invested in the protagonists' relationship. Whether the secrets bring conflict or connection, they become catalysts for growth and self-discovery. Ultimately, the love story becomes a testament to the power of truth, trust, and forgiveness in shaping the characters' hearts and the course of their love. The resolution of the secrets offers a sense of closure and healing, leaving readers captivated by the emotional journey of the protagonists and the transformative power of love.

Unexpected Challenges

Surprise the characters and readers with unexpected challenges that disrupt their plans and force them to adapt. These surprises can test their commitment to each other and reveal the strength of their bond. Think of it as forging bonds amid turmoil. Introducing unexpected challenges can add depth and unpredictability to the narrative. Here's how to craft unexpected challenges that captivate characters and readers:

- *External Tragedies*: Introduce unforeseen external tragedies that impact the protagonists' lives and relationship. These events become pivotal moments of emotional growth and strength.
- *Sudden Relocation*: Disrupt the characters' plans with a sudden relocation, testing their ability to maintain their love across distance and change.
- *Family Secrets*: Reveal long-buried family secrets that surface and create turmoil within the protagonists' lives.
- *Unexpected Professional Opportunities*: A career opportunity that requires one protagonist to

make a difficult choice can add tension and uncertainty to the relationship.
- *Disagreements with Friends*: Unexpected disagreements or conflicts with close friends can strain the protagonists' bond and challenge their support system.
- *Health Crises*: Introduce health crises that require the characters to confront mortality and make life-altering decisions together.
- *Ethical Dilemmas*: Craft ethical dilemmas that force the protagonists to reevaluate their values and beliefs, adding complexity to their relationship.
- *Unplanned Responsibilities*: Unplanned responsibilities or obligations can disrupt the characters' plans, putting their love to the test.
- *Miscommunications with Consequences*: Show how miscommunications, even innocuous ones, can lead to unforeseen consequences and emotional conflicts.
- *Moments of Growth and Solidarity*: As the characters navigate unexpected challenges, highlight moments of growth and solidarity, revealing the strength of their bond.

Incorporating unexpected challenges in a lesbian love story adds intrigue and emotional depth to the protagonists' journey. Whether they face external tragedies, sudden relocations, or family secrets, these challenges test their commitment and resilience. As the characters adapt to unexpected circumstances, moments of growth and solidarity become the driving force behind their emotional journey. The love story serves as a reminder of the unpredictability of life and the power of love to forge unbreakable bonds amid turmoil. Ultimately, the resolution becomes a testament to the protagonists' strength and determination, leaving readers captivated by the emotional roller coaster of their love story.

Emotional Distance – Bridging the Divide, Rediscovering Love

In a compelling lesbian love story, exploring moments of emotional distance between the protagonists adds depth and tension to their relationship. Temporary emotional detachment becomes a catalyst for introspection, enabling the characters to confront their feelings and reassess their priorities. Here's how to skillfully navigate emotional distance to create a powerful narrative:

- *Internal Struggles*: Establish internal struggles that lead to emotional distance between the characters. These struggles can be related to past traumas, personal insecurities, or conflicting desires.
- *Communication Breakdown*: Illustrate instances where communication breaks down, leading to misunderstandings and emotional barriers between the protagonists.
- *External Stressors*: Introduce external stressors that contribute to emotional distance, such as work pressures, family conflicts, or unforeseen challenges.
- *Self-Reflection*: Allow the characters to engage in self-reflection during periods of emotional distance, prompting them to question their feelings and desires.
- *Reassessing Priorities*: The emotional distance can prompt the protagonists to reevaluate their priorities and what they truly want from their

relationship.
- *Vulnerable Moments*: Craft vulnerable moments where the characters confront their feelings and fears, fostering a deeper emotional connection.
- *Growth Through Space*: Explore how emotional distance can lead to personal growth for the characters, providing them with space to discover themselves.
- *Seeking Support*: Show how the characters seek support from friends or mentors during times of emotional distance, gaining valuable insights into their relationship.
- *Rediscovering Love*: As the emotional distance is bridged, depict the characters rediscovering their love for each other, leading to a stronger and more resilient bond.
- *Mutual Understanding*: Ultimately, the resolution should emphasize mutual understanding and a renewed commitment to their relationship.

Exploring emotional distance in a lesbian love story allows the characters to face their internal struggles and confront the complexities of their relationship. Communication breakdowns, external stressors, and moments of self-reflection create tension that paves the way for emotional growth. As the characters reassess their priorities and seek support from their friends or mentors, they rediscover the depth of their love for each other. The resolution becomes a celebration of their mutual understanding and a testament to the power of love to overcome emotional barriers. The love story serves as a reminder that confronting emotional distance can lead to personal growth and a deeper emotional connection, leaving readers captivated by the transformative journey of the protagonists' love.

Timing and Sacrifices – A Test of Commitment and Emotional Tension

In a poignant lesbian love story, timing can become a source of tension, challenging the characters with decisions that demand sacrifices or compromises for the sake of their relationship. These emotionally charged moments test the depth of their commitment and love for each other. Here's how to skillfully utilize timing and sacrifices to create a compelling narrative:

- *Opposing Life Paths*: Introduce situations where the protagonists' life paths seem to diverge, leading to difficult decisions about their future together.
- *Personal Aspirations*: Highlight the characters' personal aspirations that may conflict with the timing of their relationship, creating inner turmoil.
- *Long-Distance Relationships*: Explore the challenges of maintaining a long-distance relationship due to career opportunities or personal commitments.
- *Fear of Missing Out*: Show how the characters wrestle with the fear of missing out on other opportunities or experiences if they prioritize their relationship.
- *Emotional Crossroads*: Craft pivotal moments where the characters face emotional crossroads, forcing them to make sacrifices or compromises that impact their future.
- *Supportive Friends*: Utilize the support of friends or mentors who offer advice and guidance, adding depth to the characters' decision-making process.

- *Heartfelt Conversations*: Include heartfelt conversations where the characters candidly express their fears, hopes, and desires, revealing the depth of their emotions.
- *Internal Conflict*: Illustrate the internal conflict the characters experience as they weigh the cost of sacrifices against the potential rewards of their love.
- *Tests of Commitment*: The timing-related decisions become tests of the characters' commitment and determination to prioritize their relationship.
- *Growth and Solidarity*: Ultimately, showcase the growth and solidarity that emerge from the sacrifices and compromises made, reinforcing the strength of their love.

Timing and sacrifices in a love story create emotional tension that resonates with readers. As the characters confront opposing life paths, personal aspirations, and long-distance challenges, they face difficult decisions about their future together. These pivotal moments become emotional crossroads that test the depth of their commitment and love. Heartfelt conversations and internal conflicts add authenticity to their emotional journey. As the characters seek support and engage in introspection, they grow individually and as a couple. The resolution becomes a testament to the power of love to navigate the complexities of timing and sacrifices, leaving readers captivated by the transformative journey of the protagonists' relationship. The love story serves as a reminder that true love requires sacrifices and compromises, but in doing so, it becomes even more profound and resilient.

Ethical Dilemmas – Confronting Moral Choices, Testing Bonds

Ethical dilemmas force the protagonists to confront difficult moral choices. These dilemmas can impact their relationship and lead to internal conflicts that need resolution. Introducing ethical dilemmas adds complexity and depth to the narrative. Here's how to skillfully incorporate ethical dilemmas to create a powerful and thought-provoking story:

- *Conflicting Values*: Establish conflicting values or beliefs between the protagonists that lead to ethical dilemmas, highlighting their different perspectives.
- *Challenging Circumstances*: Present the characters with challenging circumstances that force them to make tough moral choices, putting their bond to the test.
- *Sacrifice vs. Self-Interest*: Explore dilemmas that revolve around sacrifice for the greater good versus pursuing self-interest or personal desires.
- *Loyalty and Truth*: Create dilemmas where loyalty to each other conflicts with the truth, leading to internal struggles over honesty and trust.
- *Moral Consequences*: Illustrate the moral consequences of the characters' choices, showcasing the impact on their relationship and personal growth.
- *Seeking Advice*: Allow the characters to seek advice from trusted friends or mentors, deepening the ethical exploration within the story.
- *Emotional Turmoil*: Depict the emotional

turmoil the protagonists experience as they grapple with the weight of their moral decisions.
- *Growth and Redemption*: Show how confronting ethical dilemmas leads to personal growth and potential opportunities for redemption.
- *Mutual Understanding*: Emphasize the importance of mutual understanding and compromise as the characters navigate their ethical conflicts together.
- *Resolution and Growth*: Ultimately, the resolution should offer a sense of growth and emotional resolution, solidifying their bond through the ethical journey.

Incorporating ethical dilemmas in a love story presents the protagonists with moral choices that deeply impact their relationship and sense of self. Conflicting values, challenging circumstances, and dilemmas of sacrifice versus self-interest create internal conflicts that demand resolution. As the characters grapple with loyalty, truth, and the consequences of their choices, emotional turmoil becomes a driving force of their emotional journey. Seeking advice from trusted friends and mentors adds depth to their ethical exploration.

The resolution showcases their growth and mutual understanding, ultimately solidifying their bond. The love story serves as a reminder that confronting ethical dilemmas can lead to personal growth and strengthened relationships, leaving readers captivated by the transformative journey of the protagonists' love. It also challenges readers to reflect on their own moral choices and the impact they have on their relationships and sense of self.

Incorporating conflict and tension in a lesbian romance novel is essential for keeping readers engaged and emotionally invested in the love story. By weaving personal insecurities, external challenges, miscommunication, and unexpected obstacles, authors create a dynamic narrative that showcases the protagonists' growth, resilience, and the transformative power of love. Balancing conflict and resolution allows for a satisfying and emotionally resonant love story that captivates readers from start to finish.

Creating a Compelling Plot – Balancing Romance with Other Plot Elements

In a lesbian romance novel, striking the right balance between the romantic storyline and other plot elements is crucial to create a well-rounded and engaging narrative. While the romance is the heart of the story, incorporating other plot elements enhances the depth and complexity of the novel. Here are some tips for achieving this balance:

Establish Clear Story Goals – Beyond the Romance, Navigating Life's Journey

In a well-crafted love story, it's essential to identify main story goals beyond the romantic plot. These goals add depth and dimension to the narrative, guiding the pacing and structure of the novel. Whether it's solving a mystery, pursuing a career goal, or navigating personal challenges, well-defined storyline goals enrich the protagonists' journey. Here's how to establish clear story goals:

- *Personal Growth*: Make personal growth a central goal for both protagonists. Show how they evolve as individuals throughout the story, independent of their romantic relationship.
- *Career Aspirations*: Integrate career aspirations that impact the characters' lives, aspirations

they strive to achieve while also navigating their love story.
- *Overcoming Obstacles*: Establish specific challenges and obstacles that the characters must overcome on their journey, creating a compelling subplot alongside the romance.
- *Solving a Mystery*: Incorporate a mystery or puzzle that captures the characters' attention, leading them on a journey of discovery and intrigue.
- *Family Dynamics*: Explore family dynamics and conflicts that influence the protagonists' decisions, showcasing how family relationships intersect with their romantic journey.
- *Embracing Identity*: Make embracing one's identity a significant goal for the characters. This could involve exploring their sexual orientation, cultural background, or personal beliefs.
- *Building Support Systems*: Develop the goal of creating strong support systems for the protagonists. Show how they rely on friends and mentors to navigate life's challenges.
- *Self-Discovery*: Emphasize self-discovery as a goal, with the characters seeking to understand their true desires and aspirations.
- *Overcoming Prejudices*: Introduce the goal of overcoming prejudices and societal barriers that impact the characters' relationship and sense of self.
- *Achieving Harmony*: Ultimately, the main story goals should align with achieving harmony and balance in the characters' lives, where personal growth and romance converge.

In a love story, establishing clear story goals beyond the romantic plot adds depth and complexity to the narrative. Personal growth, career aspirations, overcoming obstacles, solving mysteries, and embracing identity become pivotal aspects of the protagonists' journey. Exploring family dynamics, building support systems, and navigating prejudices further enrich the storyline. The ultimate goal is achieving harmony and balance in the characters' lives as they navigate the ups and downs of their personal and romantic journeys. Well-defined story goals guide the pacing and structure of the novel, leading to a captivating and transformative narrative. The love story becomes a powerful exploration of life's challenges and triumphs, leaving readers captivated by the multifaceted journey of the protagonists' love.

Intertwine Themes with Romance – Crafting a Cohesive Narrative

Interweaving the romantic storyline with the other plot elements by connecting them thematically adds depth and coherence to the narrative. The romantic relationship can mirror or enhance the protagonist's personal growth or external challenges, making the narrative more cohesive. Here's how to skillfully intertwine themes with romance:

- *Personal Growth and Love*: Make personal growth a central theme and show how the romantic relationship serves as a catalyst for the protagonists' individual development. As they fall in love, they also discover new aspects of themselves and overcome personal obstacles.
- *Overcoming External Challenges Together*: Connect the romantic relationship with external challenges that the protagonists face. As they navigate these obstacles together, their love

becomes a source of strength and resilience.
- *Embracing Identity and Finding Acceptance*: Intertwine themes of embracing one's identity and finding acceptance with the romantic plot. The characters' journey to self-acceptance mirrors their journey to embracing their love for each other.
- *Support and Belonging*: Show how the romantic relationship provides a sense of support and belonging for the protagonists. This theme can also extend to their broader support systems, such as friends and LGBTQ+ communities.
- *Sacrifice and Commitment*: Explore the theme of sacrifice and commitment in both the romantic relationship and other plot elements. The characters' willingness to make sacrifices for each other and their personal goals enhances the emotional depth of the narrative.
- *Love and Resilience*: Connect the theme of love with resilience, showcasing how the protagonists' love for each other helps them persevere through challenges and setbacks.
- *Truth and Communication*: Intertwine the importance of truth and effective communication in the romantic relationship and the characters' interactions with others. Misunderstandings and honesty become pivotal themes.
- *Family Dynamics and Acceptance*: Explore family dynamics and the theme of acceptance as the characters navigate their romantic relationship in the context of family approval or disapproval.
- *Redemption and Forgiveness*: Connect the themes of redemption and forgiveness, showing how characters learn to forgive themselves and others, fostering growth in their personal and romantic lives.

- *Journey to Fulfillment*: Ultimately, connect the journey to fulfillment with the characters' pursuit of personal goals and their romantic bond, making the resolution feel satisfying and harmonious.

Intertwining themes with romance in a lesbian love story creates a cohesive and emotionally resonant narrative. Personal growth, overcoming external challenges, and embracing identity become integral to the characters' romantic journey. Themes of support, sacrifice, love, and resilience enrich the emotional depth of the story. By connecting the romantic storyline with other plot elements thematically, the novel becomes a powerful exploration of life's complexities and triumphs. The love story serves as a reflection of the characters' personal growth, the challenges they face, and the power of love to overcome obstacles. Readers are captivated by the cohesive and transformative journey of the protagonists' love, leaving them moved and inspired by the interconnected themes that drive the narrative forward.

Create Multidimensional Characters – Crafting Rich and Engaging Personal Journeys

Each character should have their own motivations, dreams, and subplots that align with the overall plot while contributing to the romantic development. Here's how to develop multidimensional characters:

- *Protagonists' Distinct Personalities*: Create protagonists with unique personalities, each bringing their strengths, weaknesses, and quirks to the story.

- *Individual Motivations*: Give each character their own distinct motivations and desires that drive their actions and decisions beyond their romantic interest.
- *Backstories and Histories*: Develop detailed backstories and histories for the characters, delving into their past experiences and how they shaped their current selves.
- *Subplots*: Introduce subplots for each protagonist that align with the main story but are independent of the romantic plot, allowing them to grow as individuals.
- *External Challenges*: Design external challenges for each character that they must face and overcome, providing opportunities for personal growth and development.
- *Internal Conflicts*: Explore internal conflicts that the characters grapple with, such as fears, insecurities, and unresolved emotions.
- *Relationships with Others*: Showcase the characters' relationships with other supporting characters, friends, and family members, highlighting how these connections influence their personal journeys.
- *Individual Goals*: Give the protagonists their own individual goals and aspirations, showcasing their ambitions and dreams beyond the romantic relationship.
- *Compelling Character Arcs*: Craft compelling character arcs for each protagonist, showing how their personal growth aligns with the romantic development.
- *Parallel Growth*: Illustrate how the characters' individual journeys align and intertwine with their romantic bond, reinforcing the depth of their connection.

Developing multidimensional characters in a love story

adds depth and complexity to the narrative. Through distinct personalities, motivations, and subplots, each character becomes a fully realized individual. Their unique backstories, challenges, and relationships with others enrich the overall plot and contribute to the romantic development. With external challenges and internal conflicts, the characters undergo personal growth and transformation. Individual goals and aspirations add depth to their journey, while compelling character arcs reinforce the emotional resonance of the story. The alignment of the protagonists' personal growth with the romantic bond creates a powerful and engaging narrative, leaving readers captivated by the multifaceted journey of the protagonists' love.

Parallel Development – Interweaving Romance and Main Plot

Showcase the parallel development of the romantic relationship and the main plot. Parallel development is a powerful narrative technique that showcases the interweaving of the romantic relationship and the main plot. As the protagonists face challenges in both aspects of their lives, their growth and resolution complement each other, creating a cohesive and emotionally resonant story. Here's how to showcase parallel development:

- *Establishing Common Themes*: Introduce common themes that resonate in the romantic relationship and the main plot, such as resilience, acceptance, or the pursuit of dreams.
- *Mirroring Emotions*: Reflect the emotional journey of the protagonists in their romantic

bond and the challenges they encounter in the main plot, allowing readers to empathize with their experiences.
- *Impact on Each Other*: Show how the events and growth in one aspect of their lives impact the other. Their emotional development in the romance influences their decisions and actions in the main plot, and vice versa.
- *Overlapping Obstacles*: Create overlapping obstacles that the protagonists must face in their romantic relationship and the main plot, deepening the connections between the two elements.
- *Supporting Each Other*: Demonstrate how the protagonists' support for each other in their romantic relationship spills over into their efforts to overcome challenges in the main plot, fostering unity and strength.
- *Symbolism and Metaphors*: Utilize symbolism and metaphors that represent the romance and the main plot, tying their journeys together in a meaningful way.
- *Shared Goals*: Develop shared goals between the protagonists in their romantic relationship and the main plot, reinforcing their alignment and interconnectedness.
- *Resolutions Converging*: As the story reaches its climax, ensure that the resolution of the romantic relationship and the main plot converge, emphasizing the significant impact they have on each other.
- *Character Growth in Tandem*: Allow the characters' personal growth in the romantic relationship and the main plot to progress in tandem, showing how their journeys reinforce and complement each other.
- *Emotional Impact*: Emphasize the emotional impact of their experiences in both aspects of

their lives, making the connections between the romance and the main plot resonate deeply with readers.

Showcasing parallel development in a love story enhances the narrative's cohesiveness and emotional resonance. By establishing common themes, mirroring emotions, and intertwining the challenges and growth of the protagonists in the romantic relationship and the main plot, the story becomes a powerful exploration of their interconnected journeys. The characters' support for each other and shared goals reinforce their unity, while the resolution of both aspects of their lives converges, leaving readers captivated by the transformative power of their love and personal growth. Parallel development enhances the impact of the story, making it a moving and immersive experience that explores the depth of human emotions and relationships.

Subplots and Supporting Characters – Enriching the Narrative

Incorporate subplots that involve supporting characters, providing depth and additional layers to the story. These subplots should add value to the overall narrative and influence the protagonists' decisions. Here's how to effectively incorporate subplots and supporting characters:

- *Individual Journeys*: Develop subplots that explore the individual journeys of supporting characters. These subplots can shed light on their own challenges, aspirations, and relationships, offering a broader perspective on

the story.
- *Impact on the Protagonists*: Ensure that the subplots of supporting characters have a meaningful impact on the protagonists' lives and decisions. This can include providing advice, offering contrasting perspectives, or presenting moral dilemmas.
- *Personal Connections*: Create personal connections between the protagonists and the supporting characters involved in the subplots. These connections deepen the emotional bonds between characters, influencing their interactions and choices.
- *Themes of Acceptance and Friendship*: Utilize subplots to explore themes of acceptance, friendship, and community. Supporting characters can serve as a source of support and understanding for the protagonists as they navigate their love journey.
- *Conflict and Collaboration*: Introduce conflicts and collaborations between the supporting characters and the protagonists, showing how these interactions shape the overall narrative and contribute to character development.
- *External Challenges*: Develop subplots that introduce external challenges that the protagonists and supporting characters must face together, fostering a sense of unity and camaraderie.
- *Foils and Mirrors*: Use supporting characters as foils or mirrors to the protagonists, highlighting different aspects of their personalities and motivations.
- *Symbolic Relationships*: Explore symbolic relationships between supporting characters and the main plot, using these connections to reinforce thematic elements.
- *Growth Opportunities*: Allow the subplots

involving supporting characters to provide growth opportunities for the protagonists, challenging their beliefs and prompting self-reflection.
- *Resolutions and Closure*: Ensure that the subplots find satisfying resolutions and closure, adding to the overall sense of fulfillment and completion in the story.

Incorporating subplots involving supporting characters elevates a lesbian love story, providing depth and layers to the narrative. As these subplots impact the protagonists' lives and decisions, they contribute value to the overall plot and enrich the character development. By exploring individual journeys, personal connections, and themes of acceptance and friendship, the story becomes more immersive and emotionally resonant. The interactions and conflicts between supporting characters and the protagonists offer growth opportunities and foster a sense of unity within the narrative. The inclusion of subplots with satisfying resolutions adds to the overall sense of fulfillment, leaving readers captivated by the interconnected journeys of the protagonists and supporting characters in the story.

Use Conflict to Drive the Plot – Creating Tension and Growth

Conflict is a powerful tool in crafting a compelling love story. By introducing conflicts and obstacles related to the main plot that impact the romantic relationship, the narrative becomes more engaging and emotionally resonant. These challenges not only create tension, but also provide opportunities for character growth and development. Here's how to effectively use conflict to drive the plot:

- *External Challenges*: Introduce external challenges that the protagonists and their romantic relationship must confront. These challenges can include societal prejudices, family opposition, or professional conflicts that strain their ability to be together.
- *Internal Conflicts*: Explore internal conflicts within the characters that affect their romantic bond and personal growth. These internal struggles, such as self-doubt or fear of vulnerability, add depth to the characters and their journey.
- *Miscommunication and Assumptions*: Play with the idea of characters making assumptions or failing to communicate effectively, leading to conflicts that need to be resolved. Misunderstandings can create tension and drive the plot forward.
- *Past Traumas and Insecurities*: Address past traumas or insecurities that impact the characters' actions and decisions in the present. Confronting these issues can be pivotal to their romantic relationship and personal growth.
- *Sacrifices and Compromises*: Introduce dilemmas that require sacrifices or compromises for the sake of the relationship. These moments can be emotionally charged and test the depth of their commitment.
- *Love Triangles*: Consider incorporating a love triangle where one or both protagonists have to choose between two potential love interests. This adds complexity and heightened emotions to the story.
- *Ethical Dilemmas*: Introduce ethical dilemmas that force the protagonists to confront difficult

moral choices. These dilemmas can impact their relationship and lead to internal conflicts that need resolution.
- *Emotional Distance*: Explore moments of emotional distance between the protagonists, where they must confront their feelings and reassess their priorities.
- *Secrets and Reveals*: Incorporate secrets or undisclosed information that can alter the course of the relationship. Revealing these secrets at pivotal moments can heighten tension and create additional conflicts to resolve.
- *Unexpected Challenges*: Surprise the characters and readers with unexpected challenges that disrupt their plans and force them to adapt. These surprises can test their commitment to each other and reveal the strength of their bond.

Using conflict to drive the plot in a love story adds depth and tension to the narrative. External challenges, internal conflicts, miscommunications, and past traumas impact the romantic relationship and drive character growth. Sacrifices, ethical dilemmas, and unexpected challenges create emotional resonance and opportunities for the protagonists to confront their feelings and priorities. As the characters navigate these conflicts, their love and commitment are put to the test, leading to personal growth and a stronger emotional connection. Conflict becomes the driving force behind the plot, captivating readers and immersing them in the complex and transformative journey of the protagonists' love story.

Strategic Placement of Romantic Moments – Balancing Intimacy and Plot Progression

The placement of romantic moments is crucial to maintain a balance between the development of the romantic relationship and other plot elements. By strategically interspersing moments of intimacy and emotional connection with the progression of the overall plot, the narrative remains engaging and avoids overwhelming or overshadowing other essential aspects of the story. Here's how to achieve this balance:

- *Plot-Relevant Intimacy*: Ensure that romantic moments are relevant to the plot and character development. Intimacy should arise naturally from the protagonists' emotional journeys, enhancing their growth and the overall narrative.
- *Build Anticipation*: Space out the romantic moments to build anticipation and emotional investment. Allow the tension to simmer and the emotional connection to deepen gradually.
- *Intimacy and Conflict*: Pair moments of intimacy with conflict or challenges in the main plot. This creates contrast and emphasizes the emotional stakes of the relationship amid external struggles.
- *Reflective Moments*: Use romantic moments as opportunities for reflection and introspection. Let the characters share their vulnerabilities and feelings, deepening the emotional connection between them and readers.
- *Emotional Pacing*: Balance the intensity of romantic moments with the pacing of the overall plot. Avoid consecutive highly emotional scenes, instead spreading them out to maintain a steady rhythm.
- *Subtle Gestures*: Incorporate subtle romantic gestures and actions throughout the narrative to continuously reinforce the bond between the

protagonists.
- *Character-Driven Intimacy*: Ensure that romantic moments are driven by the characters' choices and actions, reflecting their growth and emotional arcs.
- *Intimacy and Conflict Resolution*: Use intimate moments as opportunities for conflict resolution, where the characters can find comfort and support in each other during challenging times.
- *Intimacy in Quiet Moments*: Include romantic moments in quieter, more introspective scenes, where the emotional connection takes center stage.
- *Emotional Balance*: Keep the emotional balance in mind while planning romantic scenes. Consider the overall emotional trajectory of the story to maintain coherence and impact.

Strategic placement of romantic moments in a lesbian love story is essential to maintain a balanced and engaging narrative. By ensuring the relevance of intimacy to the plot, spacing out emotional moments and aligning them with conflicts and character growth, the story becomes a powerful exploration of love and personal development. Balancing intimacy with other plot elements allows the emotional connection between the protagonists to flourish without overshadowing the larger narrative. The result is a well-crafted love story that captivates readers, evokes a range of emotions, and weaves a beautiful tapestry of romantic and plot-driven moments that intertwine to create a satisfying and immersive reading experience.

Maintain Consistent Tone – Harmonizing Romance and Plot Elements

Consistent tone is vital to create a seamless blend of romance and non-romantic elements. Whether the tone is lighthearted and comedic or emotionally charged and dramatic, ensuring its continuity throughout the novel enhances the readers' engagement and emotional connection to the narrative. Here's how to maintain a consistent tone:

- *Establish Tone Early*: Set the tone of the story early on, preferably in the opening chapters. This allows readers to acclimate to the emotional atmosphere and prepares them for the journey ahead.
- *Character-Centric Tone*: Ensure that the tone aligns with the personalities and experiences of the main characters. The tone should reflect their emotions and the overall themes of the story.
- *Balance Romantic and Non-Romantic Elements*: Strive for a harmonious balance between romantic and non-romantic elements. While the romance is central, supporting plotlines and conflicts should complement the overall tone.
- *Emotional Resonance*: Maintain emotional resonance throughout the story, regardless of the tone. Even in lighthearted moments, emotions should be authentic and relatable, allowing readers to connect with the characters on a deeper level.
- *Transitions and Scene Shifts*: Smoothly transition between scenes with different tones. Consider how each scene connects to the broader narrative while retaining the established emotional atmosphere.
- *Use of Humor*: In stories with a lighter tone, incorporate humor organically. Humorous

moments can enhance the chemistry between the characters and provide levity amid emotional challenges.
- *Emotional Impact*: In emotionally charged stories, ensure that the emotional impact remains consistent. Readers should feel the depth of the characters' feelings and empathize with their struggles throughout.
- *Subtle Tone Shifts*: If the tone needs to shift at certain points in the story, do so gradually and purposefully. Subtle changes in tone can add complexity and dimension to the narrative.
- *Themes and Messages*: Align the tone with the themes and messages of the story. A consistent tone reinforces the overall message and enhances the readers' understanding and emotional connection.
- *Beta Readers*: Seek feedback from beta readers to ensure the tone resonates with the intended emotions. Beta readers can offer valuable insights into how the tone affects their reading experience.

Maintaining a consistent tone in a love story is essential to create a cohesive and immersive reading experience. By establishing the tone early, balancing romantic and non-romantic elements, and ensuring emotional resonance throughout, the narrative becomes a seamless blend of romance and plot-driven moments. As characters navigate their emotional journeys, the tone should authentically reflect their experiences and personalities. Whether the tone is lighthearted and comedic or emotionally charged and dramatic, its consistency enhances the readers' emotional connection to the story, making it a captivating and resonant exploration of love, growth, and personal discovery.

Vary the Pace – Balancing Intensity and Introspection

Varying the pace is key to keeping readers engaged and invested in the narrative. By alternating between slower-paced, introspective moments and high-energy action or tension-filled scenes, the story gains depth and richness. Here's how to effectively vary the pace:

- *Intimate Interludes*: Introduce slower-paced, intimate interludes where the protagonists share reflective and emotionally charged moments. These scenes deepen the emotional connection between the characters and provide insight into their thoughts and feelings.
- *Action-Packed Sequences*: Alternate with action-packed sequences that heighten the stakes and create tension. These scenes may involve external conflicts or challenges that test the protagonists' relationship.
- *Breath-Catching Reprieves*: Offer breath-catching reprieves after intense scenes, allowing readers and characters to take a moment to process the emotions and events. These moments of pause can enhance the impact of subsequent scenes.
- *Subplots and Side Stories*: Incorporate subplots and side stories that have different pacing from the central romantic plot. This adds variety to the narrative and keeps readers engaged in multiple aspects of the story.
- *Emotional Climaxes*: Build emotional climaxes that escalate the intensity and then transition to quieter, more introspective moments for emotional release and character growth.

- *Moments of Tension*: Create moments of tension and suspense, such as romantic misunderstandings or external challenges, followed by resolutions that bring relief and satisfaction.
- *Emotional Peaks and Valleys*: Craft a narrative with emotional peaks and valleys, allowing the characters to experience a range of emotions throughout their journey.
- *Pace Shifts with Story Arcs*: Align pace shifts with different story arcs. The pacing may be faster during the climax of the central conflict and slower during the characters' introspective and transformative moments.
- *Use of Dialogue and Action*: Balance dialogue-heavy scenes with action-driven sequences to maintain a dynamic flow in the narrative.
- *Emotional Impact*: Consider how pacing influences the emotional impact on readers. Varying the pace can enhance the emotional resonance of the story.

Varying the pace in a love story is a powerful technique to keep readers engaged and emotionally invested. By alternating between slower-paced, introspective moments and high-energy action or tension-filled scenes, the narrative gains depth and complexity. Intimate interludes deepen the emotional connection between the characters, while action-packed sequences heighten the stakes and create tension. Breath-catching reprieves offer moments of reflection and emotional release. By carefully balancing the pacing throughout the story, the reader's emotional journey mirrors that of the protagonists, creating a captivating and fulfilling reading experience.

Satisfying Resolutions for All Plotlines – Fulfilling the Reader's Journey

Providing satisfying resolutions for all plotlines is crucial to leaving readers with a sense of closure and completion. Each plotline, including the romantic relationship and other narrative threads, should be thoughtfully resolved, ensuring that the reader's emotional journey feels fulfilled. Here's how to achieve satisfying resolutions:

- *Romantic Relationship*: Ensure the romantic relationship reaches a point of emotional growth and stability. Let the protagonists confront their obstacles, communicate openly, and deepen their connection, leading to a satisfying culmination of their love journey.
- *External Conflicts*: Resolve external conflicts that have impacted the protagonists' relationship. Address societal prejudices, family opposition, or professional challenges in a manner that reflects the characters' growth and fortifies their bond.
- *Character Arcs*: Allow each character to complete their individual character arcs. Ensure their personal growth aligns with their goals and desires, contributing to the overall emotional resonance of the story.
- *Subplots*: Provide closure for subplots and side stories, addressing their relevance to the main narrative. Readers should feel that every aspect of the story has been thoughtfully explored and resolved.
- *Emotional Closure*: Offer emotional closure for characters and readers alike. Emotional journeys should be acknowledged and celebrated,

allowing characters to embrace their true selves and find acceptance.
- *Reflection and Growth*: Allow moments of reflection for the characters, highlighting the progress they've made and the lessons they've learned. This introspection adds depth to the resolutions and underscores the transformative nature of their experiences.
- *Final Test of Love*: Present a final test of the protagonists' love and commitment, reinforcing the strength of their relationship as they overcome challenges together.
- *Emotional Impact*: Ensure that the resolutions have an emotional impact on readers, evoking a range of feelings, from joy and relief to catharsis and satisfaction.
- *Closure for Supporting Characters*: Tie up loose ends for supporting characters, showing how their journeys intertwine with the main plot and emphasizing the interconnectedness of the story.
- *Hopeful Outlook*: End the story on a hopeful note, leaving room for readers to imagine the protagonists' future beyond the last page.

Providing satisfying resolutions for all plotlines is a crucial aspect of crafting a captivating lesbian love story. Readers should feel a sense of closure and completion for the romantic relationship, as well as other plot elements. By addressing external conflicts, character arcs, subplots, and emotional closure, the narrative becomes a fulfilling and memorable experience for readers. A well-crafted ending that leaves room for hope and possibility reinforces the power of love, growth, and self-acceptance, resonating long after the final page is turned.

Balancing romance with other plot elements in a romance novel enriches the narrative, creating a more immersive and compelling reading experience. By developing multidimensional characters, intertwining themes, and strategically placing romantic moments, authors can seamlessly integrate the romantic plot with other elements, offering a well-rounded and emotionally resonant story. Ultimately, finding the right balance ensures that readers are invested in the romantic journey and the overall narrative, making for a memorable and satisfying reading experience.

Establishing a Captivating Setting – Choosing the Right Location and Atmosphere

The setting of a lesbian romance novel plays a crucial role in immersing readers in the story and enhancing the overall atmosphere. A well-chosen location and carefully crafted atmosphere can evoke emotions, create a vivid backdrop for the romance, and add depth to the narrative. Here are some tips for establishing a captivating setting:

Consider the Genre and Themes – Aligning Setting with Tone and Mood in Your Romance Novel

The setting plays a significant role in enhancing the tone and mood of the story, complementing the genre and themes. The setting should align with the tone and mood you want to convey. For example, a contemporary romance might be set in a bustling urban city, while a historical romance might be in a picturesque countryside or a vibrant city of the past. By carefully selecting the setting, authors can immerse readers in a world that resonates with the characters' emotions and the overarching narrative. Here's how to align the setting with the tone and mood of your lesbian romance novel based on the genre and themes:

- *Contemporary Romance*: For a contemporary

lesbian romance, consider setting the story in an urban city. The diverse cityscape can reflect the fast-paced nature of modern relationships and offer a backdrop for the characters to navigate the complexities of love in a rapidly changing world.
- *Historical Romance*: If writing a historical lesbian romance, opt for a picturesque countryside or a vibrant city of the past. This setting lends itself to a slower pace and a nostalgic atmosphere, evoking the beauty and charm of bygone eras while adding a sense of timelessness to the romance.
- *Fantasy or Paranormal Romance*: In a fantasy or paranormal lesbian romance, create a rich and immersive world that matches the magical or supernatural elements of the story. Inventive realms, enchanted forests, or mystical cities can set the stage for an extraordinary love story that transcends the boundaries of reality.
- *Young Adult Romance*: For a young adult lesbian romance, consider a setting that resonates with the experiences of young people. High school or college campuses, small towns with tight-knit communities, or summer retreats can provide a backdrop for youthful love and self-discovery.
- *Dramatic Romance*: In a dramatic lesbian romance, choose a setting that amplifies emotions and conflicts. A moody, stormy coastal town or a secluded mountain cabin can heighten the tension and add an atmospheric dimension to the story.
- *Romantic Comedy*: For a lighthearted romantic comedy, set the story in a charming small town or a thriving city filled with quirky locales. Playful and enchanting

- *LGBTQ+ Spaces*: Incorporate LGBTQ+ spaces and communities into the setting, creating an inclusive and affirming environment for the characters. These spaces can serve as sources of support, friendship, and understanding, enhancing the authenticity of the story.
- *Themes and Symbolism*: Choose a setting that aligns with the themes and symbolism of the novel. For example, a beach setting can symbolize the ebb and flow of love, while a snowy mountain retreat can represent the characters' journey to find inner peace and clarity.

Selecting the right setting is a crucial element of crafting a compelling romance novel. The chosen setting should align with the genre, themes, and mood of the story, enhancing the emotional resonance and immersing readers in the world of the characters. Whether it's a contemporary urban city, a picturesque countryside of the past, or a fantastical realm, the setting should enrich the narrative and contribute to the overall authenticity and enjoyment of the love story.

Research the Location – Enhancing Authenticity in a Real-World Setting

If your novel is set in a real-world location, conducting thorough research to accurately portray the setting is essential to bring the setting to life and create an authentic and captivating experience for readers. Pay attention to details like geography, culture, landmarks, and local customs. This authenticity will resonate with readers and make the setting more captivating. Here's how to enhance the authenticity of the setting through research:

- *Geography and Landmarks*: Familiarize yourself with the geography of the location, including its natural features such as mountains, rivers, and coastlines. Research prominent landmarks, iconic buildings, and popular tourist attractions to incorporate them seamlessly into the story.
- *Culture and Customs*: Immerse yourself in the local culture to accurately depict the customs, traditions, and way of life. Understand the social norms, greetings, dining etiquette, and celebrations specific to the region, infusing them into the characters' interactions and experiences.
- *Language and Dialect*: If the location has a distinct language or dialect, incorporate authentic phrases or expressions sparingly, creating a sense of place and adding realism to the dialogue.
- *Historical Context*: If your story has historical elements, research the region's history during the chosen time period. This will inform the characters' backgrounds, societal expectations, and cultural references.
- *Climate and Seasons*: Consider the location's climate and how it affects daily life and activities throughout the seasons. Use weather patterns to enhance the mood and atmosphere of different scenes.
- *Local Cuisine*: Explore the local cuisine, traditional dishes, and dining customs. Integrating authentic food experiences can

add sensory richness and cultural depth to the narrative.
- *LGBTQ+ Acceptance*: Research the LGBTQ+ acceptance and rights in the chosen location. Understand the legal and social landscape to depict the characters' experiences accurately.
- *Local Events and Festivals*: Incorporate local events and festivals into the story, providing opportunities for the characters to interact with the community and experience the region's cultural celebrations.
- *Community and Neighborhoods*: Understand the dynamics of different neighborhoods and communities within the location. Highlighting these distinct areas can add depth to the characters' experiences and interactions.
- *Sensitivity and Respect*: Approach the portrayal of the real-world location with sensitivity and respect, avoiding stereotypes and misrepresentations. Be mindful of cultural sensitivities and seek feedback from sensitivity readers if possible.

Thoroughly researching the real-world location of your romance novel is vital to creating an authentic and captivating setting. Pay attention to geographical details, culture, landmarks, customs, and local events. By infusing the narrative with these authentic elements, readers will be transported to the location, connecting with the characters and their experiences on a deeper level. Accurate portrayal of the setting adds richness to the story, making it a memorable and immersive reading experience for your audience.

Use Descriptive Language – Bring the Setting to Life

Utilize descriptive language to paint a vivid picture of the setting. Engage the readers' senses by describing the sights, sounds, smells, and textures, allowing them to feel like they are experiencing the location alongside the characters. Immerse readers in the setting and create a vivid and sensory experience. Here are some tips on using descriptive language effectively:

- *Sight*: Describe the visual elements of the setting in detail. Use evocative imagery to paint a picture of the landscapes, architecture, and surroundings. Whether it's the towering city skyline, the sun setting over a tranquil lake, or the quaint streets of a historical town, capture the sights with rich and colorful language.

Example: "The bustling urban streets of the city were adorned with neon lights, casting a radiant glow upon the towering skyscrapers that seemed to touch the heavens."

- *Sound*: Create an auditory experience for the readers by describing the sounds of the location. Whether it's the cacophony of city traffic, the gentle rustling of leaves in the countryside, or the distant crashing of waves on a beach, use onomatopoeia and descriptive language to evoke the atmosphere.

Example: "The symphony of car horns, laughter, and chatter filled the air, creating an energetic pulse that resonated through the heart of the city."

- *Smell*: Engage readers' sense of smell by describing the scents that permeate the location. Whether it's the aroma of freshly baked pastries in a local café, the salty tang of the ocean breeze, or the earthy scent of a forest, use descriptive adjectives to transport readers.

Example: "The air was tinged with the mouthwatering fragrance of spices and herbs, wafting from the street food vendors."

- *Texture*: Bring the setting to life by describing the tactile sensations the characters encounter. Whether it's the coarse texture of cobblestone streets, the softness of sand between toes, or the smoothness of polished wood, use tactile language to create a sensory experience.

Example: "She ran her fingers along the rough, weathered bark of the ancient oak tree, feeling a sense of grounding and strength."

- *Emotions*: Intertwine the characters' emotions with the description of the setting to enhance the atmosphere. Use metaphors and similes to create emotional connections between the characters and their surroundings.

Example: "The sun dipped below the horizon, casting a warm, golden glow over the two women, mirroring the warmth they felt in each other's presence."

By utilizing descriptive language to engage the readers' senses, authors can create a vibrant and immersive experience of the setting in a romance novel. The rich imagery of sights, sounds, smells, textures, and emotions allows readers to feel like they are part of the characters' world, deepening their connection to the story. Through descriptive writing, the setting becomes more than just a backdrop; it becomes a dynamic and integral part of the narrative, enriching the overall reading experience.

Establish Mood and Atmosphere – Mood and Atmosphere through Setting

The setting should contribute to the mood and atmosphere of the story. A gloomy, misty forest might set a mysterious or eerie tone, while a sunlit beach could evoke a sense of serenity and romance. By carefully choosing and describing the setting, authors can evoke specific emotions and set the tone for the narrative. Here's how to establish mood and atmosphere through setting:

- *Mysterious and Eerie*: For a mysterious or eerie tone, consider a setting like a gloomy, misty forest shrouded in shadows. Describe the twisted branches, the sound of rustling leaves, and the faint glow of moonlight filtering through the canopy. This atmospheric setting can add an element of intrigue and anticipation to the romance.
- *Serene and Romantic*: To evoke a sense of serenity and romance, opt for a sunlit beach with gentle waves caressing the shore. Describe the golden sand, the scent of salty sea breeze, and the distant cry of seagulls. This tranquil setting sets the stage for heartfelt moments and tender connections between the characters.
- *Intense and Passionate*: For an intense and passionate mood, consider a setting with a fiery sunset or a lively urban cityscape. Describe the vibrant colors of the sky, the bustling streets, and the electric energy in the air. This dynamic setting can heighten the emotions and chemistry

between the protagonists.
- *Melancholic and Reflective*: To create a melancholic and reflective atmosphere, choose a rainy day in a quaint town or a serene countryside. Describe the sound of raindrops tapping on windows, the misty landscapes, and the melancholic beauty of nature. This setting can add depth to introspective moments and emotional revelations.
- *Adventurous and Exciting*: For an adventurous and exciting tone, consider a setting like a busy market in a foreign city or an untamed wilderness. Describe the brilliant colors, the lively crowds, and the sense of adventure in the air. This setting can heighten the excitement of the characters' journey together.
- *Whimsical and Magical*: To create a whimsical and magical atmosphere, opt for a setting like a hidden garden or a whimsical fairy-tale land. Describe the enchanting flora, the twinkling fairy lights, and the sense of wonder that permeates the air. This setting can add an element of fantasy and enchantment to the romance.

By carefully selecting and describing the setting, authors can establish the mood and atmosphere of their romance novel. Whether it's a mysterious forest, a romantic beach, a bustling cityscape, or a magical garden, the setting plays a vital role in shaping the emotions and tone of the narrative. Through evocative descriptions of the surroundings, readers can feel immersed in the characters' world, enhancing their emotional connection to the story.

Make the Setting an Active Participant – Making

Setting a Character in the Story

Treat the setting as an active participant in the story. By infusing the environment with life and influence, authors can deepen the connection between the characters and their surroundings. Here's how to make the setting an active participant in the story:

- *Reflecting Emotions*: Use the setting to reflect the characters' emotions. If the protagonists are experiencing joy and love, describe the sunlit meadows or crowded city streets teeming with life. Conversely, during moments of conflict or sadness, evoke a sense of gloom in the surroundings, such as a stormy sky or a deserted, desolate place.

Example: "As they strolled hand in hand through the park, the golden sunlight streaming through the leaves seemed to mirror the warmth they felt for each other."

- *Influencing Actions*: Allow the setting to influence the characters' actions. A breathtaking sunset on the beach might inspire the characters to share heartfelt confessions, or a secluded cabin in the woods might encourage moments of intimacy and vulnerability.

Example: "The secluded cabin cocooned them in a world of their own, where the crackling fireplace and the gentle rustle of leaves outside seemed to coax them closer together."

- *Symbolism and Metaphor*: Utilize symbolic elements in the setting to enhance the story's themes and character development. A blooming garden could symbolize the protagonists' blossoming love, while a winding river might represent the ebb and flow of their relationship.

Example: "As they stood at the edge of the cliff overlooking the vast ocean, it was as if the endless horizon mirrored the possibilities that lay ahead for their love."

- *Foreshadowing*: Employ the setting to foreshadow events or challenges in the story. A looming thunderstorm might hint at impending conflicts, while a picturesque garden could foreshadow moments of respite and growth.

Example: "The distant rumble of thunder echoed in the air, hinting at the storm that was about to brew between them."

- *Mirroring Internal States*: Use the setting to mirror the characters' internal states. If a protagonist is feeling lost or uncertain, describe a labyrinthine cityscape or a dense forest, emphasizing their emotional journey.

Example: "The labyrinth of streets seemed to reflect the tangle of thoughts in her mind as she navigated the complexities of her feelings."

- *Evolving with the Plot*: Allow the setting to evolve with the plot and the characters. As their relationship develops and faces challenges, describe how the environment changes or adapts alongside them.

Example: "As winter turned to spring, the once barren garden bloomed with life, just like the love that flourished between them."

By treating the setting as an active participant in the story, authors can add depth and significance to the narrative. The environment can reflect emotions, influence actions, symbolize themes, and even foreshadow events. Through its dynamic interaction with the characters, the setting becomes an integral part of the story, contributing to the readers' emotional investment in the romance and enriching the overall reading experience.

Use Setting to Reflect Characters

Choose a setting that reflects the personalities and desires of the characters. For example, a character who values adventure and freedom might thrive in an exotic, adventurous location, while someone seeking solace may find comfort in a tranquil, natural setting. By carefully selecting a setting that aligns with the protagonists' traits, authors can enhance the readers' understanding of the characters and create a more immersive and resonant story. Here's how to use the setting to reflect the characters:

- *Adventurous Spirit*: For a character with an adventurous and free-spirited nature, consider a setting that offers excitement and exploration. An exotic destination like a bustling city in a foreign country, a tropical island paradise, or a mountainous landscape with breathtaking vistas could align with her daring personality.

Example: "Amid the busy streets of an enchanting foreign city, she felt her adventurous spirit come alive, each new corner revealing a world of possibilities she longed to explore."

- *Seeker of Solace*: A character who craves solace and introspection might find peace in a tranquil and natural setting. A secluded cabin in the woods, a serene countryside with rolling hills, or a private beach with gentle waves could resonate with her desire for quiet contemplation.

Example: "As she walked along the tranquil beach, the soft lull of the waves offered her the solace she had been yearning for, allowing her thoughts to drift into a place of serenity."

- *Urban Enthusiast*: A character with a love for the hustle and bustle of city life might thrive in an urban setting. A vibrant metropolis with its diverse culture and lively nightlife could mirror her outgoing personality.

Example: "The electrifying energy of the city enveloped her like a warm embrace, and amid the lively chaos, she felt a sense of belonging she had never experienced before."

- *Nature Lover*: A character who finds joy and connection in nature might be at home in a setting surrounded by natural beauty. A blooming garden, a serene forest, or a picturesque countryside could embody her appreciation for the environment.

Example: "She could lose herself for hours in the enchanting garden, the colorful blossoms reflecting the beauty she saw in the world around her."

- *Artistic Soul*: A character with a creative and artistic soul might be drawn to a setting rich in art and culture. A bohemian art district, an elegant museum, or a historic city with a thriving arts scene could resonate with her passion for self-expression.

Example: "The bright colors of the art district seemed to seep into her soul, igniting a spark of inspiration that fueled her artistic endeavors."

By choosing a setting that reflects the personalities and desires of the characters, authors can deepen the readers' understanding of the protagonists and enhance the overall storytelling experience. The setting becomes a mirror of the characters' traits and aspirations, creating a more immersive world in which their love story unfolds. As the characters interact with the environment, their personalities are further illuminated, allowing readers to connect on a deeper level and become fully engrossed in their journey.

Establish Cultural Nuances

If your story involves diverse cultures or locations, incorporate cultural nuances into the setting. This adds richness and authenticity to the narrative, highlighting the characters' experiences in their specific cultural contexts. Here's how to effectively integrate cultural elements into the story:

- *Research and Sensitivity*: Thoroughly research the cultures and locations depicted in the story to ensure accuracy and avoid stereotypes. Sensitivity is crucial when portraying diverse cultures, as it helps foster respectful representation.

Example: "She immersed herself in learning about her partner's cultural traditions, respecting the significance of each ritual with genuine curiosity."

- *Language and Dialogue*: Introduce phrases, expressions, or dialogue that reflect the characters' cultural backgrounds. Integrating native languages or specific idioms can enhance the authenticity of their interactions.

Example: "The characters greeted each other with warm embraces, using traditional phrases that conveyed a sense of belonging and familial ties."

- *Customs and Traditions*: Showcase cultural customs, traditions, and celebrations to provide insight into the characters' identities and beliefs. These elements can play pivotal roles in shaping the narrative and character arcs.

Example: "The lively festival brought the characters together, allowing them to bond over shared cultural experiences and creating lasting memories."

- *Cuisine and Culinary Traditions*: Describe traditional dishes and culinary customs that the characters enjoy. Sharing meals and exploring local delicacies can become meaningful moments of connection and cultural exchange.

Example: "As they savored the rich flavors of traditional cuisine, their love blossomed amid the laughter and shared appreciation for cultural delicacies."

- *Family and Community Dynamics*: Explore family structures and community values that influence the characters' decisions and relationships. Highlighting these dynamics can deepen the readers' understanding of the protagonists' cultural contexts.

Example: "Their love story unfolded amid the backdrop of close-knit family gatherings and a supportive community that celebrated and embraced their relationship."

- *Local Landmarks and Trademarks*: Include references to iconic landmarks, historical sites, or local customs that are significant to the characters' cultural backgrounds. These details anchor the characters' experiences in their respective environments.

Example: "The characters found solace in the shadow of a historic monument, contemplating the significance of their love story within the context of their shared cultural heritage."

By incorporating cultural nuances into the setting of a romance novel, authors can add richness and authenticity to the narrative. Respectful portrayal of diverse cultures, traditions, and customs enhances the readers' connection with the characters and fosters a more immersive and meaningful reading experience. Cultural elements provide depth to the storyline and allow readers to empathize with the characters as they navigate their love journey within their specific cultural contexts.

Balance Familiarity and Novelty

Creating a setting that strikes the right balance between

familiarity and novelty is essential in a romance novel. By incorporating familiar and new elements, authors can create a captivating world that resonates with readers while also offering them the excitement of exploring uncharted territories. Here's how to achieve this balance:

- *Familiar Settings*: Start with familiar settings that readers can easily relate to. This can include everyday places like a cozy coffee shop, a bustling city neighborhood, or a small-town community. Familiar settings ground the story in a relatable reality, making it easier for readers to connect with the characters and their emotions.

Example: "The coffee shop, with its comforting aroma of freshly brewed coffee, became their sanctuary—a place where love bloomed amid the familiar sounds of clinking mugs and soft chatter."

- *Unique Twists*: Add unique twists to the familiar settings to inject novelty into the story. This could be a quirky barista with an infectious personality, a hidden garden behind the coffee shop that becomes their secret meeting spot, or a special event that brings unexpected opportunities for romance.

Example: "The coffee shop's whimsical décor, adorned with art and colorful murals, set the stage for their love story—a story that found magic in the most ordinary of places."

- *Unexplored Locations*: Introduce new and unexplored locations that readers can discover alongside the characters. This could be an enchanting bookstore tucked away in an old alley, an exotic travel destination, or an otherworldly fantasy realm that adds a touch of wonder and adventure.

Example: "Their journey took them to the mesmerizing pages of a hidden bookstore, where love blossomed amid the allure of uncharted literature and shared passions."

- *Cultural Exploration*: Incorporate cultural exploration to provide readers with fresh experiences. This could involve immersing the characters in a cultural festival, exploring diverse traditions, or embarking on a culinary adventure through various cuisines.

Example: "In the heart of a vibrant cultural festival, they found themselves entwined in a celebration that not only opened their hearts, but also expanded their horizons."

- *Emotional Connection*: Regardless of the setting's novelty, maintain an emotional connection between the characters and their surroundings. The setting should complement and enhance their love story, evoking emotions that resonate with readers.

Example: "As they ventured into the unexplored wilderness, their hearts raced with excitement, mirroring the intensity of their growing love for each other."

In a lesbian romance novel, a balanced mix of familiarity and novelty in the setting enriches the reader's experience. Familiar settings provide a relatable foundation for the love story, while unique and unexplored locations add freshness and excitement to the narrative. The emotional connection between the characters and their surroundings ties everything together, creating a captivating world that readers can immerse themselves in and cherish alongside the protagonists.

Symbolic Settings

Incorporating symbolic settings in a romance novel adds depth and layers to the narrative, allowing the physical environment to mirror the emotional journey of the characters. By infusing specific locations with symbolic meaning, authors can enhance the storytelling and evoke powerful emotions. Here are some ways to use symbolic settings effectively:

- *The Dilapidated House*: A dilapidated house can symbolize the characters' past traumas, unresolved emotions, or broken relationships. As the protagonists explore the house and renovate it, it represents their efforts to heal and rebuild their lives together.

Example: "The dilapidated house stood as a poignant reminder of their shared past—its crumbling walls reflecting the emotional wounds they needed to mend. As they restored the house, they also repaired their hearts, transforming it into a sanctuary of hope and renewal."

- *The Blooming Garden*: A blooming garden represents newfound love, growth, and the blossoming of the characters' relationship. As the protagonists tend to the garden, their love deepens and flourishes, mirroring the beauty and potential of their union.

Example: "Within the bright, blooming garden, they found a metaphor for their love story—each tenderly nurtured flower reflecting the care they poured into their relationship. Amid the blossoms, they discovered the joy of love's growth and the promise of a beautiful future together."

- *The Bridge*: A bridge can symbolize the connection between the characters, bridging the gaps in their lives and uniting them on their journey. Crossing the bridge together represents the emotional and metaphorical passage from one phase of their lives to another.

Example: "The bridge, spanning a divide that separated their worlds, became a powerful symbol of their love. As they crossed it hand in hand, they bridged the gaps in their hearts and found solace in the embrace of their shared dreams."

- *The Open Sea*: The vastness of the open sea can represent the unknown and the uncertainties of their love journey. Sailing together, facing storms and serene waters, signifies the resilience and strength of their relationship.

Example: "The open sea, with its boundless expanse, reflected the uncharted territory of their love. Sailing through tempestuous waves and calm waters, they discovered the depths of their commitment and the courage to navigate life's uncertainties together."

- *The Starlit Sky*: A starlit sky can symbolize the

sense of wonder, hope, and endless possibilities in their relationship. Under the stars, the characters share intimate moments and make promises for their future together.

Example: "Beneath the shimmering starlit sky, they found a canvas of dreams. As they gazed at the constellations, they whispered their hopes and aspirations, knowing that their love was destined to reach new heights."

Using symbolic settings in a romance novel adds layers of meaning to the narrative, allowing the physical environment to reflect the emotional journey of the characters. Dilapidated houses, blooming gardens, bridges, open seas, and starlit skies become powerful metaphors for healing, growth, connection, resilience, and boundless love. These symbolic settings deepen the readers' engagement with the characters' emotions and experiences, creating a rich and resonant love story that lingers in their hearts.

Set the Scene for Romance

Choose a setting that enhances the romantic atmosphere. Whether it's a charming café, a dreamy seaside resort, or a cozy cabin in the woods, the setting can create an enchanting backdrop for the love story that enhances the emotional connection between the protagonists. Here are three romantic settings that can create an enchanting backdrop for the love story:

- *Charming Café*: A charming café exudes warmth and intimacy, making it an ideal setting for heartfelt conversations and tender moments.

The aroma of freshly brewed coffee and the soft glow of ambient lighting create an inviting atmosphere, perfect for kindling romance.

Example: "In the quaint café, the soft notes of background music filled the air, as their gazes met over steaming cups of coffee. With each shared laugh and lingering touch, the café became their sanctuary—a place where time seemed to slow, allowing their love to blossom like a delicate flower."

- *Dreamy Seaside Resort*: A dreamy seaside resort offers a magical setting with its breathtaking views, serene waves, and secluded spots for stolen glances. The sound of the ocean's melody and the feel of the sand between their toes set the stage for an unforgettable romance.

Example: "As the sun dipped below the horizon, casting hues of orange and pink across the sky, they strolled hand in hand along the tranquil shore. The seaside resort became their haven, where the rhythmic waves whispered love's sweetest promises."

- *Cozy Cabin in the Woods*: A cozy cabin nestled in the woods provides an intimate escape from the outside world. The crackling fireplace, soft blankets, and the scent of pine trees create an ambiance that fosters emotional closeness and vulnerability.

Example: "In the seclusion of the cabin, the world outside faded away, leaving only the sound of their laughter dancing in the air. The warmth of the fireplace mirrored the affection in their hearts as they discovered the solace of love amid the embracing arms of nature." In a romance novel, the setting plays a significant role in crafting an enchanting backdrop for the love story. Whether it's a charming café, a dreamy seaside resort, or a cozy cabin in the woods, the right location can set the stage for heartfelt connections, tender moments, and unforgettable romance. By carefully choosing a setting that enhances the emotional atmosphere, authors can create a love story that resonates with readers and transports them into a world of enchanting love and intimacy.

Establishing a captivating setting is a powerful tool for enhancing the appeal of your romance novel. By choosing the right location and atmosphere, you can immerse readers in the story, evoke emotions, and add depth to the characters' experiences. Whether real or fictional, the setting should be carefully crafted to complement the themes and tone of the narrative, ultimately making the love story even more compelling and memorable.

Establishing a Captivating Setting – Incorporating LGBTQ+ Spaces and Communities

In a lesbian romance novel, incorporating LGBTQ+ spaces and communities is not only important for authenticity, but also for celebrating the diversity and inclusivity of the LGBTQ+ experience. By including these spaces, authors can create a rich and realistic backdrop for their love story and offer readers a glimpse into the vibrant and supportive LGBTQ+ communities. Here are some ways to incorporate LGBTQ+ spaces and communities in your novel:

- *LGBTQ+ Social Venues*: Introduce LGBTQ+ social venues like gay bars, LGBTQ+ clubs, or community centers where the characters can interact and form connections. These spaces can serve as meeting points for the protagonists or places where they seek support and acceptance.

Incorporating LGBTQ+ social venues in a lesbian romance novel adds depth and authenticity to the story, allowing the characters to interact in spaces that foster support, understanding, and acceptance. These venues can serve as meeting points for the protagonists, where they forge connections with like-minded individuals who share similar experiences and struggles. Here are some LGBTQ+ social venues that can play a significant role in the love story:

- *Gay Bar*: A gay bar provides an electric and inclusive atmosphere where LGBTQ+ individuals can freely express themselves. It can be the perfect setting for the protagonists to have their first encounter or share intimate moments, surrounded by the radiant energy of the LGBTQ+ community.

Example: "Amid the pulsating music and colorful lights of the gay bar, their gazes met across the crowded dance floor. Drawn together by an invisible thread, they found comfort and joy in the shared embrace of a place where love was celebrated and identities were embraced."

- *LGBTQ+ Club*: An LGBTQ+ club offers a haven for the characters to let loose and celebrate their identities. In this safe space, they can dance, laugh, and connect with others, forming bonds that extend beyond the dance floor.

Example: "In the dimly lit LGBTQ+ club, the beat of the music matched the rhythm of their hearts. As they swayed to the music, they discovered a sense of belonging in the diverse sea of people, finding solace in a place where they could be unapologetically themselves."

- *LGBTQ+ Community Center*: An LGBTQ+ community center serves as a hub for support and resources. Here, the characters can attend workshops, support groups, and events that help them navigate their identities and relationships.

Example: "Inside the LGBTQ+ community center, they found a network of individuals who understood their unique experiences. From attending empowering workshops to sharing stories in support groups, they discovered a community that nurtured their growth and strengthened their love."

- *Pride Parade or Festival*: A Pride parade or festival becomes a momentous occasion where the characters celebrate their identities and love amid a sea of rainbow colors and jubilation.

Example: "Hand in hand, they walked proudly in the midst of the Pride parade, surrounded by a cacophony of cheers and celebration. The parade became a testament to their love—a love that blossomed despite the challenges they faced, now embraced by a jubilant crowd of allies and fellow LGBTQ+ individuals."

Introducing LGBTQ+ social venues in a lesbian romance novel not only adds authenticity to the narrative, but also creates spaces where the characters can connect, form meaningful relationships, and seek support and acceptance. Gay bars, LGBTQ+ clubs, community centers, and Pride events serve as essential backdrops that contribute to the protagonists' emotional growth and the overall sense of belonging within the LGBTQ+ community. By incorporating these venues, authors can enrich the love story with the power of community, celebrating love in all its diverse and beautiful forms. Here are some LGBTQ+ Pride events that can play a significant role in the love story:

- *Pride Parade*: The Pride parade becomes a lively and colorful spectacle where the characters join in the celebration of love and acceptance. It can be a transformative experience for the protagonists as they march proudly and unapologetically, surrounded by a diverse and supportive community.

Example: "Hand in hand, they stood at the starting point of the Pride parade, their hearts pounding with excitement. With each step they took, the cheers of the crowd enveloped them, affirming their love and unity. The parade became a joyous expression of their journey to self-acceptance and a testament to their commitment to love boldly."

- *Pride Festival*: A Pride festival provides a carnival-like atmosphere of music, art, and activism. It serves as a space where the characters immerse themselves in the rich diversity of LGBTQ+ culture, forging connections with others who share their experiences.

Example: "In the midst of the Pride festival, they explored the diverse booths and stages, surrounded by a kaleidoscope of expressions and identities. Among the rainbow flags and exuberant performances, they found a sense of belonging—a feeling of home in the heart of the LGBTQ+ community."

- *Pride March*: Participating in a Pride march can become a moment of empowerment for the characters as they raise their voices for LGBTQ+ rights and equality. It can also be a catalyst for their personal growth and commitment to making a difference.

Example: "Amid the chanting and colorful placards of the Pride march, they felt an overwhelming surge of unity. Their voices blended with the chorus of demands for equality, and they realized the power of their love extended beyond their relationship—it was a force that could spark change and touch the lives of others."

- *Pride Concert*: A Pride concert offers an opportunity for the characters to bask in the energy of live performances while being surrounded by a community that celebrates love and acceptance.

Example: "As the music filled the air at the Pride concert, they became lost in the melodies and lyrics that spoke to their hearts. In the sea of cheering faces, they discovered a shared experience of love and resilience—an experience that strengthened their bond even further."

Including LGBTQ+ Pride events in a lesbian romance novel infuses the story with moments of joy, activism, and personal growth for the characters. Pride parades, festivals, marches, and concerts become powerful settings that reflect the protagonists' emotional journey and their place within the LGBTQ+ community. These events serve as reminders of the importance of love, acceptance, and celebrating one's true self, making the love story even more powerful and resonant with readers.

LGBTQ+ Support Groups

Showcase LGBTQ+ support groups or counseling services that offer a safe space for characters to share their experiences and seek guidance. Incorporating LGBTQ+ support groups or counseling services in a lesbian romance novel provides a meaningful backdrop for the characters' personal development and relationship dynamics. These safe spaces offer solace, understanding, and guidance, becoming essential sources of support and empowerment for the protagonists. Here are some ways these LGBTQ+ support groups can be portrayed in the story:

- *LGBTQ+ Support Group*: An LGBTQ+ support group becomes a haven where the characters can openly share their experiences, fears, and triumphs with others who have faced similar challenges. Through these gatherings, the protagonists find a community that empathizes with their struggles and provides a space to grow and heal.

Example: "In the comforting circle of the LGBTQ+ support group, they took turns sharing their journeys of self-discovery and love. As she listened to others' stories, she found strength in knowing she was not alone, and the bond among the members of the group deepened."

- *LGBTQ+ Counseling Services*: Seeking counseling or therapy provides the characters with a professional and confidential outlet to address their personal struggles and relationship dynamics. The counseling sessions become a catalyst for self-reflection and growth, aiding the protagonists in understanding themselves and their feelings more deeply.

Example: "In the quiet room of the LGBTQ+ counseling service, they explored the complexities of their emotions, guided by a compassionate therapist who listened without judgment. As they delved into their vulnerabilities, they learned to embrace their true selves and the love that blossomed between them."

- *LGBTQ+ Youth Group*: For characters who may be exploring their identities during their youth, an LGBTQ+ youth group offers a safe and nurturing space to connect with peers who are going through similar experiences. These groups become vital in shaping their self-acceptance and understanding.

Example: "In the brightly decorated meeting room of the LGBTQ+ youth group, they found friends who shared their struggles and joys. Together, they learned to navigate the challenges of adolescence and love, forming a bond that fostered growth, laughter, and the unwavering support of a chosen family."

- *LGBTQ+ Couples Counseling*: As the protagonists' relationship faces its own set of challenges, seeking couples counseling becomes a means to strengthen their connection and communication. These sessions allow the characters to work through conflicts, deepen their emotional intimacy, and build a more resilient partnership.

Example: "In the calming space of LGBTQ+ couples counseling, they unraveled the knots of miscommunication and fears that had entangled their love. Through patience and understanding, they discovered the power of vulnerability and the potential for growth in the face of adversity."

Incorporating LGBTQ+ support groups or counseling services in a lesbian romance novel not only adds depth to the characters' personal development, but also highlights the significance of community and understanding within the LGBTQ+ world. These safe spaces serve as catalysts for self-acceptance, resilience, and the blossoming of love between the protagonists.

By showcasing the power of support and guidance, authors can create a narrative that celebrates the strength and beauty of love within the LGBTQ+ community.

Online LGBTQ+ Communities

Highlight the significance of online LGBTQ+ communities and forums where characters can connect, seek advice, and express themselves anonymously. These virtual spaces are vital for many LGBTQ+ individuals and can play a significant role in shaping the characters' personal journeys and romantic development. These virtual spaces become valuable resources for connection, support, and exploration of one's identity. Here's how they can be highlighted in the story:

- *Virtual Connection*: Online LGBTQ+ communities provide characters with a platform to connect with others who share similar experiences and identities. Through anonymous usernames, they can freely express themselves, finding solace in the knowledge that they are not alone in their journey.

Example: "Late at night, under the glow of her laptop screen, she joined an LGBTQ+ forum. As she scrolled through the messages and heartfelt stories of others, she discovered a community that understood her deepest feelings, sparking hope for a new chapter in her life."

- *Seeking Advice and Guidance*: Within these online spaces, characters can seek advice and guidance about various aspects of their lives, including relationships. The community becomes a virtual support system, offering valuable insights and perspectives.

Example: "With trembling fingers, she typed her question into the LGBTQ+ chatroom, seeking advice about navigating her first same-sex relationship. The responses poured in, filled with empathy and encouragement, guiding her toward embracing love with an open heart."

- *Anonymous Exploration*: For characters who may still be in the process of self-discovery, these online communities offer a safe and nonjudgmental environment to explore their identities and feelings without fear of exposure.

Example: "In the secure confines of an LGBTQ+ social media group, she anonymously asked questions that had long lingered in her heart. Exploring her identity with the supportive members, she felt empowered to be her authentic self."

- *A Space to Celebrate Love*: As the characters' romantic journey unfolds, online LGBTQ+ communities become a place to celebrate their love and milestones. Sharing their joy with like-minded individuals strengthens their emotional connection to the community.

Example: "After a whirlwind date, she couldn't wait to share the news with her online LGBTQ+ friends. Posting a heartfelt message on the platform, she basked in the warmth of congratulatory responses, cherishing the sense of belonging she had found."

In a lesbian romance novel, online LGBTQ+ communities and forums serve as powerful tools for the characters' growth, self-discovery, and romantic development. These virtual spaces offer a sense of community and understanding that are essential for LGBTQ+ individuals on their journey to self-acceptance and love. By highlighting the significance of online connections, authors can showcase the strength and impact of digital communities in fostering meaningful relationships and celebrating the beauty of love within the LGBTQ+ world.

Inclusive Workplaces and Neighborhoods

Incorporate workplaces and neighborhoods that are LGBTQ+ inclusive. Characters should feel welcomed and accepted in their professional and social environments, promoting a sense of belonging. These inclusive settings contribute to the protagonists' sense of belonging and create a backdrop for their romantic journey. Here's how they can be depicted in the story:

- *LGBTQ+ Friendly Workplace*: In the workplace, characters should encounter an environment that promotes diversity and inclusivity. Co-workers and superiors should demonstrate acceptance and support, fostering a safe space for LGBTQ+ individuals to be their authentic selves.

Example: "Walking into her LGBTQ+ friendly workplace, she was greeted with smiles and warm hellos from her colleagues. The company's commitment to inclusivity allowed her to feel comfortable expressing her identity without fear of judgment."

- *LGBTQ+ Neighborhood*: Creating a neighborhood that embraces diversity is crucial to the story's setting. Characters should find a community where LGBTQ+ individuals are celebrated and respected, fostering a sense of unity and shared experiences.

Example: "Moving into their LGBTQ+ friendly neighborhood, they felt an immediate sense of belonging. As they walked down the streets, rainbow flags waved proudly, signifying a community that embraced them with open arms."

- *Supportive Social Circles*: The characters' social circles should be diverse and accepting, comprising friends and acquaintances who celebrate their identities. These friendships provide an additional layer of support and love throughout the narrative.

Example: "Within their supportive social circle, they found friends who encouraged them to embrace their love without hesitation. In these gatherings, laughter echoed alongside heartfelt conversations about love, relationships, and acceptance."

- *Inclusive Events*: Incorporate inclusive events and gatherings in the workplace or neighborhood that celebrate LGBTQ+ identities. These events provide characters with opportunities to connect with others and showcase their pride.

Example: "At the annual LGBTQ+ Pride event organized by their workplace, the protagonists reveled in the vibrant atmosphere, surrounded by co-workers and friends who were allies of the community. The event served as a reminder that they were part of a larger movement of love and acceptance."

- *LGBTQ+ Friends and Allies*: Introduce LGBTQ+ friends and allies in the characters' social circles. These characters can provide valuable support and add diversity to the story while reinforcing the importance of allies in the LGBTQ+ community.

Representation of LGBTQ+ Issues

Address LGBTQ+ issues and challenges within the community, such as coming-out experiences, discrimination, or activism. By incorporating these themes, the story can resonate with readers who have faced similar struggles, providing a platform for empathy, understanding, and empowerment. Here are some ways to represent LGBTQ+ issues in the novel:

- *Coming-Out Experiences*: Explore the complexities of coming out and its impact on the characters' lives. Show the fear, vulnerability, and courage involved in revealing their true selves to friends, family, and society.

Example: "Her heart raced as she stood before her family, ready to share her truth. The words trembled on her lips, unsure of the reaction she would receive. The scene unfolded, illustrating the emotional roller coaster of coming out and the journey toward self-acceptance."

- *Discrimination and Prejudice*: Confront the challenges of discrimination and prejudice that LGBTQ+ individuals may face in various aspects of their lives, such as at work, in public spaces, or within their communities.

Example: "Walking hand in hand, they encountered disapproving glances and whispered remarks from strangers. Despite the hurtful words, their love remained resilient, demonstrating the strength needed to navigate a world that may not always be accepting."

- *Activism and Empowerment*: Incorporate characters who engage in LGBTQ+ activism or become advocates for their community. Show how these individuals work to create positive change and support one another in the fight for equality and acceptance.

Example: "As they joined hands at a Pride march, they felt a surge of empowerment. The characters stood side by side with fellow activists, united in their mission to spread love and understanding, emphasizing the power of solidarity and collective action."

- *Intersectionality and Allyship*: Explore the intersectionality of LGBTQ+ identities, acknowledging that characters may belong to multiple marginalized communities. Showcase the significance of allyship and the importance of understanding and supporting one another's struggles.

Example: "Within their diverse group of friends, they celebrated the beauty of intersectionality. They learned from one another's experiences and grew together, fostering an environment of compassion, empathy, and unity."

By addressing LGBTQ+ issues and challenges in a lesbian romance novel, authors can create a narrative that resonates with readers who have faced similar struggles. Through authentic storytelling, the novel becomes a platform for representation, empathy, and empowerment, shedding light on the diverse experiences within the LGBTQ+ community. Addressing themes such as coming out, discrimination, activism, and allyship adds depth and realism to the story, amplifying the emotional resonance of the characters' romantic journey and creating a meaningful connection with the readers.

Mentor Figures

Include mentor figures or older LGBTQ+ characters who offer guidance and wisdom to the protagonists. Incorporating mentor figures or older LGBTQ+ characters in a lesbian romance novel can add depth and layers to the story. These characters play a significant role in guiding and supporting the protagonists' journey of self-discovery and acceptance. Here are some ways to include mentor figures in the narrative:

- *Providing Guidance and Advice*: Introduce a wise and experienced LGBTQ+ character who becomes a trusted confidant to the protagonists. This mentor figure can offer valuable advice, share personal experiences, and help the main characters navigate the challenges they face in their romantic relationship and their identities.

Example: "Amid moments of uncertainty, they found solace in the words of their older LGBTQ+ friend. The mentor figure shared stories of their own journey, offering valuable guidance and reminding them that they were not alone."

- *Advocating Self-Discovery*: Have the mentor encourage the protagonists to explore and embrace their true selves, guiding them toward self-acceptance. The mentor's support can empower the main characters to confront their insecurities and fears, leading to personal growth.

Example: "Under the mentor's gentle encouragement, they began to explore their feelings and embrace their identities. The mentor reminded them that self-discovery is a journey worth taking, allowing the characters to blossom into their authentic selves."

- *Embracing LGBTQ+ History*: Introduce a mentor figure who has lived through significant historical events within the LGBTQ+ community. This character can share stories of resilience and activism, instilling a sense of pride and purpose in the protagonists.

Example: "Through their mentor, the characters discovered the rich history of the LGBTQ+ community. They were inspired by the struggles and triumphs of those who came before them, fueling their desire to stand up for their rights and love openly."

- *Fostering Empathy and Understanding*: The mentor can bridge generational gaps, fostering empathy between the characters and the broader LGBTQ+ community. This figure can help the protagonists understand the challenges faced by older generations and the progress that has been made.

Example: "As the mentor shared her experiences of growing up in a less accepting era, the characters gained a deeper appreciation for the strides made by the LGBTQ+ community. This newfound understanding strengthened their commitment to fighting for a more inclusive future."

Incorporating mentor figures or older LGBTQ+ characters in a lesbian romance novel adds layers of wisdom, support, and historical context to the story. These characters can play a crucial role in guiding the protagonists' journey of self-discovery and acceptance, providing valuable advice and encouragement along the way. By sharing personal experiences and advocating for self-acceptance, mentor figures foster emotional growth and empowerment in the main characters. Their presence also helps bridge generational gaps and creates a sense of unity within the LGBTQ+ community, reinforcing the importance of intergenerational connections and mentorship.

Encouraging Acceptance and Support:

In a lesbian romance novel, the portrayal of LGBTQ+ spaces and communities can serve as a powerful platform to emphasize the significance of acceptance, support, and understanding. These spaces play a vital role in nurturing love, fostering personal growth, and creating a profound sense of belonging for the characters. By showcasing the power of these environments, the narrative can send a poignant message about the transformative impact of accepting and inclusive communities. Here's how to highlight these themes:

- *Safe Havens for Love*: Illustrate how LGBTQ+

spaces and communities act as safe havens where the characters can freely express their love and affection. In these spaces, they are liberated from societal judgment and can openly embrace their romantic feelings.

Example: "In the cozy corner of the LGBTQ+ café, the characters exchanged tender glances, feeling a sense of liberation in the warmth of acceptance. Their love blossomed in the comforting knowledge that they could be themselves."

- *Nurturing Personal Growth*: Demonstrate how LGBTQ+ spaces provide an environment for personal growth and self-discovery. The characters may find support and encouragement to confront their insecurities, empowering them to embrace their true selves.

Example: "Through the LGBTQ+ support group, one character found the courage to embrace her identity, breaking free from self-doubt. The genuine care and empathy of the group inspired her to grow and thrive."

- *Creating Bonds of Belonging*: Highlight the sense of belonging that LGBTQ+ spaces foster, emphasizing the deep connections characters form with others who share similar experiences and challenges.

Example: "Amid the jubilant crowd of the Pride festival, the characters felt an instant connection with strangers who were now like family. The festival became a celebration of love, unity, and the joy of belonging."

- *Empowering Advocacy and Activism*: Show how LGBTQ+ spaces can ignite a passion for advocacy and activism. Characters may become motivated to take a stand against discrimination and fight for the rights and acceptance of their community.

Example: "Participating in the LGBTQ+ rally, they realized the power of their collective voice. The experience ignited a fire within them to become advocates for change and equal rights."

- *Allies and Understanding*: Incorporate allies within these spaces who offer understanding and support. Showcase the importance of allies in creating an inclusive environment for LGBTQ+ individuals.

Example: "An ally in the LGBTQ+ community center provided a listening ear and unwavering support. The genuine allyship they experienced helped the characters embrace their identities with newfound strength."

Through the portrayal of LGBTQ+ spaces and communities, a lesbian romance novel can beautifully highlight the importance of acceptance, support, and understanding. These spaces serve as safe havens for love, nurturing personal growth and creating bonds of belonging. By empowering characters to embrace their identities and fostering a sense of unity and advocacy, LGBTQ+ spaces demonstrate the transformative power of acceptance and inclusive communities. The novel's narrative can carry a poignant message, inspiring readers to cherish and celebrate the diversity and love within the LGBTQ+ community and beyond.

Incorporating LGBTQ+ spaces and communities in a romance novel is an opportunity to celebrate diversity, representation, and inclusivity. By showcasing these spaces, characters can find acceptance, form meaningful connections, and experience personal growth within their LGBTQ+ identities. These spaces and communities serve as important backdrops for the love story, enriching the narrative and providing readers with a deeper appreciation of the LGBTQ+ experience.

Establishing a Captivating Setting – Utilizing Descriptive Language to Bring Settings to Life

Descriptive language is a powerful tool that can transport readers into the world of a lesbian romance novel, making the settings come alive in their minds. By crafting vivid and evocative descriptions, authors can create a captivating atmosphere that enhances the overall reading experience. Here are some tips for utilizing descriptive language to bring settings to life:

Engaging the Senses in the Setting

To create an immersive reading experience, it's essential to appeal to the readers' senses by vividly describing the setting. By incorporating sensory details, the novel can transport readers to the environment, evoking a more profound emotional response. Here's how to engage the senses effectively:

- *Visual Descriptions*: Paint a vivid picture of the setting by describing its visual elements, such as colors, scenery, and architecture.

Example: "The sun dipped below the horizon, casting a warm, golden glow across the serene, turquoise waters. The quaint, pastel-hued cottages lined the shore, their vibrant façades adding to the picturesque seaside village."

- *Auditory Imagery*: Incorporate sounds to bring the setting to life, capturing the ambient noises and creating a sense of atmosphere.

Example: "The gentle lapping of waves against the boat's hull provided a soothing rhythm as seagulls called out overhead, their cries blending with the laughter of beachgoers."

- *Olfactory Sensations*: Appeal to the sense of smell to enhance the readers' connection with the environment.

Example: "The air was tinged with the salty aroma of the sea, intermingled with the sweet scent of sunscreen and the occasional waft of freshly baked pastries from a nearby bakery."

- *Gustatory Descriptions*: Describe tastes that the characters experience, adding depth to the setting and enhancing the readers' sensory experience.

Example: "The protagonists savored the tangy freshness of the tropical fruit salad, a delightful mix of pineapple, mango, and papaya, served at the open-air beachside café."

- *Tactile Elements*: Incorporate tactile details to provide a sense of texture and touch, making the setting more palpable.

Example: "As they strolled hand in hand along the sandy shoreline, the soft grains of sand slipped between their toes, and the cool breeze caressed their skin."

Example: "The salty breeze caressed their skin as they strolled along the sandy beach, the rhythmic crashing of waves creating a soothing melody in the background."

By engaging the senses, the novel not only creates a vibrant and immersive setting, but also fosters a deeper emotional connection between the readers and the characters. The sensory details enable readers to experience the environment alongside the protagonists, allowing them to feel more invested in the story's unfolding romance and overall narrative.

Use Vivid Imagery

Paint a clear picture of the setting using descriptive and vivid imagery. Show readers the unique features of the location and make them feel like they are experiencing it firsthand.

Examples:

> As the sun began to dip below the horizon, casting hues of orange and pink across the vast expanse of the tranquil lake, the characters found themselves standing on a wooden dock, its weathered planks softened by time and gentle ripples of water. Surrounding them, a dense forest of evergreen trees hugged the lake's edge, their emerald foliage swaying gracefully in the soft breeze.

> A symphony of sounds filled the air—the distant chirping of crickets, the melodic trills of songbirds hidden within the branches, and the occasional rustle of leaves underfoot as they wandered along a narrow forest path. The air was crisp and fragrant, carrying the earthy

scent of pine needles and the subtle sweetness of wildflowers blooming at the forest's edge.

Beyond the lake's surface, the majestic silhouette of snow-capped mountains stood tall, their peaks kissing the cotton candy-colored sky. The mountains seemed to guard the lake like ancient sentinels, adding to the sense of wonder and awe that enveloped the characters.

As they walked hand in hand along the shoreline, the cool, pebbly sand beneath their feet provided a grounding sensation, anchoring them to the present moment. The setting sun painted the lake's water with streaks of gold, creating a mesmerizing dance of light and shadows on its surface.

With each step they took, the characters felt the world around them come alive—the soft touch of a gentle breeze on their cheeks, the rustling of leaves above, and the faint hum of crickets harmonizing with the rhythm of their heartbeats.

In this picturesque haven, the characters found solace and a profound connection, their souls intertwining like the serenity of the lake and the grandeur of the mountains. As the evening unfolded, the setting provided the perfect backdrop for their unfolding love story—a timeless tale of two hearts finding their way together amid the enchanting beauty of nature.

The ancient castle loomed before them, its weathered stone walls standing tall against the test of time, while ivy cascaded down its sides, adding a touch of nature's elegance to its rugged exterior.

By employing vivid imagery, the setting becomes a character in itself, immersing readers in the beauty and splendor of the location. The detailed descriptions paint a clear picture, allowing readers to feel like they are walking alongside the protagonists, experiencing the setting firsthand and becoming fully engaged in the romance and its surroundings.

Show, Don't Tell

Rather than simply telling readers about the setting, show them through the characters' observations and reactions. Use their perspectives to convey the ambiance and mood of the location.

Examples:

As they stepped onto the cobblestone streets, Sarah's eyes widened with awe. The quaint European town before her was like something out of a fairy tale. Colorful buildings lined the narrow streets, each adorned with cascading flower boxes overflowing with vibrant blooms. The aroma of freshly baked bread and pastries wafted from the nearby bakery, inviting them in with its irresistible charm.

"Isn't this place just magical?" Sarah exclaimed, a smile spreading across her face as she turned to Alex, who stood beside her, equally captivated.

Alex nodded, her gaze drawn to the bustling marketplace ahead. Vendors peddled their wares, their cheerful voices blending with the melodies of street musicians playing nearby. The square was alive with laughter, the clinking of glasses, and the hum of conversations in different languages—a mosaic of cultures coming together.

As they strolled through the picturesque town, hand in hand, the ambiance shifted with each twist and turn. They passed by a serene park with a tranquil pond, where ducks glided gracefully across the water's surface. The air seemed to hold a sense of peace and contentment, an invitation to slow down and savor the moment.

A sudden gust of wind swept through, carrying the salty tang of the sea from the nearby coast. They followed the scent, arriving at a breathtaking seaside cliff that overlooked the vast ocean below. Waves crashed against the rocks, their rhythm echoing the beating of their hearts. The expanse of water stretched endlessly into the horizon, instilling a sense of wonder and vastness that left them feeling both humbled and exhilarated.

The setting seemed to whisper tales of history and romance, its ancient buildings and cobbled streets bearing witness to countless love stories that had unfolded here over the years.

As the sun began its descent, casting a warm, golden glow over the town, Sarah and Alex found themselves at a charming café nestled in a quiet corner. The soft murmur of conversation and the clinking of cups provided a soothing backdrop as they settled at a small table on the cobblestones. The flickering candles on the table added a touch of intimacy to the already enchanting atmosphere.

Their gazes met, and in that moment, no words were needed. The setting itself spoke volumes—the magic of the town, the beauty of the seaside cliff, and the intimacy of the café all intertwined, reflecting the unspoken connection between them.

Through the characters' observations and reactions, the reader is immersed in the ambiance and mood of the location. The use of sensory details and the characters' emotional responses create a vivid and engaging portrayal of the setting, allowing readers to experience the charm and magic of the town along with the protagonists.

Choose Descriptive Adjectives

Select descriptive adjectives and powerful language

to create a sense of atmosphere and emotion. Well-chosen words can evoke specific feelings and make the setting more memorable.

Examples:

> The secluded cabin nestled among the towering pines exuded an aura of tranquility, offering them a private haven where their love could bloom like the wildflowers outside.
>
> As they entered the mysterious forest, a thick canopy of ancient trees enveloped them in a shadowy embrace. Sunlight filtered through the dense foliage, casting dappled patterns on the forest floor. The air was heavy with the earthy scent of damp moss and pine, creating an atmosphere of tranquility and enchantment.
>
> The forest was a labyrinth of winding paths and hidden nooks, each corner holding the promise of discovery. Soft, velvety moss cushioned their footsteps as they ventured deeper into the heart of nature's sanctuary. Shafts of golden light pierced through the leaves, creating a mesmerizing dance of shadows and illumination.
>
> Birds sang sweetly above, their melodies echoing through the ancient woods. The gentle rustling of leaves and the distant babbling of a nearby brook added to the symphony of nature's orchestra. The forest seemed to pulse with life, as if every tree and creature held its

own secret to share.

As they explored farther, they stumbled upon a small clearing bathed in a warm, ethereal glow. Wildflowers of every color carpeted the ground, their delicate petals swaying with a graceful rhythm in the soft breeze. Butterflies fluttered by, painting the air with hues of iridescent brilliance.

In this enchanting setting, they found solace from the outside world—a sanctuary of peace and serenity. The forest seemed to whisper ancient tales of love and longing, its very presence urging them to embrace the beauty of the moment.

With each step, their connection deepened, their hearts beating in harmony with the heartbeat of the forest. Time seemed to stand still as they reveled in the magic of the setting and the magic of their love.

In this evocative and emotive description, powerful adjectives and language were used to create a sense of atmosphere and emotion. Words like "mysterious," "enchanting," "tranquility," "ethereal," and "solace" evoke specific feelings, allowing readers to experience the forest's charm and the protagonists' emotions on a deeper level. The setting becomes more memorable as the carefully chosen words paint a vivid picture of the enchanting and magical world within the forest.

Create Contrast

Utilize contrast to highlight the uniqueness of the setting by juxtaposing different elements in the narrative. Contrasting elements can add depth and intrigue to the environment, drawing the readers' attention to specific details. Here are some ways to achieve this:

- *Descriptive Language*: Use descriptive language to vividly portray the contrasting features of the setting. For example, contrast a bustling urban city with a serene countryside, or a gloomy, misty forest with a vibrant, sunlit beach. Describe the differences in scenery, architecture, weather, and atmosphere to emphasize the distinctiveness of each location.
- *Mood and Tone*: Establish different moods and tones in contrasting settings. A thriving city might evoke a sense of excitement and fast-paced energy, while a tranquil countryside may exude a feeling of peace and simplicity. The contrast in mood can create a powerful impact on the readers' emotions and perception of the settings.
- *Cultural and Historical Contrasts*: If the story involves different cultures or historical periods, explore the contrasts in customs, traditions, and societal norms between the settings. This can add richness to the narrative and showcase the diversity of the world in which the characters exist.
- *Symbolism*: Utilize symbolic elements to represent the contrast between settings. For example, a dilapidated house may symbolize past struggles and hardship, while a blooming garden represents growth and new beginnings. Symbolism can enhance the thematic depth of the story and highlight the distinct qualities of each setting.

- *Character Reactions*: Show how the characters react differently to various settings. Their responses to the contrasting environments can reveal their personalities, preferences, and emotional states, providing insight into their inner world.
- *Plot and Conflict*: Introduce plot elements and conflicts that arise due to the contrasts in settings. These differences can create challenges and opportunities for the characters, shaping the plot and adding complexity to the story.
- *Shift in Perspectives*: If the story switches between different settings, consider using shifts in perspectives or narrative styles to highlight the contrast. This can provide a fresh and engaging reading experience and emphasize the uniqueness of each setting.
- *Foreshadowing*: Use foreshadowing to hint at the contrasts between settings early in the story. Foreshadowing can pique readers' curiosity and anticipation, encouraging them to pay attention to the differences that will be explored later in the narrative.

By skillfully utilizing contrast, writers can effectively emphasize the distinctiveness of various settings, making them more memorable and impactful. The use of contrast adds depth and complexity to the story, enriching the overall reading experience for the audience.

Examples:

> The city streets hummed with life and energy, contrasting sharply with the serene, starlit rooftop where they found solace in each other's arms.

As they stepped into the bustling city, the contrast between old and new was striking. Towering skyscrapers adorned the skyline, their sleek glass façades reflecting the modernity and innovation that had swept through the urban landscape. The city's heartbeat echoed with the buzz of traffic and the cacophony of city life.

Amid the gleaming towers, however, pockets of history still clung to the streets. Narrow cobblestone alleys wound through the maze of high-rises, leading to hidden courtyards and quaint, centuries-old buildings. Ivy climbed the weathered walls, adding a touch of rustic charm to the hopping metropolis.

As the sun dipped below the horizon, a transformation occurred. The city's vibrant energy gave way to a magical glow, with city lights twinkling like stars against the dark canvas of the sky. The neon signs blended with the warm glow of streetlamps, creating an enchanting juxtaposition of old and new.

The city's contrasts extended to its people, as well. Diverse faces and cultures mingled on the crowded streets, each person contributing their unique story to the city's tapestry. Amid the fast-paced rush, moments of connection and compassion could be found, reminding them that humanity still thrived amid the concrete and steel.

> In the heart of the city, a hidden gem revealed itself—an oasis of green amid the urban sprawl. A lush park offered respite from the chaos, with ancient trees providing shade and comfort. The scent of freshly cut grass mingled with the aroma of street food, creating an intoxicating blend of nature and urban life.

As the protagonists navigated the bustling cityscape, the contrasts were a constant reminder of the city's rich and diverse tapestry. From towering modernity to hidden historical nooks, the setting became a character in its own right—a place where opposites converged, and the beauty of diversity thrived. In this world of contrasts, the characters' journey of self-discovery and love unfolded, influenced by the dynamic and ever-changing environment they called home.

Capture Time and Seasons

Incorporate details about the time of day, weather, and seasons to set the mood and reflect the characters' emotions. The changing scenery can mirror the characters' journey and emotional arc.

Examples:

> As the autumn leaves fell gently around them, they found themselves wrapped in the warmth of each other's embrace, the colors of the season mirroring the blooming love in their hearts.

As the sun dipped below the horizon, casting hues of orange and pink across the sky, the city took on a different energy. The once bustling streets now seemed quieter, as if the world was taking a collective breath after a busy day. Streetlights flickered to life, illuminating the paths ahead and creating a warm, cozy ambiance.

It was autumn, and the crisp air carried the faint scent of fallen leaves. The trees that had once been lush with greenery were now adorned with hues of red, gold, and brown. The sound of leaves crunching underfoot added a comforting rhythm to their footsteps as they strolled through the city park.

In the distance, the soft glow of café lights beckoned, promising a refuge from the chill. The characters stepped inside, and the warm aroma of freshly brewed coffee enveloped them. They settled into a corner booth, savoring the cozy atmosphere as raindrops gently tapped against the windows. The pitter-patter of the rain created a soothing backdrop for their conversation, inviting intimacy and vulnerability.

As the days grew shorter, winter arrived, blanketing the city with a soft layer of snow. The cold air nipped at their cheeks, but the warmth of each other's company made it bearable. They sought solace in the city's holiday festivities, surrounded by twinkling lights and the joyful laughter of strangers.

With the arrival of spring, the city transformed once again. Cherry blossoms adorned the parks, signaling new beginnings and fresh starts. The characters' relationship also bloomed, and they found themselves drawn even closer as they explored the city's colorful gardens and embraced the promise of growth and renewal.

The passing of time was evident in the changing seasons, mirroring the characters' emotional journey. Each moment captured a different mood and atmosphere, reflecting the ebbs and flows of their love story. Time became an essential element, marking their growth, their challenges, and the eventual resolution they found in each other's arms. Through the cycle of seasons, the setting became a poignant reminder of the passage of time and the beauty of love's evolution.

Use Metaphors and Similes

Enhance the descriptive language with metaphors and similes to add richness and depth to the setting. These literary devices can create powerful and imaginative comparisons.

Examples:

> The old library smelled of dusty pages and forgotten stories, like a treasure chest of secrets

waiting to be unlocked by curious minds.

The city skyline rose like a majestic crown, its skyscrapers piercing the sky like proud sentinels. The lights of the city glittered like a thousand stars, casting a shimmering blanket over the urban landscape.

The park was a sanctuary of tranquility, its lush greenery a tapestry of life. The trees swayed like dancers in the breeze, their leaves whispering secrets to the wind. The soft babble of the nearby creek was like a soothing lullaby, inviting the characters to lose themselves in its melody.

Inside the café, the atmosphere was warm and inviting, like a comforting embrace from an old friend. The aroma of fresh coffee wafted through the air, enveloping them in a cocoon of comfort and familiarity. The chatter of patrons and the clinking of cups provided a symphony of sounds, creating a harmonious backdrop for their conversation.

As the rain fell outside, it was as if the heavens themselves were weeping tears of joy. The raindrops danced on the windowpane like shimmering crystals, reflecting the city's lights in a dazzling display. The characters huddled close, finding solace in each other's presence, like two souls seeking shelter from life's storms.

In winter, the city was a frozen wonderland, like

a painting brought to life. The snow-covered streets were like a blank canvas, waiting to be adorned with the footprints of their journey. The city lights glowed like beacons in the winter night, guiding them through the darkness with a sense of hope and warmth.

In spring, the city burst into bloom like a canvas splashed with a riot of colors. The cherry blossoms were like delicate clouds of cotton candy, swirling gently in the breeze. The city's heartbeat seemed to quicken, like the pulse of love awakening from its winter slumber.

Through the changing seasons, the city became a living metaphor for their love story. It mirrored the highs and lows, the beauty and challenges, and the ever-changing nature of their emotions. The setting was not just a backdrop; it was a living, breathing part of their journey, entwined with their hearts and forever etched in their memories.

Descriptive language is a powerful tool that can breathe life into the settings of a romance novel. By engaging the readers' senses, using vivid imagery, and incorporating various literary devices, authors can create captivating atmospheres that transport readers into the world of their characters. Through evocative descriptions, the settings become more than mere backdrops; they become immersive experiences that enrich the overall narrative and leave a lasting impression on the readers' hearts and minds.

Writing Intimate and Emotional Scenes – Portraying Emotional Connection and Chemistry

Intimate and emotional scenes are the heart of any lesbian romance novel, where the protagonists' emotional connection and chemistry come to life. These scenes deepen the readers' investment in the characters' love journey and evoke powerful emotions. To craft compelling intimate and emotional scenes, consider the following tips:

Build Emotional Tension

Create anticipation and emotional tension leading up to the intimate scene. Foreshadow the characters' desires and feelings, heightening the readers' curiosity and engagement.

As the characters' romantic journey unfolds, the writer carefully weaves a tapestry of emotional tension, setting the stage for the intimate scene that lies ahead. It is a delicate dance, where every interaction, glance, and word exchanged adds to the building anticipation, drawing the readers deeper into the characters' desires and emotions.

In the moments leading up to the intimate scene, the writer employs subtle hints and foreshadowing to pique the readers' curiosity. Perhaps the characters

share lingering glances, their gazes locking for just a moment longer than necessary. Or their conversations take on a deeper, more meaningful tone, hinting at the unspoken emotions that simmer beneath the surface.
The characters' thoughts and inner monologues also contribute to the emotional tension. They find themselves inexplicably drawn to each other, their minds preoccupied with thoughts of the other person. Emotions swirl within them, a whirlwind of excitement and nervousness as they wrestle with their growing attraction.

The writer strategically places moments of closeness and intimacy that, while innocent on the surface, carry an undercurrent of desire. A brief touch of the hand or a brush of shoulders sends shivers down their spines, leaving them yearning for more. Each interaction leaves the characters and readers hungry for the next, wondering when their hearts will finally collide.

The setting itself becomes a catalyst for emotional tension. Perhaps they find themselves in a secluded spot, the world around them fading away as they are drawn to each other. Or the atmosphere is charged with electricity, the air thick with anticipation and unspoken words. Nature might mirror their emotions—a sun setting on the horizon, a gentle breeze caressing their skin, or raindrops tapping against the window, setting the mood for what is to come.

As the characters' emotional connection deepens, the emotional tension escalates, reaching its peak just before the intimate scene. Their chemistry crackles like electricity, their hearts beat in sync, and their souls

yearn for union. The weight of their unspoken desires hangs in the air, almost tangible, as they stand at the precipice of a moment that will change everything.
In the culmination of emotional tension, the writer delicately leads the characters to the edge of vulnerability. The barriers they once held up start to crumble, leaving them bare and exposed to each other. Their unyielding yearning merges with the readers' anticipation, creating a captivating and emotionally charged atmosphere.

When the moment finally arrives, the intimate scene becomes a breathtaking release of the emotional tension that has been building throughout the story. It is a culmination of desires and emotions, a union of hearts and souls, as the characters find solace and passion in each other's arms.

By building emotional tension and anticipation leading up to the intimate scene, the writer crafts a captivating and emotionally resonant experience for the readers. It allows them to be fully immersed in the characters' journey, feeling the depth of their desires and the intensity of their emotions, creating a truly unforgettable and powerful love story.

Show Vulnerability

Reveal the characters' vulnerability and raw emotions during intimate moments. Allow them to share their fears, hopes, and insecurities, strengthening the emotional connection between them.

During intimate moments, the writer skillfully reveals

the characters' vulnerability and raw emotions through a delicate interplay of actions, thoughts, and dialogue. Rather than explicitly stating their emotions, the writer lets their body language and inner thoughts paint a vivid picture of their emotional state.

For instance, as the characters draw closer, their trembling hands betray their nervousness, and their eyes convey a mix of desire and uncertainty. A faint blush spreads across their cheeks, revealing their vulnerability as they step into the unknown territory of intimacy.

In these tender moments, the writer delves into the characters' inner worlds, offering glimpses of their thoughts and emotions. Through inner monologues, the characters share their fears and hopes, exposing the insecurities that have long haunted them. These inner revelations create a powerful emotional connection between the characters and the readers as they witness the vulnerability of the protagonists firsthand.

Dialogue also plays a crucial role in revealing their vulnerability. The characters' words may quiver or stumble as they try to articulate their feelings, showcasing their rawness and openness. They may express their fears of being judged or rejected, their yearning for acceptance, and their desire for a deeper connection. Through these authentic conversations, the writer brings the characters' emotional journey to life, making it relatable and heartfelt.

Furthermore, the writer incorporates sensory details to evoke the characters' emotional states. Descriptions of the touch of their skin against each other or the softness of their whispered words add depth to the scene, creating an intimate atmosphere that resonates with the characters' vulnerability.

In sum, the writer reveals the characters' vulnerability and raw emotions during intimate moments through subtle yet powerful techniques. By showing rather than telling, readers are invited to experience the characters' emotional journey, making the romance more engaging and heartfelt.

Examples:

> In the tender embrace of the moonlit night, the characters find themselves entwined in each other's arms, hearts pounding in sync with the rhythm of the universe. As they delve deeper into the intimate moment, vulnerability surfaces like a fragile bloom seeking the warmth of the sun.
>
> Their gazes lock, and a whirlpool of emotions swirls within. In the safety of each other's presence, they shed their armor, revealing the rawness of their souls. Their breaths mingle, hesitant and uncertain, as unspoken words linger on their lips, waiting to be set free.
>
> The weight of their past traumas and insecurities rests upon their shoulders, woven into the fabric of their beings. With a tremor in her voice, one character softly admits, "I've spent so long hiding, afraid of who I am. But with you, I feel

like I can finally be myself."

In the intimate cocoon they've created, they dare to be vulnerable, to expose the tender fragments of their hearts. The other character listens with unwavering compassion, her touch gentle and reassuring. "You don't need to hide from me," she whispers. "I see you, all of you, and I cherish every part."

Their fears and hopes intertwine like the delicate threads of a tapestry. With every passing moment, they unravel the layers of self-doubt, replacing them with newfound courage and acceptance. It's a dance of emotions, where vulnerability is met with tenderness and vulnerability blooms into strength.

In the quiet of the night, they share their dreams and fears, confiding in each other like the closest confidants. The walls they once built to protect their hearts come tumbling down, and they find solace in the safety of vulnerability. It is a revelation, a freeing of the spirit, and a strengthening of the bond that unites them.

As they traverse the landscape of emotions, the characters discover that vulnerability is not a weakness, but a testament to their humanity. In each other's presence, they find acceptance and understanding, a refuge from the storm of their past. Together, they explore the uncharted territory of their souls, unearthing the hidden treasures within.

Their vulnerability becomes the foundation upon which their emotional connection is built. It fosters an intimacy that transcends the physical, a connection that weaves their hearts and souls into an unbreakable tapestry of love and acceptance.

In the aftermath of the intimate moment, they lay bare before each other, stronger than ever before. Their vulnerabilities have become their strengths, a testament to their resilience and capacity to love. And as they bask in the afterglow of vulnerability embraced, they know that their love is boundless, and their hearts are forever entwined.

Use Inner Dialogue

Incorporate inner dialogue to showcase the characters' internal thoughts and feelings. This allows readers to understand their perspectives, doubts, and the emotional significance of the moment. Here are some techniques and examples to showcase characters' internal thoughts and feelings:

- *Stream of Consciousness*: Writers can employ a stream-of-consciousness style to reveal the characters' unfiltered thoughts and feelings as they happen. This approach allows readers to experience the characters' inner monologue in a raw and immediate manner.
- *Italicized Thoughts*: Writers may italicize the characters' thoughts to differentiate them from

regular narrative or dialogue. This stylistic choice draws attention to the characters' inner musings and helps readers understand their perspectives.
- *First-Person Narration*: In stories with a first-person perspective, the main character narrates her own thoughts and emotions, giving readers direct access to her internal world. This creates an intimate connection between the character and the reader.
- *Third-Person Limited Point of View*: Even in third-person limited point of view, writers can delve into a character's thoughts and feelings by providing internal insights within the narration. This allows readers to connect with the character on a deeper level.
- *Reflective Moments*: Writers can incorporate reflective moments where the character takes a pause to contemplate their feelings and thoughts. This allows readers to witness their emotional growth and the significance of the moment.
- *Dialogue Tags and Actions*: Including descriptive dialogue tags or character actions can convey the characters' inner emotions indirectly. For example, a character may clench their fists to show anger or blush to demonstrate embarrassment.
- *Interior Monologues*: Characters may engage in interior monologues where they have a more extended, introspective conversation with themselves. These monologues can reveal their doubts, fears, and desires.
- *Showing Reactions*: When characters experience an emotional moment, writers can show their reactions through physical responses or facial expressions. These nonverbal cues can give readers a glimpse into the characters' internal

state.

By skillfully incorporating inner dialogue and internal emotional exploration, writers enable readers to understand the characters' perspectives, doubts, and emotional significance of the moment. This deeper connection with the characters enhances the overall emotional resonance of the story.

Examples:

> As their lips brushed against each other, Sarah's heart raced, and a flurry of thoughts flooded her mind. *Is this right? Can I allow myself to feel this way?* Her inner dialogue echoed with uncertainty and vulnerability. For years, she had buried her true self under the weight of societal expectations and the fear of judgment. Now in this intimate moment, she was confronted with the raw truth of her desires.
>
> Amelia caressed Sarah's cheek, sensing the hesitation in her touch. In her own thoughts, Amelia understood the significance of this moment. She knew the courage it took for Sarah to open her heart, to let herself be seen and loved for who she truly was. She longed to reassure her, to let her know that she was accepted, cherished, and that they could navigate this journey together.
>
> Amelia leaned in, looking into Sarah's eyes, silently communicating her support and love. In those unspoken moments, their connection deepened, and the walls around Sarah's heart

began to crumble. She felt a sense of safety and acceptance she had never experienced before. The intimacy of the moment was not just physical but emotional—a connection that went beyond the surface.

As their bodies moved closer, Sarah's inner dialogue shifted from doubt to acceptance. This was her truth, her heart laid bare before Amelia. And in that vulnerability, she found strength—the strength to embrace her identity and the love that had blossomed between them.

In the tender space between them, where words weren't needed, Amelia sensed Sarah's transformation. The tears in Sarah's eyes spoke of the weight lifted off her shoulders, of the journey she had embarked on, and the self-acceptance she was gradually embracing. Amelia felt honored to witness this profound moment of growth and vulnerability.

In the midst of their passionate embrace, Sarah and Amelia experienced a shared inner dialogue—an unspoken understanding of the significance of their love. Their hearts were laid bare, and in that vulnerability, they found solace and strength in each other's arms. The emotional depth of their connection transcended physical touch, solidifying their bond and paving the way for a love that was genuine and authentic.

Focus on Body Language

Nonverbal communication, such as gentle touches, eye contact, and breaths taken, can convey the depth of their emotional connection. A writer can focus on body language to convey the characters' emotions during intimate scenes in several ways:

- *Descriptive Language*: Use descriptive language to portray the characters' body language in intimate detail. Describe the gentle touches, the softness of their caresses, the intensity of their eye contact, and the way their bodies respond to each other.
- *Sensory Details*: Include sensory details to enhance the intimacy of the scene. Describe how the characters' bodies feel against each other, the warmth of their breaths mingling, and the rapid beating of their hearts.
- *Actions and Reactions*: Show the characters' actions and reactions to each other's touch. For example, describe how they lean in closer, how their fingers intertwine, or how they tremble with anticipation.
- *Breath and Heartbeat*: Use breath and heartbeat to convey the characters' emotional state. For instance, mention how their breaths become shallow with desire or how their hearts race with excitement.
- *Eye Contact*: Emphasize the significance of eye contact during intimate moments. Describe how the characters stare into each other's eyes, conveying unspoken emotions and a profound connection.
- *Posture and Body Movement*: Pay attention to the characters' posture and body movement during intimate scenes. Show how they instinctively lean toward each other or how

they seek physical closeness.
- *Dialogue Interruptions*: Use body language to interrupt dialogue during intimate moments. For example, characters may pause midsentence, captivated by each other's presence, or lean in for a kiss, silencing their words.
- *Emotional Gestures*: Include emotional gestures like tender smiles, blushing cheeks, or the brushing away of tears. These small actions can speak volumes about the depth of their emotional bond.
- *Symbolic Gestures*: Utilize symbolic gestures that carry emotional meaning, such as offering a comforting embrace or tracing a heart shape on each other's palm.
- *Build Gradually*: Gradually build the intensity of the characters' body language as the emotional connection deepens throughout the story. This allows readers to experience the growing intimacy between the characters.

By focusing on body language and physical cues during intimate scenes, a writer can create a powerful and evocative portrayal of the characters' emotional connection. These nonverbal expressions enrich the narrative and provide readers with a deeper understanding of the characters' feelings and desires.

Examples:

> In the dimly lit room, Emma and Olivia stood face to face, their bodies drawn together by an invisible force. The air crackled with tension as they exchanged glances filled with longing and vulnerability. Slowly, Emma reached out, her fingers trembling slightly, to brush a strand of hair

from Olivia's face. The gentle touch sent shivers down Olivia's spine, and she let out a soft sigh.

Their gazes locked, and time seemed to stand still. In that moment, words were unnecessary as their looks spoke volumes, revealing the depth of their emotions and the unspoken connection between them. With each passing second, their breaths synchronized, the rhythm of their hearts beating in unison.

As the anticipation grew, Emma's hand found its way to Olivia's cheek, cradling it gently. Olivia leaned into the touch, her eyes fluttering closed, surrendering to the intensity of the moment. Their faces drew closer, their lips almost touching, and then they paused, their breaths mingling as they savored the magnetic pull between them.

The room seemed to fade away, leaving only the two of them enveloped in a cocoon of intimacy. Emma's thumb traced Olivia's lower lip, and she felt the softness of it against her skin. The desire to close the distance overwhelmed them, and finally, their lips met in a tender and electrifying kiss.

Their bodies pressed together, seeking comfort and solace in each other's embrace. The warmth of their skin against each other sent a rush of sensations through their bodies, intensifying the connection between them. It was as if their bodies had known each other forever, and every touch felt like coming home.

In that moment of vulnerability, they let go of their fears and insecurities, allowing themselves to be seen and accepted for who they truly were. The physical intimacy they shared mirrored the depth of their emotional connection, and they knew they had found something rare and precious.

As they held each other close, their bodies spoke a language that went beyond words. In the quiet of that intimate space, they found solace and belonging, knowing that they had discovered a love that was authentic and true. Their bodies entwined, they embarked on a journey of emotional connection, trust, and profound love that would forever bind their hearts together.

Develop Trust and Consent

Developing trust and consent between characters requires careful and thoughtful writing to create an authentic and respectful portrayal. Here are some tips for effectively writing about how characters develop trust and consent:

- *Establish Emotional Connection*: Before diving into intimate moments, focus on developing a strong emotional connection between the characters. Show how they bond over shared experiences, open up to each other, and build a foundation of trust through honesty and vulnerability.
- *Prioritize Communication*: Emphasize the

importance of open and honest communication between the characters. Let them have candid conversations about their desires, boundaries, and comfort levels. This dialogue should be ongoing and not limited to a single scene.
- *Show Active Listening*: Highlight the characters' active listening skills during their interactions. Let them respond sensitively to each other's concerns and desires, showing that they genuinely care about each other's feelings and comfort.
- *Consent as a Continuous Process*: Portray consent as an ongoing and active process, rather than a one-time agreement. Characters should continually check in with each other and respect each other's choices throughout their intimate moments.
- *Respect Boundaries*: Illustrate how characters respect and honor each other's boundaries. If one character expresses discomfort or hesitation, the other should respond with understanding and stop any activity immediately.
- *Avoid Coercion*: Avoid any scenes where one character pressures or coerces the other into intimacy. Consent should be freely given without manipulation.
- *Showcase Affirmative Consent*: Demonstrate that characters explicitly give affirmative consent before engaging in intimate activities. Affirmative consent means an enthusiastic "yes" rather than the absence of a "no."
- *Portray Characters' Growth*: Show how the characters' trust and consent evolve over time as their relationship deepens. Let them learn from their mistakes and communicate more effectively as they grow together.
- *Address Past Traumas*: If relevant, explore how past traumas or negative experiences may

impact a character's ability to trust and give consent. Approach this topic with sensitivity and show how characters support each other in healing and moving forward.
- *Encourage Mutual Respect*: Emphasize the importance of mutual respect in any romantic relationship. Characters should treat each other as equals and respect each other's autonomy.

Examples:

In the intimate space they shared, trust and consent were paramount. As their bodies drew closer, their gazes locked in a silent agreement, knowing that they were on the same page. Emma's hand hesitated near Olivia's waist, and she looked into her eyes for any sign of hesitation or discomfort.

Olivia's gaze was unwavering, and she gave a subtle nod, a nonverbal confirmation that she was ready to proceed. Emma's heart swelled with admiration for Olivia's open communication and respect for her boundaries. It was a powerful reminder that trust was the foundation of their connection.

Their bodies moved in sync, each touch deliberate and purposeful. As they explored each other, they did so with the utmost care and sensitivity, ensuring that each gesture was met with acceptance and reciprocation. They understood that vulnerability came with trust, and they held each other's hearts with tenderness and reverence.

Throughout their intimate moments, they frequently checked in with each other, asking simple yet profound questions like, "Are you okay?" and "Is this okay?" Their words were laced with consideration, ensuring that both partners felt comfortable and safe.

Emma searched Olivia's face for any sign of discomfort or uncertainty. Olivia smiled softly, her eyes filled with affection and gratitude for Emma's thoughtful approach. The love they shared went beyond physical desire; it was a love that valued consent and prioritized their emotional connection.

Their words and actions communicated a profound understanding that consent was not just a one-time agreement but a continuous conversation. They embraced the vulnerability that came with expressing their desires and boundaries, knowing it was an integral part of fostering a loving and respectful relationship.

In the afterglow of their intimate moments, they held each other close, basking in the warmth of their emotional connection. It was not just about the physical act; it was about the emotional intimacy they had cultivated. The trust they had built was the foundation of their love, allowing them to be their most authentic selves with each other.

In their journey of love and intimacy, they

found that trust and consent were not just buzzwords but pillars of their connection. With open communication and a deep understanding of each other's needs, they embraced the beauty of consent and trust, creating a love that was empowering, respectful, and truly fulfilling.

By incorporating these elements into your writing, you can create a story that portrays the development of trust and consent in a realistic and respectful manner. This will allow readers to connect with the characters' journey and appreciate the importance of trust and consent in healthy relationships.

Utilize Sensory Details

Engage the readers' senses by describing sensory details, such as the taste of a kiss, the warmth of a touch, or the scent of the surroundings. Sensory imagery intensifies the emotional impact of the scene. Here are some tips for effectively using sensory details:

- *Engage Multiple Senses*: Go beyond visual descriptions and engage all the senses to create a more immersive experience. Describe the taste of a kiss, the warmth of a touch, the scent of the surroundings, and the sound of their breathing or heartbeat.
- *Be Specific*: Use precise and vivid language to describe sensory experiences. Instead of generic terms, use specific adjectives to paint a clear picture for the readers.
- *Connect Sensory Details to Emotions*: Tie sensory details to the characters' emotions and

feelings. For example, describe how the warmth of a touch sparks a sense of comfort or how the scent of a partner's perfume evokes a rush of affection.
- *Show the Characters' Reactions*: Use sensory details to showcase the characters' reactions and responses to each other's touch, taste, or scent. This helps readers understand the depth of their emotional connection.
- *Vary the Intensity*: Adjust the intensity of sensory descriptions based on the emotional tone of the scene. A tender and intimate moment may require softer and gentler sensory imagery, while a passionate scene may call for more intense and heightened sensations.
- *Use Metaphors and Symbolism*: Employ metaphors and symbolism to amplify the emotional impact of sensory details. For example, compare the taste of a kiss to a sweet indulgence or the warmth of a touch to a comforting embrace.
- *Integrate Sensory Details into the Narrative*: Seamlessly integrate sensory details into the narrative to enhance the overall flow of the scene. Avoid interrupting the natural progression of the moment with overly lengthy descriptions.

Balance Sensory Descriptions

Strike a balance between sensory descriptions and emotional insights. Sensory details should complement and deepen the emotional impact of the scene rather than overshadow it. To effectively utilize sensory details in writing, including the taste of a kiss, the warmth of a touch, or the scent of the surroundings, follow these tips:

- *Engage Multiple Senses*: Incorporate sensory details that engage multiple senses to create a vivid and immersive experience. Describe not only what the characters see and hear, but also what they taste, feel, and smell.
- *Be Specific and Descriptive*: Use specific and descriptive language to convey sensory experiences. Instead of simply mentioning a "sweet kiss," describe the taste of strawberries or honey on their lips.
- *Focus on Emotional Impact*: Connect the sensory details to the characters' emotions and feelings in the scene. For example, describe the warmth of a touch as comforting or the scent of the surroundings as reminiscent of a happy memory.
- *Use Metaphors and Similes*: Enhance sensory descriptions with metaphors and similes to add depth and creativity. Compare a kiss to the sweetness of nectar or a touch to the warmth of sunshine.
- *Show Characters' Reactions*: Use sensory details to illustrate the characters' reactions and emotional responses. Describe how a gentle touch sends shivers down their spine or how the scent of flowers makes their heart flutter.
- *Balance Sensory Imagery*: Strike a balance between sensory imagery and other narrative elements. While sensory details intensify the emotional impact, they should complement the overall plot and character development.
- *Integrate Sensory Details Seamlessly*: Integrate sensory details seamlessly into the narrative without overwhelming the reader. Sensory descriptions should flow naturally within the context of the scene.
- *Consider the Setting*: Tailor sensory details

to the setting of the scene. For example, in a romantic outdoor setting, describe the scent of blooming flowers and the feel of soft grass beneath their feet.
- *Avoid Clichés*: Be original in your sensory descriptions and avoid using clichés. Instead of relying on overused phrases, find unique and evocative ways to convey the characters' experiences.
- *Use Sensory Details Sparingly*: While sensory details can enhance the emotional impact, use them sparingly to avoid overwhelming the reader. Choose the most poignant moments to employ sensory imagery for maximum effect.

By effectively utilizing sensory details in your writing, you can intensify the emotional impact of intimate scenes, making them more immersive and resonant for readers. These details will enrich the readers' experience and allow them to connect deeply with the characters and their journey of love and intimacy.

Show Emotional Growth

Demonstrate emotional growth in the characters throughout their love journey. The level of emotional intimacy should deepen as they grow closer and develop a stronger bond. As the characters embark on their love journey, they begin to undergo profound emotional growth, shaped by their experiences and the deepening bond between them. Initially, they may harbor uncertainties and reservations, unsure of where their feelings might lead. However, as they spend more time together, their emotional intimacy gradually unfolds.

Through their interactions, the characters begin to reveal glimpses of vulnerability, allowing each other into the innermost corners of their hearts. They learn to trust and confide in each other, breaking down the barriers that once shielded their true selves. As their connection strengthens, so does their ability to understand and support each other's emotions. The characters learn from past misunderstandings and confrontations, using those lessons to communicate more openly and honestly. Their conversations become more profound, touching on fears, dreams, and aspirations, fostering a profound sense of understanding and empathy between them.

As they face challenges and obstacles together, their emotional bond deepens even further. They find solace in each other's presence, seeking comfort during moments of distress. Their emotional growth is evident in how they handle conflicts with newfound patience and compassion, resolving issues with respect and consideration.

Shared experiences forge an unbreakable emotional connection, creating memories that bind them together. They cherish joyous and challenging moments, finding strength in the support they provide each other. Gradually, they become attuned to each other's emotions, able to discern feelings unspoken, fostering a profound sense of unity. The characters' emotional growth reflects in their evolving actions. They take risks for the sake of their love, stepping out of their comfort zones to demonstrate their commitment to the relationship. The transformation is visible in how they prioritize each other's happiness, offering unwavering support and encouragement in pursuing their dreams. Throughout their love journey, they reflect on their progress, appreciating the positive impact of their emotional growth on their bond. They find contentment in knowing that the love they share is built on mutual respect, trust, and an ever-deepening emotional intimacy. As the characters grow closer and their connection solidifies, their emotional growth becomes the foundation upon which their love story unfolds. It is through this profound emotional intimacy that they discover the true depth of their feelings and find solace in the arms of their beloved, forming an unbreakable bond that stands the test of time.

To effectively portray emotional growth in characters throughout their love journey, writers can use the following techniques:

- *Show Vulnerability*: Allow the characters to show vulnerability and open up about their feelings, fears, and insecurities. As they become more comfortable with each other, they should gradually share their emotional burdens.
- *Inner Monologues*: Include inner monologues to reveal the characters' internal thoughts and emotions. This allows readers to witness their introspection and personal growth as they navigate their feelings for each other.
- *Evolving Communication*: Illustrate how the characters' communication evolves over time. As their emotional bond strengthens, they should become more open and honest with each other, leading to more profound and meaningful conversations.
- *Learning from Past Mistakes*: Demonstrate that the characters learn from their past mistakes

and apply that knowledge to their relationship. This growth should reflect in their actions and decisions, showing they are evolving as individuals.
- *Handling Conflict*: Show how the characters handle conflicts and disagreements differently as their emotional connection deepens. They should be more willing to listen, understand, and find compromise, fostering a healthier relationship.
- *Overcoming Insecurities*: As the characters grow emotionally, they should work on overcoming their insecurities and trust issues. This progress can be portrayed through their interactions and how they respond to challenges.
- *Supporting Each Other*: Illustrate how the characters support each other's emotional well-being. They should be each other's pillars, providing comfort, encouragement, and understanding during difficult times.
- *Emphasize Shared Experiences*: Showcase how shared experiences and moments of vulnerability contribute to the characters' emotional growth. Through these shared moments, they develop a deeper connection and understanding of each other.
- *Gradual Intimacy*: Let the level of emotional intimacy grow gradually, reflecting the characters' increasing trust and affection for each other. Show how they become more attuned to each other's emotions and needs.
- *Reflect on Progress*: Provide opportunities for characters to reflect on their emotional growth and the positive impact it has on their relationship. This reflection can happen through conversations, internal thoughts, or even journaling.

By using these techniques, writers can effectively portray emotional growth in characters throughout their love journey. The characters' evolving emotional connection will resonate with readers, making the romance more authentic and compelling.

Balance Physical and Emotional Intimacy

Writers can achieve a balance between physical and emotional intimacy by prioritizing the characters' emotional connection and using it as the driving force behind their physical interactions. Balance physical intimacy with emotional intimacy. Here are some tips on how to achieve this balance:

- *Establish Emotional Chemistry*: Lay the groundwork for a strong emotional connection between the characters before delving into physical intimacy. Allow them to bond emotionally through shared experiences, meaningful conversations, and genuine understanding of each other's feelings.
- *Develop Trust and Communication*: Showcase the characters communicating openly about their desires, boundaries, and insecurities. This level of trust and honest communication builds a foundation for a deeper emotional connection that enriches their physical interactions.
- *Use Inner Monologues*: Incorporate inner monologues to reveal the characters' internal thoughts and emotions during intimate moments. This provides insight into their feelings, fears, and vulnerabilities, making the scene more authentic and meaningful.
- *Connect Actions to Emotions*: Ensure that physical intimacy is intertwined with the

characters' emotions. Show how their touches, kisses, and gestures are driven by their love, affection, and desire for each other.
- *Focus on Sensory Details*: Use sensory details to enhance the emotional impact of physical intimacy. Describe the characters' sensations and emotions, such as the racing of their hearts, the warmth of their touch, or the intensity of their gazes.
- *Emphasize Aftermath and Emotional Processing*: After an intimate scene, explore the characters' emotional aftermath. Show how they process their feelings, deepen their emotional bond, and share their thoughts with each other.
- *Avoid Gratuitous Content*: Be mindful of the purpose and relevance of each intimate scene. Avoid gratuitous or explicit content that may overshadow the emotional aspect of the relationship.
- *Show Vulnerability*: Reveal the characters' vulnerability and emotional investment during physical intimacy. Allow them to share their fears, hopes, and insecurities, strengthening the emotional connection between them.
- *Focus on Consent*: Highlight the importance of consent and mutual respect during intimate moments. Characters should communicate their comfort levels and boundaries, ensuring a respectful and consensual experience.
- *Use Symbolism*: Utilize symbolism and metaphors to enhance the emotional depth of physical intimacy. Symbolic elements can add richness and resonance to the scene, further reinforcing the emotional connection between the characters.

By prioritizing emotional intimacy and using it as a guiding force in physical interactions, writers can create love scenes that are meaningful and authentic, resonating with readers on a deeper level. The balance between physical and emotional intimacy adds depth and complexity to the characters' relationship, making their love journey all the more captivating and relatable.

- *Use Metaphors and Symbolism:* Incorporate metaphors and symbolism to enhance the emotional depth of the scene. Symbolic elements can evoke powerful emotions and add layers of meaning to the characters' experiences.
- *Emphasize Emotional Connection:* Focus on the emotional connection and chemistry between the characters, rather than solely on physical actions. The emotional bond is what makes the intimate scenes truly impactful.
- *Gradual Escalation:* Allow the intimacy between the characters to escalate gradually, reflecting the development of their relationship. This gradual progression builds anticipation and emotional resonance.
- *Aftercare and Reflection:* Consider including scenes of aftercare and reflection following intimate moments. Show how the characters support each other emotionally and process their feelings.

Writing intimate and emotional scenes in a lesbian romance novel requires careful attention to the characters' emotional connection and chemistry. By building emotional tension, showing vulnerability, and utilizing sensory details, authors can create powerful and authentic intimate scenes that resonate with readers. Balancing physical and emotional intimacy while emphasizing trust, consent, and emotional growth ensures that these scenes contribute to the protagonists' love journey and the overall depth of the narrative. Ultimately, well-crafted intimate and emotional scenes strengthen the readers' emotional investment in the characters' romance, leaving a lasting impact long after the final page.

Writing Intimate and Emotional Scenes – Navigating Sexual and Romantic Tension

Intimate and emotional scenes play a crucial role in revealing the depth of the protagonists' connection and the evolution of their love story. Navigating sexual and romantic tension in these moments requires the utmost sensitivity and thoughtfulness to create a compelling and respectful portrayal.

When crafting these scenes, it's essential to focus on the characters' emotions and the emotional journey they are experiencing. Instead of relying solely on physical descriptions, delve into their thoughts, desires, and vulnerabilities. Show how their feelings for each other deepen and how their connection grows stronger with each interaction.

Consent is paramount in any intimate scene. Both characters must willingly participate and express their desire for each other explicitly. By portraying clear and enthusiastic consent, the scene becomes empowering, fostering a sense of trust and respect between the characters.

Avoiding stereotypes and clichés is crucial. Each character's experiences and expressions of intimacy should be unique and authentic to their personalities and backgrounds. Avoid using offensive language or reducing the characters to mere stereotypes, as this can undermine the emotional depth of the scene and the overall narrative.

Incorporate emotional intimacy alongside physical connection to create a well-rounded portrayal of their relationship. Show how their emotional bond enhances their physical intimacy and how they find comfort and solace in each other's arms. Navigating sexual tension can be an intricate dance between desire and restraint. By using subtle cues, body language, and dialogue, you can heighten the anticipation and build up to a powerful and intimate moment. The tension should be a natural progression of their emotional connection, never forced or rushed.

Ultimately, creating intimate and emotional scenes in a lesbian romance novel requires empathy, sensitivity, and a profound understanding of the characters' journeys. When done thoughtfully, these moments can evoke a range of emotions in readers and leave a lasting impact, making the love story all the more compelling and meaningful.

Lastly, keep in mind that these scenes are not meant for gratuitous content but rather to deepen the readers' understanding of the characters and their love story. Handle them with care and respect, ensuring that they serve the narrative's purpose and contribute to the overall growth and development of the characters and their relationship.

Here are some tips for writing intimate and emotional scenes while handling sexual and romantic tension:

- *Establish Consent and Communication:* Prioritize consent and open communication between the characters during intimate moments. Show that they trust and respect each other's boundaries, making the scene consensual and empowering.

In a lesbian romance, establishing consent and communication during intimate moments is of utmost importance. It is essential to portray the characters as being respectful of each other's boundaries and showing mutual trust, ensuring that the scenes are consensual and empowering for both individuals involved.

To achieve this, depict the characters engaging in open and honest conversations about their feelings, desires, and comfort levels. Prioritize verbal communication, where they explicitly express their consent and discuss any boundaries they may have. Avoid portraying situations where one character pressures or coerces the other into intimacy, as this can be harmful and perpetuates harmful stereotypes.

In intimate scenes, demonstrate that both characters actively participate and are enthusiastic about their connection. Show them checking in with each other and ensuring that they are both comfortable and willing to proceed. Remember that consent is an ongoing process and can be withdrawn at any point if one or both characters feel uncomfortable.

Incorporate nonverbal cues, as well, such as body language and facial expressions, to convey the characters' mutual understanding and consent. Depict moments of tenderness and respect, where they listen to each other's needs and desires, fostering a sense of safety and empowerment in the relationship.

Furthermore, avoid presenting intimate moments in a sensationalized or explicit manner that objectifies the characters. Instead, focus on the emotional connection and the depth of their feelings for each other. Let the intimacy be a natural and meaningful expression of their love and trust.

By prioritizing consent and communication in intimate scenes, you not only promote healthy relationships, but also contribute to a positive and respectful representation of lesbian romance. Portraying consensual and empowering relationships sends a powerful message of respect, equality, and trust, and allows readers to connect with the characters on a deeper emotional level.

Examples:

> In the dimly lit room, their gazes met, and an unspoken understanding passed between them. They had shared many intimate moments before, but tonight felt different, a sense of vulnerability and trust hanging in the air.
>
> She reached out, her fingers gently brushing against her love interest's cheek, seeking permission without words. The slight nod and soft smile that followed were all she needed to know that they were on the same page.
>
> Their bodies moved closer, hearts beating in sync

as they held each other, their breaths mingling in the space between them. With each touch, they ensured that the other was comfortable, never pushing beyond the boundaries set by their partner.

In the quiet moments, they communicated through soft whispers, sharing their desires and fears, baring their souls to each other. There were no assumptions or expectations, only a genuine desire to understand and connect on a deeper level.

As their love deepened, so did their communication. They learned each other's love languages, knowing that a gentle touch or a lingering gaze could convey emotions more than words ever could. They allowed each other to be vulnerable, knowing that it was through this vulnerability that their connection grew stronger.

In the midst of passion, they continued to check in with each other, ensuring that their partner was comfortable and fully present in the moment. They understood that consent was not just a one-time agreement but an ongoing conversation that evolved with their relationship.

In the aftermath of their intimate encounter, they lay tangled in each other's arms, their hearts overflowing with love and gratitude. They knew that their journey of consent and communication was an integral part of their love story, an expression of trust, respect, and empowerment that bound them together.

As their romance blossomed, they continued to prioritize consent and communication in every aspect of their relationship. It became the foundation upon which they built their love, a cornerstone of trust and understanding that allowed them to navigate the highs and lows of their journey together. And in doing so, they created a love story that was not only passionate and intense, but also consensual, empowering, and deeply meaningful.

Build Sexual and Emotional Anticipation

Building sexual and emotional anticipation is crucial to creating a captivating and engaging love story. To achieve this, focus on gradually developing the characters' desires and feelings, allowing their emotions to simmer and intensify over time. By doing so, readers become emotionally invested in their love journey, making the unfolding romance even more compelling.

To build sexual anticipation, use subtle cues and moments of attraction between the characters. Small gestures, lingering glances, and accidental touches can all contribute to the growing sense of desire and chemistry. However, avoid rushing into physical intimacy too quickly; instead, let the anticipation build organically, making the eventual moment of intimacy even more powerful and meaningful.

Emotional anticipation is equally important in a lesbian romance. Allow the characters to open up to each other gradually, sharing their fears, hopes, and vulnerabilities. As their emotional bond deepens, readers will become more invested in their emotional journey and root for their love to flourish.

One effective way to create anticipation is to use alternating points of view between the protagonists. By offering insights into their thoughts and emotions, readers can see the growing attraction from both perspectives, heightening the anticipation and emotional investment.

Additionally, use pacing strategically to control the flow of the romance. Slow down during significant moments of connection and emotional revelation, allowing readers to savor the depth of the characters' feelings. Conversely, pick up the pace during moments of tension and conflict to keep the readers engaged and curious about the outcome.

Remember that building anticipation is about allowing the relationship to develop naturally. Don't rush the process or force the characters into situations that don't align with their emotional arcs. Let their connection and intimacy grow in a way that feels authentic and true to their personalities.

By gradually building sexual and emotional tension, you create a more immersive and emotionally resonant love story. Readers will be drawn into the characters' desires and feelings, making the ultimate fulfillment of their romance more rewarding and satisfying.

Use Subtle Gestures and Descriptions

Using subtle gestures and descriptive language can be a powerful way to heighten tension and convey the intensity of the characters' emotions. Show how the characters respond to each other's touch or gaze, conveying the intensity of their emotions. These small, nuanced moments can add depth and authenticity to the romantic relationship, allowing readers to feel more immersed in the love story.

When describing the characters' interactions, pay attention to their body language and nonverbal cues, whether it's a lingering hand on the small of the back, a gentle brush of fingers, or an intense gaze that lingers a moment too long. These gestures can speak volumes about their feelings and the chemistry between them. Incorporate sensory details to enhance the emotional impact of these moments. Describe how the characters' hearts race, how their breath catches, or how their skin tingles with excitement when they are near each other. These visceral reactions can reveal the depth of their connection and attraction.

Additionally, use metaphorical language to evoke the characters' emotions. Compare their feelings to natural elements, like the warmth of the sun on a cool day or the rush of a tidal wave. Metaphors can beautifully capture the intensity of their emotions in a way that resonates with readers.

Examples:

As Alex and Riley stood in the softly lit room,

their gazes locked in a wordless conversation. The air seemed to hum with anticipation, and a delicate shiver ran down Riley's spine as Alex's fingertips brushed against her forearm. It was a fleeting touch, but it sent a rush of warmth through her veins.

They exchanged a knowing smile, their unspoken attraction simmering just below the surface. Every movement felt charged with meaning, as if the world had slowed down to capture this intimate moment. Riley's heart pounded in her chest, and she could feel her cheeks flush with a mix of excitement and nervousness.

As Alex leaned closer, the air between them crackled with electricity. Their breaths mingled, and Riley felt a gentle brush of Alex's lips against her earlobe. It was a tender gesture, filled with unspoken promises and a desire to be closer.

Their gazes met again, and Riley could see the intensity of Alex's emotions reflected in those deep, soulful eyes. It was as if they were dancing on the edge of something profound, a connection that went beyond words.

A soft, hesitant hand reached out, fingers grazing the curve of Riley's cheek. The touch was so delicate, yet it sent her heart soaring. In that moment, everything else faded away, and all that mattered was the magnetic pull drawing them together.

As they inched closer, the space between them seemed to disappear. Their lips brushed against each other, a feather-light touch that sent a jolt of electricity through both of them. It was a simple kiss, yet it held the promise of so much more.

Their bodies moved closer, instinctively seeking the comfort and warmth of each other. Riley felt a rush of emotions flood her heart—desire, vulnerability, and a sense of being seen and accepted for who she truly was.

In the quiet stillness of the room, they embraced, their bodies fitting together like two pieces of a puzzle. They didn't need to say anything; their actions spoke volumes. With each touch and caress, they conveyed their deep affection and longing.

As they shared this intimate moment, the world outside seemed to fade away, leaving only the two of them in their own little universe. In each other's arms, they found solace, understanding, and a love that transcended everything else.

The subtlety of their gestures and the intensity of their emotions created a magnetic pull, drawing them together in a dance of passion and tenderness. It was a moment of connection that would forever linger in their hearts, sparking the beginning of a love story that would leave an indelible mark on their souls.

Remember to strike a balance between subtlety and explicitness. While you want to convey the emotions and tension between the characters, it's important to avoid overly graphic or explicit descriptions. Instead, let the power of suggestion and innuendo create an air of sensuality and intimacy.

Overall, incorporating subtle gestures and descriptive language adds layers of depth to the romantic relationship, making the love story more compelling and engaging for readers. It allows them to feel the characters' emotions and experience the unfolding romance in a vivid and evocative way.

Inner Monologues and Emotions

Include inner monologues to reveal the characters' internal thoughts and emotions. This provides insight into their desires and anxieties, making the scene more intimate and relatable by providing insight into the characters' thoughts, feelings, and internal struggles. Here are some techniques to achieve this:

- *Use First-Person Narration*: If the story is written in the first-person perspective, the writer can directly convey the protagonist's inner thoughts and emotions. This approach allows readers to experience the story through the character's eyes and gain a deep understanding of their perspective.
- *Employ Third-Person Limited Point of View*: In third-person limited point of view, the narration follows the thoughts and emotions of a single character. This allows the writer to

delve into the character's mind and explore their inner world while maintaining a degree of objectivity.
- *Utilize Free Indirect Discourse*: Free indirect discourse is a narrative technique that blends the character's thoughts with the narrator's voice. It creates a seamless transition between the character's inner monologue and the external narrative, providing a more intimate look into their emotions.
- *Create Introspective Scenes*: Incorporate scenes that allow characters to reflect on their feelings and motivations. These introspective moments provide opportunities to explore their emotional growth and internal conflicts.
- *Show, Don't Tell*: Rather than outright stating the character's emotions, show their feelings through their actions, body language, and reactions to situations. This technique allows readers to interpret and connect with the emotions on a deeper level.
- *Use Descriptive Language*: Employ vivid and evocative language to describe the characters' emotional states. Use sensory details to engage readers' senses and immerse them in the characters' feelings.
- *Employ Inner Dialogue*: Introduce inner dialogue to reveal the characters' internal thoughts and conversations with themselves. This technique allows readers to witness the characters' doubts, hopes, and fears firsthand.
- *Depict External Triggers*: Use external events or interactions to trigger the characters' emotional responses. Show how they react to these triggers and how it influences their thoughts and decisions.
- *Explore Subtext*: Utilize subtext in conversations and interactions to imply underlying emotions

and thoughts. Readers can infer the characters' true feelings through subtle cues and nonverbal communication.
- *Develop Character Arcs*: Create well-defined character arcs that showcase the evolution of the characters' emotions and perspectives throughout the story. This progression allows readers to witness their growth and development.

By skillfully incorporating inner monologues and emotions, writers can provide a window into the characters' inner worlds, adding depth and authenticity to their experiences. This level of emotional insight enhances the readers' connection to the characters and makes the storytelling more compelling and relatable.

Examples:

> As they moved closer, their lips finally meeting in a soft and tentative kiss, their inner monologues quieted, replaced by the unspoken language of love and vulnerability. In that moment, they both knew that their hearts were in sync, and the journey they were embarking on was one filled with hope, possibility, and the promise of a love that would change their lives forever.

> As their fingers lightly intertwined, Mia's heart raced with a mixture of anticipation and apprehension. She couldn't believe how much she longed for this moment, to feel Liz's touch, to be close to her like this. A part of her yearned to lean in, to deepen the connection between

them, while another part hesitated, afraid of what it all meant.

I can't believe how much I want this, Mia thought, her mind filled with uncertainty and desire. Is she feeling the same way? What if I'm misreading her signals? I don't want to ruin our friendship, but I can't deny these feelings.

As Liz leaned in, her breath softly brushing against Mia's cheek, a shiver ran down her spine. She could feel the intensity of their connection, the electricity that seemed to crackle between them. But she also sensed Mia's hesitancy, and she didn't want to push too far, too fast.

Does she feel what I feel? Liz wondered, her heart pounding in her chest. I want to be closer to her, to show her how much she means to me. But I need to be patient, to let her lead the way. I don't want to rush things and risk scaring her off.

In that moment, their gazes met, and Mia could see the same mix of emotions mirrored in Liz's eyes. It was as if they were both standing on the edge of a precipice, uncertain of what lay ahead but drawn irresistibly toward each other.

I need to trust my heart, Mia thought, a surge of determination replacing her doubts. I can't let fear hold me back. If there's a chance for something beautiful between us, I want to take it.

As they leaned in, their lips finally meeting in a tender, hesitant kiss, their inner monologues faded away, replaced by the shared language of emotions and desires. In that moment, they both knew that this was the beginning of something extraordinary, a love that had the power to transform their lives in ways they could never have imagined.

Focus on Emotional Connection

Emphasize the emotional connection between the characters, ensuring that their bond drives the intimacy. Show how their emotional intimacy enhances the physical aspect of their relationship.

Examples:

> In the quiet moments they shared together, it was the depth of their emotional connection that truly set their hearts ablaze. As their fingers intertwined, a rush of warmth spread through both their bodies, and they felt as though they could communicate without uttering a word.

> Their conversations were filled with laughter, vulnerability, and the sharing of their dreams and fears. They found solace in each other's embrace, seeking refuge in the safety of their love. It was the way Mia could look into Sarah's eyes and see her soul laid bare or the way Sarah could sense Mia's every mood shift with just a

gentle touch that made their emotional bond so profound.

Every touch, every caress, and every whispered word were infused with the weight of their emotions, each gesture an expression of their love and devotion. When they kissed, it was not merely a physical act, but a merging of souls, an affirmation of the connection that bound them together.

Their emotional intimacy enhanced every aspect of their physical relationship. When they made love, it was not simply a union of bodies, but a dance of hearts, a symphony of passion and tenderness. Each touch ignited a spark of longing, a yearning to be closer, to become one.

In the quiet moments after, they lay entwined, their hearts beating in unison, their breaths mingling as they reveled in the afterglow of their love. It was in these moments that their emotional connection deepened even further, as they shared their hopes for the future, their dreams of what their love could become.

Their emotional connection was the foundation of their romance, the anchor that held them steady through the storms of life. It was the driving force that propelled them forward, that gave them the strength to face whatever challenges came their way.

As they journeyed together, hand in hand,

their love grew stronger with each passing day. They knew that as long as they held on to their emotional connection, their love would continue to flourish, and they would always find their way back to each other, no matter what life threw their way. For in each other's arms, they had found a love that was pure, unconditional, and everlasting.

Sensory Details and Imagery

Engage the readers' senses with sensory details and vivid imagery. Describe the characters' physical sensations and the atmosphere surrounding them, enhancing the readers' emotional experience.

Examples:

> The air was thick with the scent of blooming flowers as Mia and Sarah wandered through the vibrant garden, their fingers brushing against soft petals. Sunlight dappled through the leaves, casting a warm, golden glow on their faces. The gentle breeze played with Sarah's hair, and she turned to see Mia's eyes shining like stars, reflecting the beauty of the moment.
>
> As they strolled along the cobblestone path, their steps resonated with a rhythmic melody, the soft crunch of gravel beneath their feet. The sound of distant laughter from other parkgoers

added to the cheerful atmosphere, creating a sense of shared joy and happiness.

Mia felt a flutter of excitement in her chest, her heart beating faster with every stolen glance at Sarah. She marveled at the way Sarah's eyes sparkled with affection and how her lips curved into a gentle smile that reached her eyes.

Their hands found each other naturally, their fingers interlocking like puzzle pieces. The contact sent a jolt of electricity through both of them, igniting a familiar warmth that spread from their hands to their hearts. Mia couldn't help but notice the way Sarah's grip tightened ever so slightly, as if to hold on to the fleeting moment forever.

They found a secluded bench beneath a sprawling oak tree, its branches offering a protective canopy over them. The shade provided a respite from the midday sun, and they settled in, their bodies drawn close in an intimate cocoon of affection.

As they spoke, their voices mingled with the rustling of leaves overhead, forming a harmonious symphony. They shared their dreams and aspirations, their voices filled with passion and vulnerability, weaving a tapestry of emotions that wrapped around them like a warm embrace.

Sarah's fingers traced absentminded patterns on Mia's arm, leaving a trail of tingling sensations in their wake. Mia leaned into the touch, savoring the soft caress, feeling a sense of security and contentment enveloping her.

The world around them seemed to fade into the background, leaving only the two of them in their bubble of bliss. They were lost in each other, their souls entwined in a dance of connection that defied space and time.

As the sun began its descent, casting a golden hue across the sky, they knew this day would forever be etched in their memories. The garden had witnessed the birth of something special, a love that bloomed as brightly as the flowers surrounding them.

In that moment, Mia and Sarah knew that their love story was only just beginning, and they couldn't wait to explore the depths of their emotions and connection. For it was in these sensory details, in the gentle touch of their hands, the sound of their laughter, and the warmth of their hearts, that their love story unfolded with every beat of their hearts.

Avoid Gratuitous or Exploitative Content

Exercise caution to avoid gratuitous or exploitative content. Intimate scenes should serve the narrative and contribute to the characters' emotional development rather than being solely for titillation, unless you are writing an erotic romance, then there still needs to be respectful consent, but the titillation factor is the reason readers pick up an erotic romance.

In a romance, it's crucial to approach intimate scenes with sensitivity and respect for the characters and the readers. Intimacy should be depicted in a way that enhances the emotional connection and character development.

These scenes should serve the narrative by revealing the characters' vulnerabilities, desires, and emotional depth. They offer a window into the characters' hearts and minds, providing insight into their growth, fears, and hopes.

By carefully crafting these intimate moments, the focus remains on the emotional bond between the characters and the journey of their love. It's about portraying the tenderness, passion, and genuine affection they share, rather than using explicit content for shock value.

Moreover, consent and communication remain at the forefront during these moments. Characters must openly express their desires and boundaries, fostering an environment of trust and empowerment. This ensures that the intimacy depicted is consensual and respectful, strengthening the connection between the characters.

Ultimately, the goal is to create a meaningful and authentic portrayal of their relationship, one that resonates with readers and fosters a deeper understanding and appreciation for love in all its forms.

Portray Realistic Reactions

Portray realistic reactions to intimacy, including nervousness, vulnerability, and emotional connection. This authenticity allows readers to connect with the characters on a deeper level. By capturing the characters' genuine emotions, such as nervousness, vulnerability, and emotional connection, the story becomes relatable and emotionally resonant for readers.

Intimate moments can be transformative experiences, and it's essential to show the characters' authentic reactions as they navigate this aspect of their relationship. Nervousness and vulnerability are natural responses to opening oneself up to another person in such an intimate way. Readers can empathize with these emotions, as they may have experienced similar feelings in their own lives.

Moreover, emphasizing the emotional connection during these scenes enhances the depth of the characters' bond. Intimacy goes beyond physical attraction; it's about sharing trust, affection, and understanding. By portraying this emotional aspect, readers can witness the characters' love evolving and deepening.

Realistic reactions also include moments of tenderness, comfort, and joy. It's essential to depict the characters' shared moments of bliss and the intimacy that strengthens their emotional connection. These moments remind readers that love is about vulnerability and finding solace in each other.

By crafting intimate scenes with realism and authenticity, the characters become more relatable, and their journey toward love and intimacy becomes more powerful. Readers can connect on an emotional level, forming a meaningful and lasting bond with the story and its characters.

Be Mindful of Readers' Comfort

Acknowledge that readers may have different comfort levels when reading intimate scenes. Handle the content with sensitivity, ensuring that it is appropriate for the target audience. Different readers may have varying sensitivities and boundaries when it comes to reading about romantic and intimate moments. It's crucial to handle such content with sensitivity and care, ensuring that it aligns with the expectations and appropriateness for the target audience. Here are some considerations to keep in mind while writing intimate scenes:

- *Target Audience*: Understand the target demographic for your lesbian romance novel.

Consider the age group, cultural backgrounds, and preferences of your readers. Tailor the content to suit the sensibilities of your intended audience.
- *Gradual Progression*: If your novel is intended for a younger or more conservative audience, you might choose to focus on emotional intimacy rather than explicit physical descriptions. Allow the relationship to develop gradually, emphasizing the emotional connection and building anticipation.
- *Fade-to-Black Approach*: For readers who prefer a more subtle approach to intimate scenes, consider using a "fade-to-black" technique. This means implying that the intimate moment occurs without describing it in explicit detail. The focus can shift to the emotions and aftermath of the scene.
- *Provide Warnings*: If your novel contains mature content, consider adding content warnings or age recommendations on the book cover or in the book's description. This helps readers make an informed decision about whether the content is suitable for them.
- *Balance with Other Themes*: While intimacy is an essential aspect of a romance novel, ensure that it is balanced with other themes and plotlines. A well-rounded story will engage readers and offer more than just intimate moments.
- *Beta Readers*: If possible, seek feedback from beta readers who represent your target audience. Their insights can help you gauge the comfort level of your readers and make necessary adjustments.

By being sensitive to readers' comfort and preferences, you can create a safe and enjoyable reading experience for everyone while still maintaining the emotional depth and authenticity of the romance in your lesbian novel.

Use Metaphors and Symbolism

Utilizing metaphors and symbolism during intimate moments can add depth and resonance to the characters' emotional journey. Here are some ways a writer can incorporate these literary devices:

- *Describing Physical Sensations*: Use metaphorical language to describe the characters' physical sensations during intimate moments. For example, comparing the fluttering of their hearts to the wings of butterflies or their breathless anticipation to a tidal wave building up inside them can evoke a sense of heightened emotion and excitement.
- *Symbolic Objects*: Introduce symbolic objects that represent the characters' emotional connection. For instance, a piece of jewelry that holds special meaning for both characters or a shared memento from a significant moment in their relationship can serve as a tangible symbol of their love.
- *Natural Imagery*: Incorporate natural imagery to mirror the characters' emotional states. For instance, describing the moon emerging from behind clouds just as the characters share an intimate moment can symbolize the unveiling of hidden emotions and desires.
- *Weather and Setting*: Use weather and setting as symbolic elements. A sudden rain shower can signify cleansing and renewal, while a warm, sunny day can represent the warmth and happiness they bring to each other's lives.

- *Colors*: Assign specific colors to represent the characters' emotions or the tone of the scene. For example, use vibrant colors like red or gold during passionate moments and softer hues like blue or lavender during tender and affectionate scenes.
- *Metaphorical Language in Dialogue*: Allow the characters to use metaphorical language when expressing their feelings. This can add an extra layer of meaning to their words and create a poetic and intimate atmosphere.
- *Recurring Symbols*: Establish recurring symbols throughout the story that relate to the characters' emotional journey. These symbols can be tied to their personal growth, changing relationship dynamics, or pivotal moments in their romance.
- *Nature's Rhythms*: Symbolize the characters' connection through nature's rhythms, such as the ebb and flow of the tide, the changing of seasons, or the rising and setting of the sun. These natural cycles can mirror the evolving nature of their relationship.
- *Metaphorical Actions*: Use metaphors to describe the characters' actions during intimate moments. For instance, describing their lips meeting like the meeting of two stars in the night sky or their fingers entwining like the roots of two trees growing together.
- *Shared Dreams and Visions*: Incorporate shared dreams or visions that hold symbolic meaning for the characters. These dreams can act as a manifestation of their emotional bond and shared aspirations.

By skillfully integrating metaphors and symbolism into the intimate moments, a writer can elevate the emotional depth of the characters' journey and create a more profound and resonant reading experience for the audience.

Examples:

> As the two women stood facing each other, the air around them seemed to crackle with anticipation. The room was dimly lit, and a soft, flickering candle cast dancing shadows on the walls. The warmth of the candle's glow mirrored the warmth in their hearts as they tentatively reached out to touch each other.
>
> Their hands met, and it felt like an electric current surged through their bodies. Time seemed to slow as they gazed into each other's eyes, and in that moment, the rest of the world faded away. They were lost in each other, their connection so intense that it felt like they were the only two people in existence.
>
> As they drew closer, their breaths mingled like a gentle breeze rustling through the leaves of a blossoming tree. Each touch, each caress was like a delicate petal unfurling, revealing the beauty within. They were like two flowers, blooming in each other's presence, basking in the sunlight of love.
>
> The room seemed to be holding its breath, waiting for the culmination of their desire. They moved together like two stars dancing in the night sky, their bodies aligned in perfect harmony. It was as if the universe itself had

conspired to bring them together in this moment of profound connection.

Their lips met, and it was like a spark igniting a wildfire within their souls. The intensity of their emotions surged like a river rushing downstream, unstoppable and unyielding. They surrendered to the current, allowing it to carry them away to a place where there was no past or future, only the present, and the overwhelming love they felt for each other.

In that moment, they were no longer two separate beings but one soul entwined in an eternal embrace. The room was filled with the music of their hearts beating in sync, a symphony of love that echoed through the ages.

As they finally parted, a soft, contented smile played on their lips. They knew that this was just the beginning of their journey together, a journey filled with love, passion, and the beauty of two souls finding solace in each other's embrace.

The symbolism of their intimate moment was not lost on them. They had become each other's safe haven, their love a beacon of hope in a world that sometimes felt dark and uncertain. And as they looked into each other's eyes, they knew that they had found something truly precious—a love that was pure, profound, and everlasting.

Focus on Emotional Aftermath

Explore the emotional aftermath of intimate scenes, depicting how the characters process their feelings and strengthen their bond. After intimate scenes in a lesbian romance novel, the emotional aftermath becomes a pivotal moment for the characters. As the passion and intensity subside, a profound sense of vulnerability and intimacy lingers between the protagonists. They find themselves entangled in a web of emotions, processing the depth of their feelings and the significance of their connection.

In the aftermath, the characters may experience a mixture of emotions—awe, tenderness, and even a hint of trepidation. They might exchange soft glances, their eyes communicating what words cannot express. The intimacy they shared has opened a door to a new level of emotional closeness, and they find themselves unraveling their true selves before each other.

The vulnerability that comes with intimacy can create a unique sense of trust and understanding. The characters feel seen and cherished, knowing that they have laid bare not only their bodies, but also their hearts and souls. This newfound emotional intimacy strengthens the bond between them, forging a connection that is built on mutual respect and affection.

In the quiet moments that follow, the characters may engage in intimate conversations, sharing their thoughts and fears. They speak of dreams and aspirations, as well as the vulnerabilities they have been hesitant to reveal. As they confide in each other, the barriers that once stood between them begin to crumble, leaving space for a deeper sense of emotional connection.

The emotional aftermath is an opportunity for the characters to reaffirm their feelings and intentions. They might express their affection through gentle touches, holding hands, or stealing glances that convey a world of unspoken sentiments. These small gestures speak volumes about the depth of their bond and the tenderness they share.

At times, the emotional aftermath might also bring forth challenges. Past traumas or insecurities may resurface, and the characters must navigate their way through these emotions together. Their intimate connection becomes a source of strength, empowering them to confront their fears and insecurities with the knowledge that they are not alone.

Throughout the emotional aftermath, the characters' relationship continues to evolve. They learn to lean on each other for support, finding solace in the understanding that they are loved and accepted for who they are. Their intimacy becomes a safe space where they can be unapologetically themselves, knowing that they are cherished in all their vulnerabilities and strengths.

As the emotional aftermath unfolds, readers witness the characters' growth and transformation. They embrace their desires and emotions and the love that has blossomed between them. The emotional intimacy they share becomes a driving force in their journey, propelling them forward as they navigate the challenges and joys of their romantic relationship.

In a lesbian romance novel, exploring the emotional aftermath of intimate scenes allows readers to delve deeper into the characters' emotional landscape. It showcases the profound impact of their connection, emphasizing the power of love and emotional intimacy in shaping their journey toward self-discovery, acceptance, and a love that knows no bounds.

Writing intimate and emotional scenes requires delicacy and thoughtfulness in navigating sexual and romantic tension. Prioritize consent, emotional connection, and realistic portrayals while being mindful of readers' comfort levels. By creating anticipation, utilizing sensory details, and focusing on the characters' emotional journey, authors can craft intimate and emotional scenes that add depth and authenticity to the lesbian romance novel. Ultimately, well-written intimate scenes can deepen the readers' emotional investment in the characters' love journey, creating a powerful and unforgettable reading experience.

Exploring Themes in Lesbian Romance – Identity, Self-acceptance, and Coming Out

Lesbian romance novels often delve into powerful themes that resonate with readers from all walks of life. Among the most prevalent and impactful themes are identity, self-acceptance, and coming out. These themes are central to the characters' emotional journeys and play a significant role in shaping their love stories. Here's an exploration of each theme:

Identity

Identity is a fundamental theme in lesbian romance novels, as characters grapple with understanding and embracing their sexual orientation. Protagonists may struggle to define their lesbian identity, especially if they have previously identified as heterosexual or faced societal expectations of heteronormativity. Exploring their authentic selves is a key step toward personal growth and genuine connections with others.

In lesbian romance novels, the theme of identity plays a crucial role in shaping the characters' emotional journeys. The protagonists often find themselves on a path of self-discovery as they grapple with understanding and embracing their sexual orientation. This exploration of their authentic selves becomes a pivotal step toward personal growth and forging genuine connections with others.

For some protagonists, coming to terms with their lesbian identity may be a challenging process. Societal pressures can lead to inner conflicts and feelings of confusion as they question their true desires and feelings.

As the story unfolds, readers witness the characters' internal struggles and emotional turmoil. Through their inner monologues and reflections, the protagonists may voice their uncertainties, fears, and hopes. This vulnerable portrayal allows readers to empathize with their journey and understand the complexity of self-discovery.

Throughout the narrative, supportive LGBTQ+ spaces, such as online communities, LGBTQ+ support groups, or LGBTQ+ social venues, can serve as invaluable sources of comfort and understanding. These spaces offer a sense of belonging and acceptance, providing the protagonists with the support they need to explore their identity in a safe environment.

As the characters delve deeper into their authentic selves, they gradually shed the weight of societal expectations and emerge stronger and more confident. This process of self-acceptance empowers them to embrace their lesbian identity unapologetically, leading to a greater sense of self-awareness and personal fulfillment.

In addition to the protagonists' individual journeys, the romance itself becomes a catalyst for growth. The emotional connection they share serves as a mirror for their evolving identities, enabling them to be vulnerable and open with each other. Through this genuine connection, the characters find the strength to confront their fears and insecurities, further solidifying their understanding of who they are and what they want in life.

The theme of identity in lesbian romance novels ultimately underscores the significance of being true to oneself. It highlights the importance of embracing one's sexual orientation and finding love and acceptance within oneself and in a partner. By authentically exploring the characters' journeys of self-discovery, these novels resonate with readers who may have faced similar challenges, fostering a sense of camaraderie and understanding within the LGBTQ+ community and beyond.

Self-acceptance

Self-acceptance is an essential aspect of the characters' development in lesbian romance novels. Many protagonists experience internal conflicts and insecurities surrounding their sexual orientation. Accepting and embracing their identity allows them to build confidence, form healthy relationships, and find love. Self-acceptance also empowers characters to confront external challenges, such as judgment from family, friends, or society.

In lesbian romance novels, the theme of self-acceptance holds significant importance in the protagonists' emotional journey. The characters often grapple with internal conflicts and insecurities related to their sexual orientation. These struggles can hinder their ability to embrace their true selves fully.

Throughout the story, readers witness the protagonists' inner battles as they come to terms with their lesbian identity. They may wrestle with feelings of shame, fear of judgment, or societal pressures to conform to heteronormative norms. These internal struggles create a sense of vulnerability and authenticity, allowing readers to connect with the characters on a deeply emotional level.

As the narrative unfolds, pivotal moments of self-reflection and personal growth emerge. The protagonists gradually begin to confront their doubts and insecurities, taking small steps toward self-acceptance. These moments of self-discovery serve as transformative experiences, enabling the characters to build confidence in their identity.

In their journey toward self-acceptance, the characters may find solace and support in LGBTQ+ spaces or through the guidance of mentor figures who have navigated similar challenges. These sources of understanding offer a sense of belonging and validation, reaffirming the importance of embracing their authentic selves.

As the characters embrace their true identities, they grow in self-assurance, paving the way for healthier relationships and deeper emotional connections. The romance between the protagonists becomes a beacon of hope and acceptance, reflecting the transformative power of self-love.

In addition to internal conflicts, external challenges often test the characters' newfound self-acceptance. They may encounter judgment from family, friends, or society, facing adversity and prejudice. However, the inner strength they have cultivated through self-acceptance equips them to confront these external challenges with resilience and grace.

As the story progresses, self-acceptance becomes a driving force behind the protagonists' choices and actions. It empowers them to stand firm in their identity, making decisions that align with their true selves and prioritize their happiness and well-being. Ultimately, self-acceptance serves as a catalyst for personal growth, emotional fulfillment, and finding love. The characters' journeys of self-discovery inspire readers to embrace their own identities and celebrate their uniqueness. Through these stories, lesbian romance novels encourage a message of acceptance, understanding, and love, fostering a positive and empowering representation of LGBTQ+ experiences.

Coming Out

Coming out is a deeply emotional and transformative process depicted in lesbian romance novels. Characters may face fear, uncertainty, and vulnerability as they consider whether and how to reveal their sexuality to loved ones. The coming-out journey can be filled with heartache and liberation, and it often impacts the characters' relationships and personal growth. The support, or lack thereof, from friends and family plays a significant role in shaping the characters' experiences.

In lesbian romance novels, the theme of coming out holds a profound emotional weight, representing a pivotal moment in the characters' lives. The protagonists grapple with the decision of whether and when to reveal their true selves to their loved ones. This process is fraught with fear, uncertainty, and vulnerability, as they navigate the potential consequences of sharing their sexual orientation.

As the story unfolds, readers witness the characters' internal struggle as they grapple with the idea of coming out. They may fear rejection, judgment, or a loss of acceptance from those they hold dear. This fear creates a sense of emotional turmoil, leaving the characters torn between their desire for authenticity and their fear of potential repercussions.

The coming-out journey is a transformative process that elicits a range of emotions, from anxiety and hesitation to courage and empowerment. For some characters, the decision to come out is a liberating experience, a moment of embracing their true selves and stepping into their authentic identity. For others, it can be a heartbreaking and challenging ordeal, especially if they face opposition or lack of understanding from their friends and family.

The reactions of the characters' loved ones play a significant role in shaping their coming-out experiences. Supportive and accepting reactions can be a source of comfort and validation, fostering an environment of love and understanding. In contrast, negative reactions or rejection can lead to feelings of isolation and hurt, underscoring the importance of chosen family and supportive LGBTQ+ communities. Throughout the coming-out process, the characters' relationships undergo significant changes. Some friendships may deepen and strengthen as they reveal their true selves, while others may falter or become strained due to prejudice or misunderstanding. Similarly, the characters' romantic relationships may also evolve as they navigate the challenges and joys of coming out together.

Coming out is not a one-time event but a continuous journey of self-discovery and growth. As the characters embrace their identities openly, they experience a newfound sense of liberation and self-acceptance. Their coming-out experiences become instrumental in shaping their personal growth and emotional development, paving the way for healthier and more authentic connections with others.

In lesbian romance novels, the theme of coming out is a powerful portrayal of the complexities of identity and the resilience of the human spirit. These stories showcase the courage and vulnerability of characters as they navigate their paths to self-discovery and acceptance, inspiring readers to embrace their own identities and celebrate the uniqueness that makes them who they are.

Through the exploration of these themes, lesbian romance novels offer readers a chance to connect with the characters' emotions and experiences. The journey of identity, self-acceptance, and coming out mirrors the real-life struggles of LGBTQ+ individuals, fostering empathy and understanding among readers.

In lesbian romance novels, themes of identity, self-acceptance, and coming out serve as powerful drivers of character development and emotional depth. The protagonists' journeys to embrace their authentic selves, find love, and navigate the challenges of coming out resonate with readers, creating narratives that are relatable and empowering. By exploring these themes, lesbian romance authors contribute to positive representation and offer valuable insights into the complexities of LGBTQ+ relationships and experiences.

Exploring Themes in Lesbian Romance – Overcoming Obstacles and Prejudices

Overcoming obstacles and prejudices is a central theme in many lesbian romance novels. As characters navigate their love journey, they encounter various challenges arising from societal biases, personal insecurities, and external pressures. Here's a closer look at how this theme unfolds in such stories:

- *Societal Prejudices*: Lesbian romance novels often address the societal prejudices and discrimination faced by LGBTQ+ individuals. Characters may encounter judgment, homophobia, or rejection from family, friends, or the community. Overcoming these prejudices requires resilience and the strength to stay true to oneself despite the external negativity.
- *Internal Struggles*: Characters in lesbian romance novels may battle internal struggles stemming from self-doubt and fear of rejection. These internal obstacles can hinder their ability to embrace their true selves and form meaningful connections with their love interests. Overcoming these struggles is often a significant part of their character growth.
- *Family and Cultural Expectations*: The clash between family or cultural expectations and a character's authentic identity can present a significant obstacle. Some characters may fear disappointing their families or fear losing

their cultural connections if they embrace their lesbian identity. Overcoming these expectations may lead to a journey of self-discovery and finding a balance between personal and cultural identities.
- *Fear of Vulnerability*: Fear of vulnerability and past emotional wounds can create obstacles in forming and maintaining intimate relationships. Characters may struggle to open up emotionally due to past traumas or heartbreaks. Overcoming this fear involves taking risks and learning to trust others with their hearts.
- *Legal and Workplace Challenges*: Lesbian romance novels may also explore legal and workplace challenges faced by LGBTQ+ individuals, such as discrimination, lack of legal protections, or difficulties in securing equal opportunities. Overcoming these hurdles may involve advocating for change and fighting for equal rights.
- *Building a Supportive Community*: Overcoming obstacles often involves finding and building a supportive community. Characters may seek like-minded friends or join LGBTQ+ support groups, finding strength and encouragement from others who have faced similar challenges.
- *Challenging Stereotypes*: Lesbian romance novels can challenge stereotypes associated with LGBTQ+ relationships and characters. By depicting diverse and multidimensional characters, authors break away from harmful clichés and offer authentic and empowering representations.

Overcoming obstacles and prejudices is a recurring and transformative theme in lesbian romance novels. As characters confront external biases, internal struggles, and personal insecurities, they experience profound growth and self-discovery. These stories portray the resilience and strength of LGBTQ+ individuals in the face of adversity, while highlighting the importance of finding acceptance, love, and support within themselves and their communities. Ultimately, overcoming obstacles and prejudices is not only pivotal to the characters' love journey, but also reflects the real-life triumphs of LGBTQ+ individuals in their pursuit of happiness and equality.

Exploring Themes in Lesbian Romance – Celebrating Love and Relationships

Celebrating love and relationships is at the heart of every lesbian romance novel. These stories beautifully capture the emotional journey of characters as they discover, embrace, and nurture their love for each other. Here's how lesbian romance novels celebrate love and relationships:

- *Authentic Representation*: Lesbian romance novels celebrate love by offering authentic representation of LGBTQ+ relationships. By portraying diverse and relatable characters, these stories reflect the experiences of real-life LGBTQ+ individuals, fostering empathy and understanding.
- *Unconditional Acceptance*: Love in lesbian romance novels often triumphs through unconditional acceptance. Characters embrace each other for who they are, supporting and cherishing their partner's unique qualities and quirks.
- *Emotional Intimacy*: The celebration of love goes beyond physical attraction. Emotional intimacy is a key aspect of lesbian romance, where characters connect on a deep, soulful level. These emotional bonds strengthen the love story and resonate with readers.
- *Empowering Relationships*: Lesbian romance novels often feature empowering relationships

where partners lift each other up, encourage personal growth, and stand as equals in their love journey. These relationships serve as inspirations for healthy and supportive partnerships.
- *Overcoming Adversity Together*: Celebrating love in lesbian romance novels involves characters overcoming challenges together. Their love becomes a source of strength, empowering them to face external obstacles and prejudice with courage and resilience.
- *Expressions of Affection*: Expressions of affection, whether grand gestures or small moments, are celebrated in these novels. From passionate kisses to heartfelt declarations of love, these moments evoke powerful emotions in the characters and readers.
- *Finding Love in Unexpected Places*: Lesbian romance novels often explore the theme of finding love in unexpected places. Characters may stumble upon each other when they least expect it, leading to transformative and heartfelt connections.
- *Positive Role Models*: Love stories in lesbian romance novels serve as positive role models for LGBTQ+ readers and allies. These stories validate the experiences and emotions of LGBTQ+ individuals, fostering a sense of pride and belonging.
- *Embracing Individuality*: In celebrating love, lesbian romance novels emphasize the importance of embracing individuality. Characters appreciate and love each other's uniqueness, understanding that it is what makes their bond special and strong.
- *Inspiring Hope and Happiness*: Ultimately, lesbian romance novels celebrate love by inspiring hope and happiness. The emotional

journey of the characters, filled with ups and downs, culminates in a satisfying and uplifting conclusion, leaving readers with a sense of joy and fulfillment.

Celebrating love and relationships is a central theme in lesbian romance novels. These stories embrace authentic representation, emotional intimacy, and unconditional acceptance to create empowering and transformative love stories. By overcoming challenges, supporting each other, and finding joy in unexpected places, characters in lesbian romance novels inspire readers with messages of hope, love, and the power of genuine connections. These narratives celebrate the beauty of love in all its forms, offering heartwarming and uplifting reading experiences for readers of diverse backgrounds.

Editing and Polishing Your Novel

Once you've crafted your story, the process of refining, editing, and polishing is essential to ensure that your lesbian romance captivates readers and delivers a seamless and immersive experience. We will explore the art of editing, refining plot elements, improving prose, and perfecting the overall presentation of your lesbian romance novel.

The Importance of Editing

- *Refining Craftsmanship:* Editing elevates your writing by refining plot inconsistencies, enhancing character development, and tightening narrative flow.
- *Reader Satisfaction:* A well-edited lesbian romance novel ensures that readers are fully immersed in the story without distractions or inconsistencies.

Elements of Effective Editing

- *Plot Consistency:* Review your plot for continuity, ensuring that clues, character actions, and events align seamlessly.
- *Character Development:* Scrutinize character arcs, motivations, and interactions to ensure they remain authentic and contribute to the narrative.

Refining Plot Twists

- *Twist Clarity:* Assess the clarity and impact of your plot twists, ensuring they

are surprising yet logically grounded.
- *Foreshadowing:* Integrate subtle foreshadowing earlier in the story to enhance the impact and credibility of major revelations.

Enhancing Pacing and Tension

- *Pacing Dynamics:* Review pacing across different story segments, adjusting the rhythm to maintain reader engagement.
- *Tension Building:* Fine-tune the balance between suspenseful scenes and moments of respite to keep readers hooked.

Polishing Prose and Dialogue

- *Eloquent Descriptions:* Evaluate your descriptions, aiming for vivid yet concise language that enhances the reader's visual experience.
- *Authentic Dialogue:* Revise dialogue to ensure it sounds natural and reflects characters' distinct voices, emotions, and motivations.

Eliminating Redundancy

- *Unnecessary Details:* Trim redundant or irrelevant descriptions, details, or scenes that don't contribute to character or plot development.
- *Repetition:* Identify and remove excessive repetition of phrases, actions, or information that can detract from a smooth reading experience.

Checking for Clarity

- *Clear Exposition:* Ensure that your explanations, clues, and revelations are

conveyed clearly, preventing confusion for readers.
- *Beta Reader Feedback:* Gather input from beta readers to identify areas where clarity may be lacking or where additional explanations are needed.

Grammar and Style

- *Grammar and Mechanics:* Review your manuscript for grammar, punctuation, and spelling errors to maintain a professional presentation.
- *Consistent Style:* Ensure consistent use of tense, point of view, and narrative style throughout the novel.

Finalizing Presentation

- *Formatting:* Format your manuscript according to industry standards, including proper chapter headings, margins, fonts, and spacing.
- *Proofreading:* Conduct a final proofread or enlist a professional proofreader to catch any lingering errors or inconsistencies.

Crafting an Engaging Opening and Closing

- *Compelling Introduction:* Polish your opening scenes to immediately engage readers and establish the tone and atmosphere of your lesbian romance.
- *Satisfying Conclusion:* Craft a satisfying and resonant conclusion that ties up loose ends while leaving room for reflection and interpretation.

Preparing for Publication

- *Agent or Publisher Queries:* If seeking

traditional publishing, research and follow submission guidelines for agents or publishers.
- *Self-Publishing Considerations:* If opting for self-publishing, ensure your manuscript is professionally edited and formatted before publication.

Editing and polishing are the final stages in transforming your lesbian novel from a draft into a polished masterpiece. By meticulously refining your plot, characters, prose, and presentation, you provide readers with a seamless and immersive reading experience. As you embark on the editing journey, remember that each revision brings you closer to achieving a compelling and captivating lesbian that will resonate with readers long after they've turned the final page.

Editing and Polishing Your Novel – The Importance of Multiple Drafts

Multiple drafts play a critical role in the process of crafting a compelling lesbian romance narrative. Writing is a journey that involves refining ideas, improving pacing, strengthening characters, and enhancing plot twists. We will explore the significance of multiple drafts and the techniques that will help you transform your initial concept into a polished and engaging lesbian romance story.

Iterative Refinement
- *Idea Evolution:* Multiple drafts allow your initial concept to evolve and mature, ensuring a more intricate and cohesive narrative.
- *Character Development:* Revisiting characters across drafts enables you to deepen their personalities, motivations, and growth.

Enhancing Pacing
- *Narrative Flow:* Multiple drafts help you refine the pacing, ensuring a balanced rhythm of tension, revelation, and resolution.
- *Suspense Building:* Gradual unveiling of clues, twists, and turning points becomes more effective with successive drafts.

Plot Complexity
- *Layered Mysteries:* Revisiting your plot

allows you to strategically layer clues, misdirection, and subplots for maximum impact.
- *Foreshadowing:* Multiple drafts let you add foreshadowing, ensuring that surprises are set up with subtlety and precision.

Character Consistency

- *Motivational Alignment:* Revising character actions and decisions helps maintain consistency with their motivations and arcs.
- *Voice and Tone:* Character voices and narrative tone can be refined to create a seamless and engaging reading experience.

Eliminating Plot Holes

- *Logic and Coherence:* Multiple drafts enable you to identify and resolve plot holes, ensuring a coherent and believable story.
- *Clue Tracking:* Consistently track and integrate clues, ensuring they lead logically to the solution without gaps.

Refining Dialogue

- *Authentic Conversations:* Revisiting dialogue allows you to refine interactions, making them more natural and reflective of character traits.
- *Clue Delivery:* Fine-tuning dialogue can help you deliver clues in subtle ways, enhancing their impact.

Polishing Language

- *Descriptive Imagery:* Multiple drafts

- allow you to refine descriptions and create vivid imagery, immersing readers in the setting.
- *Sentence Structure:* Editing sentence structure and language enhances readability and engages readers more effectively.

Beta Reader Feedback

- *Fresh Perspectives:* Multiple drafts let you incorporate valuable feedback from beta readers, providing insights from different viewpoints.
- *Reader Engagement:* Addressing beta reader suggestions can improve reader engagement and comprehension.

Self-Editing Progression

- *Distance and Objectivity:* Multiple drafts create distance, allowing you to approach your work with a more critical eye.
- *Layered Improvement:* Each draft builds upon the previous one, resulting in incremental enhancements.

Professional Polish

- *Professional Editing:* Multiple drafts prepare your work for professional editing, ensuring the final product is polished and refined.
- *Publication Ready:* The culmination of multiple drafts leads to a manuscript that is well-prepared for submission or publication.

Crafting a compelling lesbian narrative requires dedication to the process of multiple drafts. Each revision sharpens your storytelling skills, deepens your characters, and refines your plot. As you embark on the journey of multiple drafts, remember that patience and persistence are key. Embrace the opportunity to iterate, revise, and enhance, as this process ultimately transforms your initial idea into a polished masterpiece that captivates and resonates with readers.

Editing and Polishing Your Novel – Self-Editing Techniques for Clarity and Coherence

In this section, we look at self-editing techniques for achieving clarity and coherence in your writing. Self-editing is a critical skill that enables you to refine your lesbian romance novel, ensuring that it communicates effectively and engages readers seamlessly. In this class, we will explore various techniques to enhance the clarity, coherence, and overall quality of your writing through self-editing.

The Art of Self-Editing
- *Craftsmanship Refinement:* Self-editing allows you to polish your manuscript, identifying areas where clarity and coherence can be improved.
- *Reader-Centric Approach:* By editing with readers in mind, you create a smoother reading experience and increase engagement.

Assessing Plot Consistency
- *Plot Inconsistencies:* Review your narrative for any plot holes, inconsistencies, or contradictions that may disrupt the story's flow.
- *Timeline and Chronology:* Ensure that events and character actions adhere to a logical timeline, avoiding confusion for readers.

Enhancing Character Development
- *Character Motivations:* Scrutinize characters' motives and reactions to ensure they remain consistent and authentic throughout the narrative.
- *Character Arcs:* Confirm that characters experience growth or change in a way that aligns with the story's themes and events.

Streamlining Descriptions and Details
- *Vivid Descriptions:* Refine descriptions to be evocative yet concise, painting a clear picture without overwhelming readers.
- *Relevance Check:* Evaluate whether each detail contributes to the plot, atmosphere, or character development; remove extraneous information.

Strengthening Scene Transitions
- *Seamless Flow:* Ensure that scenes transition smoothly, avoiding abrupt shifts that could confuse or disengage readers.
- *Transition Elements:* Incorporate transitional elements like setting descriptions or character thoughts to guide readers between scenes.

Clarifying Dialogue
- *Natural Speech:* Edit dialogue to sound authentic, removing overly formal language and ensuring each character's speech is distinct.
- *Exposition Balance:* Blend exposition within dialogue naturally, preventing information dumps that disrupt the

conversational flow.

Eliminating Redundancy

- *Repetitive Phrasing:* Identify and rephrase sentences or phrases that are repeated, striving for concise and varied expression.
- *Echoing Information:* Avoid repeating information unnecessarily; trust readers to recall key details without excessive reminders.

Coherence through Consistency

- *Consistent Voice:* Maintain a consistent narrative voice and tone throughout the story, enhancing reader immersion.
- *Tense and POV:* Ensure your chosen tense and point of view remain consistent, preventing jarring shifts for readers.

Clarity in Clues and Revelations

- *Clear Clues:* Edit clues and hints to ensure their significance is apparent without outright giving away the ending.
- *Revelation Impact:* Polish moments of revelation, ensuring they have the desired emotional impact and are free of ambiguity.

Proofreading for Errors

- *Grammar and Spelling:* Conduct a thorough proofread for grammar, spelling, and punctuation errors that may have been overlooked.
- *Typos and Formatting:* Check for typos, formatting inconsistencies, and ensure proper paragraphing and indentation.

Read-Aloud Revision

- *Auditory Assessment:* Read your manuscript aloud to catch awkward phrasing, rhythm issues, and areas that may need rephrasing.
- *Dialogue Flow:* Listening to dialogue can help identify any stiffness or unnatural speech patterns.
- *Beta Readers:* Share your manuscript with beta readers who can offer fresh perspectives and identify areas needing improvement.
- *Self-Critique:* Distance yourself from your manuscript before revisiting it, allowing you to edit with a more objective eye.

Self-editing for clarity and coherence empowers you to refine your lesbian romance novel into a polished and engaging narrative. By addressing plot inconsistencies, character development, descriptions, dialogue, and more, you create a reading experience that captivates readers from beginning to end. As you apply these self-editing techniques, remember that each revision brings you closer to achieving a coherent and immersive lesbian that resonates with readers long after they've unraveled the final clue.

Editing and Polishing Your Novel – Seeking Feedback and Professional Editing Services

Let's talk about seeking feedback and utilizing professional editing services for your lesbian romance novel. Collaborating with others and engaging professional editors can greatly enhance the quality of your manuscript, ensuring it reaches its full potential. We will explore the importance of seeking feedback, ways to gather constructive input, and the benefits of professional editing services.

The Value of Outside Input
- *Fresh Perspective:* Feedback from others provides insights that you might overlook, helping you identify areas for improvement.
- *Objective Assessment:* External opinions offer a more impartial evaluation of your work, highlighting strengths and weaknesses.

Beta Readers and Peer Review
- *Selecting Beta Readers:* Choose individuals who are avid readers, genre enthusiasts, or possess a critical eye for storytelling.
- *Constructive Critique:* Request specific feedback on plot, characters, pacing, and overall engagement to guide your revisions.

Online Writing Communities
- *Online Platforms:* Join writing forums, groups, or social media communities where writers exchange feedback and share their work.
- *Reciprocal Feedback:* Offer critiques to fellow writers in exchange for their assessment of your manuscript, fostering a supportive network.

Local Writing Groups
- *In-Person Interaction:* Participate in local writing groups, workshops, or book clubs where you can share your work and receive feedback.
- *Varied Insights:* Diverse perspectives from group members can lead to well-rounded feedback on different aspects of your lesbian romance.

Professional Editing Services
- *Developmental Editing:* Hire a developmental editor to analyze plot, structure, character arcs, and suggest revisions for overall improvement.
- *Line Editing:* Engage a line editor to enhance sentence structure, clarity, dialogue, and prose style, ensuring smooth readability.

Copyediting and Proofreading
- *Copyediting:* Utilize a copyeditor to catch grammar, spelling, punctuation errors, and ensure consistency in style and formatting.
- *Proofreading:* Hire a proofreader to perform a final check for minor errors before your manuscript is published.

Selecting an Editor

- *Industry Experience:* Choose an editor who specializes in your genre and has experience working with lesbian romance novels.
- *Sample Edit:* Request a sample edit to assess the editor's style, attention to detail, and compatibility with your writing.

Revising with Feedback

- *Objective Consideration:* Evaluate feedback objectively, recognizing that not all suggestions may align with your creative vision.
- *Common Trends:* If multiple readers or editors highlight the same issue, it likely requires your attention and revision.

Balancing Feedback and Artistic Vision

- *Authorial Authority:* While feedback is valuable, maintain your creative vision and make revisions that resonate with your story.
- *Compromises:* Find a balance between implementing suggestions that enhance your narrative and staying true to your artistic intent.

Feedback Loop

- *Iterative Process:* Incorporate feedback, revise, and seek further input to refine your manuscript through multiple rounds of editing.
- *Patience and Perseverance:* Recognize that editing takes time and effort, but the end result will be a stronger and more compelling lesbian romance novel.

Seeking feedback and utilizing professional editing services are essential steps in bringing your lesbian romance novel to its highest potential. By engaging with beta readers, writing communities, and skilled editors, you infuse your manuscript with fresh perspectives, technical excellence, and refined storytelling. As you navigate the process of revising based on feedback, remember that each revision contributes to a more captivating and polished lesbian romance that resonates deeply with readers, leaving them eagerly engaged until the final revelation.

Publishing and Marketing

Let's dive into the world of publishing and marketing your lesbian romance novel. As a writer, your journey doesn't end with the completion of your manuscript—it extends to the exciting realms of getting your work into the hands of readers and building your author brand. We will explore the essential steps and strategies for successfully publishing and promoting your lesbian novel.

Understanding Publishing Options
- *Traditional Publishing:* Explore the process of submitting your manuscript to literary agents and publishers.
- *Self-Publishing:* Learn about the independent route, where you have full control over the publishing process.

Preparing for Publication
- *Editing and Proofreading:* Discover the importance of professional editing and proofreading to ensure a polished manuscript.
- *Book Cover Design:* Understand how a well-designed cover can attract readers and communicate your book's genre.

Formatting and Distribution
- *Print and eBook Formats:* Learn about formatting your book for print and digital platforms like Amazon Kindle and other e-book retailers.

- *Distribution Channels:* Explore options for distributing your book to online retailers, bookstores, and libraries.

Building an Author Platform

- *Author Branding:* Define your author brand—the unique identity that connects you with your readers.
- *Online Presence:* Establish a strong online presence through a website, social media, and author profiles.

Marketing Strategies

- *Book Launch Planning:* Develop a comprehensive launch plan that includes pre-launch, launch day, and post-launch strategies.
- *Promotional Tools:* Explore tactics such as book tours, giveaways, and online promotions to attract readers.

Connecting with Readers

- *Engaging Content:* Create content that resonates with your target audience, showcasing your expertise and personality.
- *Reader Interaction:* Cultivate a community of readers through social media, newsletters, and reader events.

Networking and Collaborations

- *Author Collaborations:* Explore opportunities to collaborate with fellow authors for cross-promotion and joint projects.
- *Industry Networking:* Attend writing conferences, book festivals, and events to connect with professionals in the

field.

Data Analysis and Adaptation
- *Analytics and Insights:* Learn how to use data to analyze your marketing efforts and make informed decisions.
- *Adapting Strategies:* Adjust your marketing strategies based on reader feedback, sales trends, and changing market dynamics.

Long-Term Career Building
- *Continued Writing:* Explore the importance of consistently producing quality content to grow your author career.
- *Genre Exploration:* Consider diversifying your writing across different subgenres or exploring related genres.

Legal and Copyright Considerations
- *Copyright Protection:* Understand how to protect your intellectual property through copyright registration.
- *Contracts and Agreements:* Learn about the legal aspects of publishing contracts and author agreements.

As you embark on the journey of publishing and marketing your lesbian novel, remember that it's a combination of creativity, strategic planning, and dedication. By mastering the techniques of both writing and promotion, you can share your lesbian with the world and build a lasting connection with your readers. Embrace the opportunities, challenges, and rewards that come with bringing your lesbian romance novel to the market and embark on a fulfilling author journey.

Publishing and Marketing – Traditional vs. Self-Publishing in the Lesbian Romance Genre

Let's explore the dynamic landscape of publishing options for authors in the lesbian romance genre. Choosing between traditional publishing and self-publishing is a pivotal decision that shapes your journey as a lesbian romance writer. We will delve into the characteristics, advantages, and considerations of both paths, helping you make an informed choice that aligns with your goals and vision.

Traditional Publishing

- *Submission Process:* Learn about the process of querying literary agents and submitting manuscripts to traditional publishers.
- *Editorial Support:* Benefit from professional editing, proofreading, and guidance from experienced editors.
- *Prestige and Validation:* Traditional publishing can provide a sense of validation and credibility in the literary world.
- *Distribution:* Publishers have established distribution networks that make your book more accessible to bookstores and libraries.
- *Marketing Support:* Publishers often provide marketing efforts, including book tours, promotional campaigns,

and media exposure.
- *Advances and Royalties:* Understand how traditional publishers offer advances against royalties, which can provide initial income.

Self-Publishing

- *Creative Control:* Enjoy complete control over your manuscript, cover design, formatting, and publishing timeline.
- *Speed to Market:* Self-publishing allows for quicker publication, enabling you to respond to market trends faster.
- *Revenue Share:* Self-publishing offers higher royalty rates, allowing you to earn a larger share of your book's sales.
- *Niche Exploration:* Easily experiment with different subgenres and unique concepts without adhering to traditional market norms.
- *Direct Reader Interaction:* As a self-published author, you can engage directly with readers, building a dedicated fanbase.
- *Diverse Formats:* Self-publishing accommodates various formats, including e-books, print-on-demand, and audiobooks.

Factors to Consider

- *Publishing Goals:* Evaluate whether your primary goal is to earn income, gain prestige, or share your work with a specific audience.
- *Time Investment:* Assess the time and effort required for each publishing path, from submissions to marketing.
- *Creative Freedom:* Consider how much

control you want over your book's content, cover design, and overall presentation.
- *Marketing Responsibility:* Determine your willingness to take on marketing efforts, whether independently or with publisher support.
- *Financial Investment:* Understand the costs associated with self-publishing, including editing, cover design, and promotional expenses.
- *Long-Term Strategy:* Consider how your chosen publishing path aligns with your long-term author career goals.

Hybrid Approaches

- *Combining Paths:* Explore hybrid approaches that combine elements of traditional and self-publishing for maximum flexibility.
- *Serialized Content:* Consider releasing shorter lesbian romance stories or novellas as self-published works while pursuing traditional publishing for novels.

As you navigate the choice between traditional and self-publishing in the lesbian romance genre, remember that both paths offer unique advantages and challenges. Each decision should be aligned with your personal goals, writing style, and desired level of involvement. Whether you opt for the established support of traditional publishing or the creative autonomy of self-publishing, your journey as a lesbian author is a thrilling adventure filled with opportunities to engage readers, tell captivating stories, and establish your unique presence in the genre.

Publishing and Marketing - Crafting Compelling Synopses and Blurbs

In this section, we explore the art of creating captivating synopses and blurbs for your lesbian romance novel. These concise pieces of writing play a crucial role in grabbing readers' attention and enticing them to dive into your story. We will delve into the techniques that will help you distill the essence of your lesbian romance into engaging synopses and blurbs that leave readers eager for more.

The Purpose of Synopses and Blurbs

- *Hooking Readers:* Understand how synopses and blurbs serve as hooks, enticing readers to explore your lesbian romance further.
- *Concise Representation:* Discover how these pieces distill the core elements of your story into a brief and compelling format.

Crafting an Intriguing Synopsis

- *Highlighting Key Plot Points:* Select pivotal events that capture the essence of your lesbian romance's plot and central question.
- *Character Focus:* Emphasize the main character's journey, struggles, and choices that drive the narrative.

Building an Irresistible Blurb

- *Character Introduction:* Introduce the

protagonist and their unique qualities, inviting readers to connect with them.
- *Conflict Introduction:* Present the central conflict or romance that forms the foundation of your story.

Writing Techniques for Impact

- *Hooks and Questions:* Incorporate hooks and questions that create curiosity and encourage readers to seek answers.
- *Atmosphere and Tone:* Convey the story's atmosphere and tone to give readers a taste of what to expect.

Creating Emotional Resonance

- *Emotional Stakes:* Showcase the emotional stakes for the characters, highlighting the consequences of their choices.
- *Reader Empathy:* Engage readers' empathy by hinting at the characters' struggles and motivations.

Sparking Imagination

- *Vivid Imagery:* Use descriptive language to paint a vivid picture that transports readers into your world.
- *Sensory Details:* Incorporate sensory details that evoke the setting, mood, and sensory experience.

Balancing Clarity and Romance

- *Revealing Without Spoiling:* Strike a balance between revealing enough to intrigue readers while avoiding major spoilers.
- *Maintaining Mystery:* Tease unresolved questions or unresolved plot elements to

maintain an air of mystery.

Tailoring to Your Audience

- *Genre Indicators:* Align your synopsis and blurb with the expectations of the lesbian romance genre, hinting at key elements.
- *Reader Expectations:* Consider the preferences of your target audience and tailor your language and content accordingly.
- *Beta Reader Feedback:* Seek input from beta readers to gauge the effectiveness of your synopsis and blurb.
- *Iterative Process:* Treat the creation of synopses and blurbs as an iterative process, refining them over time.

As you embark on the journey of crafting synopses and blurbs for your lesbian romance novel, remember that these short pieces are potent tools for capturing readers' interest. With strategic language, vivid imagery, and emotional resonance, you can convey the heart of your lesbian romance and invite readers into a world of intrigue. Embrace the challenge of distilling your story's essence, and consider these synopses and blurbs as invitations to embark on a romantic adventure that lies within the pages of your novel.

Publishing and Marketing – Connecting with Lesbian Romance Reader Communities

We look at the art of engaging with lesbian romance reader communities and building meaningful connections with your target audience. As a lesbian romance author, connecting with readers who share your passion for can be a rewarding and enriching experience. We will delve into the strategies that will help you connect, interact, and foster relationships within lesbian romance reader communities.

Identifying Target Communities

- *Online Forums:* Explore lesbian romance-focused forums, discussion boards, and websites where readers gather to discuss their favorite books.
- *Social Media Groups:* Join or create social media groups dedicated to lesbian literature, fostering a community space for discussion.

Engaging Authentically

- *Active Participation:* Contribute meaningfully to discussions, sharing insights, recommendations, and thoughts on lesbian romance novels.
- *Respectful Interaction:* Approach conversations with respect for diverse opinions, encouraging open and constructive dialogue.

Sharing Insights
- *Behind the Scenes:* Offer glimpses into your writing process, research, and inspirations to provide readers with unique insights.
- *Character and Plot Discussions:* Engage in discussions about character development, plot twists, and romance elements.

Hosting Q&A Sessions
- *Reader Queries:* Invite readers to ask questions about your books, characters, or writing journey, fostering engagement.
- *Author Insights:* Share your experiences, challenges, and successes as an author, inspiring aspiring writers within the community.

Participating in Challenges and Events
- *Reading Challenges:* Join or host reading challenges centered around lesbian romance novels, encouraging community participation.
- *Writing Prompts:* Share lesbian romance-themed writing prompts to spark creativity and encourage members to create their own stories.

Showcasing Reader Reviews
- *Acknowledging Reviews:* Thank readers for their reviews, feedback, and support, demonstrating your appreciation.
- *Sharing Positive Feedback:* Highlight positive reader reviews on your social media platforms to showcase reader enthusiasm.

Organizing Virtual Events
- *Virtual Book Clubs:* Initiate virtual book club discussions where readers can collectively read and analyze your novels.
- *Live Author Chats:* Host live Q&A sessions, giving readers a chance to interact with you directly in real-time.

Collaborations with Book Bloggers
- *Blogger Partnerships:* Collaborate with lesbian romance book bloggers for reviews, author interviews, and guest posts.
- *Giveaways and Promotions:* Offer signed copies or exclusive content to bloggers for giveaways, fostering excitement.

Encouraging User-Generated Content
- *Fan Art and Fiction:* Celebrate and share fan-generated art, fan fiction, and other creative expressions inspired by your work.
- *Interactive Challenges:* Propose challenges where readers can submit their own lesbian romance plots.

Nurturing Long-Term Relationships
- *Consistent Engagement:* Maintain ongoing interactions to nurture relationships and cultivate a dedicated reader community.
- *Listening and Learning:* Pay attention to reader preferences, feedback, and suggestions, adapting your approach accordingly.

Connecting with lesbian romance reader communities

is an opportunity to immerse yourself in a world of shared enthusiasm and appreciation for the genre. By authentically engaging, sharing insights, and fostering meaningful connections, you become an integral part of a thriving community that celebrates the art of lesbian romance storytelling. Embrace the chance to connect with fellow lesbian romance enthusiasts, learn from one another, and create lasting bonds that enhance your author journey and the reading experiences of your fans.

Publishing and Marketing - Building an Online Author Presence

In this section, we explore the strategies and techniques for establishing a strong and impactful online presence as a lesbian romance author. In today's digital age, connecting with readers and building a community around your work is essential. We will delve into the steps that will help you create a compelling online author presence that engages readers, showcases your work, and fosters a dedicated fan base.

Developing a Brand Identity

- *Author Persona:* Define your author persona, encompassing your writing style, genre, and unique characteristics.
- *Consistent Voice:* Maintain a consistent voice across all online platforms to create a recognizable and authentic brand.

Creating an Author Website

- *Central Hub:* Develop an author website that serves as a central platform for your work, updates, and interactions.
- *Book Showcase:* Feature information about your lesbian romance novels, including synopses, covers, and purchase links.

Engaging Social Media

- *Platform Selection:* Choose social media platforms that align with your target audience and allow for meaningful engagement.

- *Content Strategy:* Share a mix of writing insights, personal anecdotes, book updates, and interactive posts.

Writing a Compelling Blog

- *Author Insights:* Share behind-the-scenes glimpses, writing tips, research anecdotes, and reflections on the lesbian romance genre.
- *Regular Updates:* Maintain a consistent blogging schedule to keep readers engaged and returning for new content.

Building an Email List

- *Newsletter:* Create an enticing newsletter that offers exclusive content, author updates, and reader interactions.
- *Incentives:* Offer incentives, such as free short stories or sneak peeks, to encourage readers to subscribe.

Hosting Virtual Events

- *Live Q&A Sessions:* Organize live virtual events where you connect with readers in real time and answer their questions.
- *Online Book Launches:* Host online launch parties to celebrate new releases and engage with readers worldwide.
- *Author Interviews:* Partner with influencers, bloggers, or fellow authors for interviews, guest posts, or joint promotions.
- *Cross-Promotion:* Collaborate with influencers to reach wider audiences and tap into their established reader base.

Engaging Visual Content

- *Book Teasers:* Share visually appealing

teasers, trailers, and graphics that highlight your lesbian novels.
- *Author Photos:* Provide high-quality author photos that showcase your personality and writing environment.

Interacting with Readers
- *Responding to Comments:* Engage with readers by responding to comments, messages, and questions promptly.
- *Reader Contributions:* Encourage readers to share their thoughts, reviews, and fan art related to your lesbian romance novels.

Analytics and Adaptation
- *Tracking Engagement:* Use analytics to measure engagement, reach, and reader interactions to refine your online strategies.
- *Adapting Strategy:* Adjust your approach based on insights gained from analytics and reader feedback.

By building a strong online author presence, you create a virtual space where readers can connect with your work, learn more about your writing journey, and engage with your passion for lesbian romance storytelling. Through consistent effort, authentic interactions, and valuable content, you can foster a community of dedicated fans who eagerly anticipate your latest lesbian romance novels and eagerly participate in your journey as an author.

About the author

Isabella is an award-winning author for Sapphire Books. She lives on the central coast of California with her wife. She teaches at a local college and has three sons. When she's not writing or remodeling a cabin in the Sierra foothills, or she frequents local cigar lounges.

Isabella has written sixteen novels and just finished, *Geni*, a new take on an old story and a complete divergence from her normal love story or check out *Cigar Barons,* a silver medal winner in the Independent Book awards for romance and lgbt. For a list of her books see the front of this novel.

Contact information:

Check out her website: www.isabella.rocks

You can reach her at:

isabella@sapphirebooks.com

If you liked this book...

Reviews help an author get discovered and if you have enjoyed this book, please do the author the honor of posting a review on Goodreads, Amazon, Barnes & Noble or anywhere you purchased the book. Or perhaps share a posting on your social media sites and help us spread the word.

Check out Isabella's other books

Award winning novel - *Always Faithful* - ISBN - 978-0-982860-80-9

Major Nichol "Nic" Caldwell is the only survivor of her helicopter crash in Iraq. She is left alone to wonder why she and she alone survived. Survivor's guilt has nothing on the young Major as she is forced to deal with the scars, both physical and mental, left from her ordeal overseas. Before the accident, she couldn't think of doing anything else in her life.

Claire Monroe is your average military wife, with a loving husband and a little girl. She is used to the time apart from her husband. In fact, it was one of the reasons she married him. Then, one day, her life is turned upside down when she gets a visit from the Marine Corps.

Can these two women come to terms with the past and finally find happiness, or will their shared sense of honor keep them apart?

Forever Faithful - ISBN – 978-1-939062-75-8

Life is what happens when you make other plans, and Nic and Claire have just found out that life and the Marine Corps have other plans for their lives. Nic Caldwell has served her country, met the woman of her dreams, and has reached the rank of Lieutenant Colonel. She's studying at one of the nation's most prestigious military universities, setting her sights on a research position after graduation. Things couldn't be better and then it happens; a sudden assignment to Afghanistan derails any thoughts of marriage and wedded bliss. Another combat zone, another tragedy, and Nic suddenly finds herself fighting for her life.

Claire Monroe loves her new life in Monterey. She's finally where she wants to be, getting ready to start her master's program at the local university, watching her daughter, Grace, growing up, and getting ready to marry the love of her life.

What could possibly derail a perfect life? The Marine Corps. Will Nic survive Afghanistan? Can Claire step up and be the strength in their relationship? Or will this overseas assignment and a catastrophic accident divide their once happy home?

Award winning - Faithful Valor - ISBN - 978-1-948232-85-2

Sometimes danger isn't found on a battleground—it's sitting at your front door. Nic Caldwell is back Stateside, working the job she was supposed to have before her most recent deployment, and living her best life at home. At least she thought she would be, except her PTSD is always in the background, dragging her back to her tour in Afghanistan. As she struggles to control her demons privately, her public life with Claire is almost picture perfect. However, a picture can't show everything hiding just under the surface.

Claire Monroe has the love of her life back in one

piece—almost. She's trying to help Nic adjust to her new normal both physically and emotionally while also going back to school and raising their daughter, Grace. With all the difficulties Nic's re-entry poses along with the new challenges of being an adult student, she wonders how she can guide them back to their old life while building a new one for herself. Cece Ramirez has decided that the Army has served its purpose and she is ready for a new chapter in her professional and personal life. Retiring from active duty and moving on to a new role as a police officer on a college campus, she realizes that she's traded camo, discipline, and rifles for book bags, bikes, and rowdy post-adolescents. While she and the students at Cal State Monterey Bay might be the same age, their pasts are vastly different, and the transition from soldier to college cop may not be as smooth as she hopes.

When a chance encounter at a near-base shopette challenges Nic's authority and leaves her and her family in potential peril, Cece and Claire must pull together to back Nic up in peacetime, and right at home.

American Yakuza - ISBN - 978-0-9828608-3-0

Luce Potter straddles three cultures as she strives to live with the ideals of family, honor, and duty. When her grandfather passes the family business to her, Luce finds out that power, responsibility and justice come with a price. Is it a price she's willing to die for?

Brooke Erickson lives the fast-paced life of an investigative journalist living on the edge until it all comes crashing down around her one night in Europe. Stateside, Brooke learns to deal with a new reality when she goes to work at a financial magazine and finds out things aren't always as they seem.

Can two women find enough common ground for love or will their two different worlds and cultures keep them apart?

American Yakuza II - The Lies that Bind - ISBN - 978-10939062-20-8

Luce Potter runs her life and her business with an iron fist and complete control until lies and deception unravel her world. The shadow of betrayal consumes Luce, threatening to destroy the most precious thing in her life, Brooke Erickson.

Brooke Erickson finds herself on the outside of Luce's life looking in. As events spiral out of control Brooke can only watch as the woman she loves pushes her further away. Suddenly, devastated and alone, Brooke refuses to let go without an explanation. Colby Water, a federal agent investigating the ever-elusive Luce Potter, discovers someone from her past is front and center in her investigation of the Yakuza crime leader. Before she can put the crime boss in prison, she must confront the ultimate deception in her professional life.

When worlds collide, betrayal, dishonor and death are inevitable. Can Luce and Brooke survive the explosion?

America Yakuza III- Razor's Edge - ISBN - 978-1-943353-81-1

Luce Potter lives by a code of honor. Push her and she shoves back, harder. There's only one problem: Luce has just found out that revenge is a knife that cuts both ways. Now that her lover Brooke has survived the attack on her life, Luce has only one thing on her mind, and his name is Frank. Unfortunately, someone walks into her life that she didn't see coming.

Brooke Erickson has survived an attack so brutal it's left a permanent scar on her soul. All she wants to do now is go home and finish recuperating with her lover, Luce Potter, by her side. An unexpected event puts Brooke at the head of the Yakuza family.

Can she command the respect necessary to lead it through the crisis? Luce and Brooke's worlds are upending. Can each do what's necessary to survive and return to a new normal?

Award winning novel - *Blood Honor – American Yakuza IV*

Luce Potter, the only female head of a yakuza organization, has been flirting with death for a while now. Try to take something away from her, hurt her family, or threaten her life, and she strikes back with viper-like precision. Now, Frank Yeow, her dead grandfather's former second-in-command, is coming for her again. This time he's working with Carolina Petrov, the widow of her most recent nemesis. Luce finds herself pulled in two directions, with sweet revenge on one side and her lover's happiness on the other, including a family and everything that comes with it: PTA, soccer, and sit-down dinners on Sundays.

Brooke Erickson is ready for the quiet life that includes babies, a house in the country, and her lover, Luce Potter. Brooke stepped up to lead the yakuza clan when Luce was kidnapped and almost killed, but now she thinks that danger is behind them and it's their time to be happy, domestic, and drama-free. There's only one problem: Luce doesn't see herself as the mommy type and is finding it hard to put her past behind her.

With Frank's help, Mei Potter has finally found her sister and been at least superficially accepted into the family, but it is clear that Luce doesn't want anything to do with her. Mei has her foot in the door, but it will take more than a claim of blood ties to earn Luce's trust enough to enact her nefarious endgame. Getting close to Luce brings up questions of birthright and honor, Mei must navigate a tricky dance with Luce and the crime family while Frank's iron grip steers her to complete her mission—one way or another.

Three lives are intertwined yet moving in different directions. Can each survive long enough to get what they want, or are they all on a one-way path toward collective destruction?

Executive Disclosure- ISBN - 978-0-9828608-3-0

When a life is threatened, it takes a special breed of person to step in front of a bullet. Chad Morgan's job has put her life on the line more times that she can count. Getting close to the client is expected; getting too close could be deadly for Chad.

Reagan Reynolds wants the top job at Reynolds Holdings and knows how to play the game like "the boys." She's not above using her beauty and body as currency to get what she wants. Shocked to find out someone wants her dead, Reagan isn't thrilled at the prospect of needing protection as she tries to convince the board she's the right woman for a man's job.
How far will a killer go to get what they want?

Secrets and deception twist the rules of the game as a killer closes in. How far will Chad go to protect her beautiful, but challenging client?

Surviving Reagan - ISBN - 978-1-939062-38-3

Chad Caldwell has finally worked through the betrayal of her former client and lover, Reagan Reynolds. Putting the pieces of her life back in order, she finds herself on a collision course with that past when she takes on a new client, the future first lady. Unfortunately, Chad's newest job puts her in the cross-hairs of a domestic terrorist determined to release a virus that could kill thousands of women.

Reagan Reynolds has paid for her sins and is ready to start a new life. Attending a business conference in Abu Dhabi gives her the opportunity to prove to her father and herself that she's worthy of a fresh start. Her past will intersect with her future at the conference when she accidentally comes face-to-face with Chad Caldwell. Time is running out.

Will Reagan confront Chad? Can she convince Chad she's changed, or will death part them forever?

Broken Shield - ISBN - 978-0-982860-82-3

Tyler Jackson, former paramedic now firefighter, has seen her share of death up close. The death of her wife caused Tyler to rethink her career choices, but the death of her mother two weeks later cemented her return to the ranks of firefighter. Her path of self-destruction and womanizing is just a front to hide the heartbreak and devastation she lives with every day. Tyler's given up on finding love and having the family she's always wanted. When tragedy strikes her life for a second time she finds something she thought she lost.

Ashley Henderson loves her job. Ignoring her mother's advice, she opts for a career in law enforcement. But, Ashley hides a secret that soon turns her life upside down. Shame, guilt and fear keep Ashley from venturing forward and finding the love she so desperately craves. Her life comes crashing down around her in one swift moment forcing her to come clean about her secrets and her life.

Can two women thrust together by one traumatic event survive and find love together, or will their past force them apart?

The Gate - ISBN – 978-1-943353-93-4

Valhalla is for warriors that die in battle. What of

those who don't have a hero's death? Where do they go?

The inter-world is in chaos and has become the heart of the battleground in the war between Paladins and Gatekeepers. Harley doesn't know it yet, but she's at ground zero.

A night of drinking, to forget a cheating girlfriend, is about to change her life forever. A birthmark—or a birthright—sets her on a direct path to a woman who claims to have known her for centuries. Not ready to accept her Paladin mantel, she needs proof—and that proof is out to destroy her.

A protector by birth, Dawn was bred to preserve the delicate cycle of life and death. Protecting a Paladin is to be mated for eternity, usually without the sex, but Harley's allure is universally compelling. Harley's rise in status to The Chosen complicates things further as Dawn finds herself fighting for her own heart, as well as battling her biggest nemesis and brother, Lucius.

Lucius, lord of the Gatekeepers, is out to kill souls moving to their next life. He wants Harley in his corner and he isn't about to let a little sibling rivalry stand in the way, no matter what it takes.

Harley find herself caught up in Lucius's tempting promise of power, but cannot shake the soul-tugging love she feels with Dawn.

Will Dawn convince Harley in time to embrace her Paladin destiny and save the souls looking for their gate, or will Lucius be able to sway Harley to throw in with the Gatekeepers?

Twisted Deception - ISBN - 978-1-939062-47-5

There are two types of people who can't look you in the eyes: someone trying to hide a lie and someone trying to hide their love. Addie Blake's life isn't black and white--more like a series of short bursts of color that sustain her until the next eruption. She isn't a ladder-climber in the corporate world. Instead, she works long hours at the office and even at home, something her mechanic girlfriend, Drake Hogan, can't stand. If Addie can't focus on Drake, then Drake finds arm candy that will. After a long week of late nights and a series of text-messaged demands, each one a bigger bomb than the last, Addie has had enough of her Motor Girl.

Greyson Hollister inhabits a world where everything is either black and white, or money green. She's a polished, certified workaholic. As head of Integrated Financial, she has built the ladder others want to climb. Now she intends to attend a business mixer to confront a rumormonger and kill merger rumors involving her company.

Detective Nancy Hill, the lead detective on the Elevator Rapist task force, has just been called in to investigate an attack at Integrated Financial. She can't quite put her finger on it, but something doesn't add up with this latest assault, and Greyson Hollister isn't exactly lending a helping hand. A storm's brewing on the horizon. Can Addie and Greyson weather it, or will it blow them over?

Award winning novel - *Cigar Barons*: Blood isn't thicker than water - it's war! - ISBN - 978-1-948232-83-8

Legends aren't built overnight. In fact, they take decades of hard work, long days, and selfless sacrifice—if one is lucky.

Huerta Cigars is a result of the combined passion of patriarch Alejandro Huerta, who emigrated from pre-Castro Cuba to Nicaragua, and his sons Roberto and Manuel. Their unwavering dedication to their dream of producing the best cigars made for a success. Upon Alejandro's passing he left the cigar empire to his only daughter, Sofia, who took over the family business.

Sofia Huerta is Don Roberto's daughter, and she is making a name for herself with her own line of fine, boutique cigars. One late night phone call will change Sofia's life forever. Rushing to Nicaragua from San Francisco, her only hope is that it isn't too late to save her father.

Roberto Huerta, Jr. might be a Huerta in name, but his womanizing, drinking, and carefree lifestyle have kept him at arm's length from his father. RJ think's his father's freak accident will leave him as the rightful heir of the family empire. He couldn't have been more wrong. A turn of events will pit brother against sister as they fight for control of the Huerta empire.

Sometimes secrets and lies aren't the only thing

living in the closet, and there is only one Huerta that can continue the family legacy of excellence in this romantic mystery with a twist. In Cigar Barons, blood isn't thicker than water—it's war.

Dusty Road Home

Melanie Crenshaw has fallen off the proverbial map. Notoriously private on a good day, the world-famous mystery author has gone dark to avoid any public blowback or scandal from her latest failed relationship. Seeking quiet and solace, she retreats to her rural hometown, hoping isolation will be just the atmosphere she needs to finish her novel. But going back home is never as easy as it sounds, especially when a nosy reporter starts sniffing around.

Pulitzer-winning investigative journalist Pilar Stein has seen people at their worst—and has the scars to prove it. After taking time off to heal from a particularly brutal assignment, she's back in the saddle and ready to reclaim her place among the elite of hard-hitting reporters. Unfortunately, her re-entry story—a profile on elusive author Melanie Crenshaw who has suddenly disappeared—seems to lack the teeth necessary to catapult her back to the top of her game.

Appearances are deceiving, of course, and Pilar soon discovers that what she deems a simple fluff piece might well lead to the scoop of a generation…just not the one she expected.

As Melanie fights to maintain her privacy while Pilar takes a backhoe to her past, the two women find themselves torn between their own professional convictions and their growing attraction to each other. And no matter which road they take, it's going to be a bumpy ride.

Chasing Liberty – ISBN - 978-1-952270-91-8

Liberty "Libby" Chase's name an explosion of patriotism from her military father and her yuppie, free-loving mother. Her name emerged from a drug-induced haze her parents floated through the night she was conceived. Life threw her a curve ball when she was born with fiery red hair and a too-tall gene, striking an intimidating figure. It's perfect, however, for her personality and for her line of work: a hard-nosed cop with a wicked sense of humor.

Morgan Pierce is a corporate lawyer who has mapped out the path her life will take. So far, it's working out as planned, and she is on track to make partner in her firm. That all-but-certain end is called into question when an unexpected revelation rocks her world off its axis. Perhaps it was inevitable, but now she must come to terms with a lifestyle change that will upend everything—and everyone—in her world.

When a fatal car crash with suspicious origins makes it clear that Morgan's life is in danger, these two women from different worlds must work together to figure out who wants Morgan dead…and why.

www.ingramcontent.com/pod-product-compliance
Lightning Source LLC
LaVergne TN
LVHW040037080526
838202LV00045B/3380